THE BIBLE:
Living Dialogue

Religious Faith in Modern Times

RABBI ABRAHAM SKORKA

DR. MARCELO FIGUEROA

Jorge Mario Bergoglio
POPE FRANCIS

COMPILED BY MARCELO FIGUEROA

Translated by Brendan Riley

 AMERICAN BIBLE SOCIETY

Philadelphia

THE BIBLE: *Living Dialogue*
Religious Faith in Modern Times

Compiled by Marcelo Figueroa
Translated by Brendan Riley

© 2015 American Bible Society
© 2012, 2013 Marcelo Figueroa (Spanish text)
All rights reserved.

ISBN 978-1-941448-98-4
LCCN 2015943999
ABS Item 124482

For nearly 200 years, American Bible Society has been providing churches of all Christian traditions with Bibles and Scripture resources to enlighten, inspire, and enrich the lives of the people they serve. Its Catholic Ministries division is pleased to make available THE BIBLE: *Living Dialogue* for English-speaking readers, trusting it will encourage Bible reading and make the encounter with the Bible more meaningful.

American Bible Society is an interconfessional Christian organization with a mission "to make the Bible available to every person in a language and format each can understand and afford, so all people may experience its life-changing message." Any specifically doctrinal positions presented in this book are those of the individuals participating in the dialogue and do not reflect the interconfessional stance of American Bible Society.

 AMERICAN BIBLE SOCIETY
101 North Independence Mall East
Philadelphia PA 19106

Printed in the United States of America
7/15—JD-5M

"I will maintain my covenant between me and you [Abraham], and your descendants after you throughout the ages as an everlasting covenant, to be your God and the God of your descendants after you."

Genesis 17:7

"For Christ himself is our peace. He united Jews and Gentiles into one people when, through his own body on the cross, he destroyed the wall of hostility that once divided us."

Ephesians 2:14

"Let brothers be united,
that law being foremost."

Martín Fierro

Contents

POPE FRANCIS AND THE GENIUS OF DIALOGUE

Introduction

It is a great privilege for American Bible Society to publish the English translation of this extraordinary record of a unique inter-faith dialogue featuring Pope Francis—then Archbishop Jorge Mario Bergoglio, S.J. of Buenos Aires—in intimate and lively conversation with a rabbi and a Protestant Scripture scholar. Here is a potent example of the Judeo-Christian embrace of the Bible as the ultimate resource to tackle the most difficult issues of our day and any age, particularly as they affect the lives of families, whose well-being is so dear to the Pope's heart.

It's particularly fitting to make this book available to American Catholics, Jews, and Protestants—and all people of good will—on the eve of Pope Francis's historic September 2015 visit to the United States! Isn't ours the land of dialogue, of different faiths and worldviews living side by side in harmony and mutual respect, despite our sometimes significant differences in belief and practice?

That aspect of the American genius is mirrored in what the world has come to discover as lying at the heart of Francis's papacy: openness to others and a readiness to look at the world from the perspective of those with different—even radically opposed—points of view. His is a relentless search for common ground, with respect for the dignity of the human person as its foundation.

This is how Pope Francis set the parameters, the ground rules for his dialogue with Rabbi Abraham Skorka and Dr. Marcelo Figueroa: "… in order to listen, my heart must be open to receive what others tell me, and have sufficient courage and candor to answer what one feels, and only there does one begin a dialogue based on respect."

Such terms are a challenge for people in all walks of life, from heads of state and religious leaders to the men and women living in the trenches of ordinary, everyday life. This is precisely where Scripture comes in. It is the inexhaustible fount of wisdom for Catholics, Jews, and Protestants alike, each tradition able—as the three partners in dialogue here demonstrate in language both practical and substantive—to find in its pages a reason for their conviction, their hope, and their joy.

Mario J. Paredes
Presidential Liaison
Roman Catholic Ministries
American Bible Society

DOCUMENTING A UNIQUE MEDIA EVENT

Prologue

This is not simply a book about a television program. I hope that it signifies for all people what it does for me, a literary document of an historic and unique media event; the only series of worldwide television broadcasts to include a Pope as a participant.

When in September 2010 I proposed to then-Cardinal Bergoglio that we record together a series of programs of inter-religious dialogue on his beloved Channel 21, his reaction was foreseeable. He did not want to use the television channel of the Archbishopric of Buenos Aires as a vehicle to spread his personality. Nevertheless, when I made it clear to him that his friend Rabbi Abraham Skorka would also be a participant in these discussions, and that between the three of us we would have a dialogue about social themes having the Bible as its epicenter, he gave it some thought. He decided to go forward with the project when he imagined that such a program could be a public example of dialogue between religions, would show a respectful encounter between those who can think differently, and would touch the hearts of those watching it. He made only one condition: "Let's record four programs and then we'll see how it's going."

In the end, between October 2010 and his trip to the conclave which anointed him as Bishop of Rome, we recorded thirty-one hour-long programs. The name of the program: *The Bible: Living Dialogue*, became, in time, a defining mark and a point of reference, even for us.

They asked me if, in addition to giving my support as an Evangelical, I would also officiate as the moderator of the series, a task which I could not refuse. And it was not difficult: the human quality and spiritual caliber of my interlocutors on the panel kept the level and centrality of the debate at a consistently high level. My work also consisted of proposing and seeking consensus on the themes to bring to the programs; we never dealt with any of them without all of us being sure that it was the opportune moment to do so. Once the theme had been selected, we all agreed to not begin discussing it until the studio lights were on and the cameras were running. The fluidity, the spontaneity, the freedom of contributions, the need to listen, the capacity for surprise, and the versatility for adapting ourselves to the different climates generated at the table, were always unwritten values that we jealously guarded.

All in all, three men of faith came together to reach, around a particular theme or topic, some agreements above and beyond our own views and individual positions. In the same way, our doctrinal and confessional differences, which we never softened or hid, actually afforded us an opportunity to learn from each other rather than giving us excuses for obstinacy and division.

Those that first heard and evaluated this televisual proposal, Julio Rimoldi and Silvia Tuosso, director and deputy director of Channel 21, were a permanent source of encouragement, tireless support, and honest advice. Eugenia Castany, as producer, and the whole team assigned to the program, simply helped to create a special climate in the recording studio. They made us feel that we were three friends having a talk around a coffee table, without feeling the pressure of the film crews.

In my acknowledgments, I mention the people who encouraged and supported me so that this book would see the light of day. I do not wish, however, to fail to mention that Pope Francis himself, having given his approval for this publication to Julio Rimoldi in Rome, had the kindness to call me within hours after traveling to Rio de Janeiro to participate in the World Youth Day, to ask how this book project was going and to offer his personal appreciations that I greatly value. In the same way, I am grateful to Rabbi Skorka for his generous encouragement and the expressions of joy that he showed when I spoke to him about this book.

The book contains the thirty-one programs in the order in which they were recorded. My literary work consisted of transforming the accurate transcriptions that contained the forms of spoken language into a written form. At the same time, due to questions of space and critical analysis of the allocutions that I witnessed and heard at various times, I took the liberty of selecting and grouping concepts and opinions. The book, then, is a faithful reflection of what was spoken during the programs and is, literarily speaking, a text to be meditated upon, re-read, and debated.

The chapters are preceded by introductions written with concern for form, content, and length. The reader will note that I have privileged some personal anecdotes which include Cardinal Jorge Mario Bergoglio and which have proven useful to me or have arisen as sources of inspiration to the themes introduced.

My hope and prayer, of which I permit myself the liberty to include Pope Francis and Rabbi Skorka, is that whoever devotes himself or herself to reading these pages will find that it does the soul good; that the book produces a desire to continue and deepen the debates set forth herein; and that minds and hearts will be opened to new avenues for exploring contemporary themes under the illumination of the Bible.

May the God of the Bible bless your life in the time and manner that he alone knows is best!

Marcelo Figueroa
Buenos Aires, 2013

1

Reason and Faith

The clock on the wall of the control room in the recording booth at Channel 21 studios read 11:00 A.M. on October 18, 2010. We found ourselves ready to begin our first program of the series *The Bible: Living Dialogue*. The three of us sat in silence, tense, pensive, and eager to begin.

We had talked at length of what the subject of discussion for the opening program should be. This was no small matter. It had to set the tone and direction for the following programs and lay the foundation for a work whose future proportions none of us was, at that moment, able to measure.

We agreed to clarify, from the start, why three men of religion wanted to engage in a dialogue about general topics from our different perspectives and faith identities.

We decided that the inaugural topic should be "Reason and Faith," and that it would explore a wide range of questions: What place does faith occupy in the analysis of social, cultural, anthropological, and sociological subjects? Is there a basic conflict between faith and reason? Do they compete with or complement one another? Can we, people devoted to religion, offer a clarifying light about secular topics? What would be our starting point?

I had dedicated many hours to researching "triggers" that would open paths of dialogue at the table, and I had planned what to say and how to present my personal point of view. Frankly, I imagined that I had the whole program neatly arranged in my mind before starting. But now, with only a few minutes to go before starting, I realized how pointless that would be. The program had to flow naturally and spontaneously. That would be the secret to our success.

BERGOGLIO: Since the world began there has been a tendency to make a separation between faith, or spiritual life, and public life. And also to foster certain antagonisms between faith and science, between faith and morality, or between faith and justice.

I was thinking of what Ortega y Gasset said: "We don't know what is happening to us, and that is precisely what is happening to us." I have the feeling that if transcendent faith ever becomes insignificant in considering the question of "what is happening to us," we will have removed a fundamental element from our concept of faith, not only individually but as a people.

SKORKA: If faith is not manifested through specific conduct, then it is not faith, but rather—if I may say—mere philosophical speculation or a mental exercise, an intellectual game. The true faith is what is taught to us by the Bible, the Torah*, or the Pentateuch, "in the beginning"—it is what we manifest through a compromise with respect to life.

What we must find, really, is a balanced dialogue between these two concepts: science and religion. In the moment when the scientist believes that he has grasped the absolute truth of existence, he is committing the sin of arrogance and, to my humble understanding, in the moment when the religious figure thinks that he carries in his pocket the exact wisdom and knowledge about the meaning of life, he is committing the sin of folly. Each one must enter into a deep dialogue with the other.

The dialogue must be complementary and neither one, neither the scientist nor the man of religion, must defend the position that declares "I have the truth in my hands," because that is a lie; only God knows the truth.

---

* **Torah:** The first five books of the Bible (Genesis, Exodus, Leviticus, Numbers, and Deuteronomy), known to Christians as the Pentateuch.

BERGOGLIO: It's curious, making that separation signifies implanting a dichotomy in human nature itself. Man, who has the mandate of dominating the world and making it advance, makes room for science, and also has an impressive thirst for transcendence deep inside his being—he has the mark of God in his heart. But then, to declare these two things to be antagonistic, to say that faith is relative while science is absolute, or to commit the folly that the Rabbi has mentioned, to suppose that religion is the only thing that matters, is to drive a wedge into the very essence of human nature.

Man has two aspects: a dimension given to him by the Lord of creation, and he has to make it grow: *"Now be fruitful and multiply, and repopulate the earth"*; and the dimension which seeks longingly for God and his mark of transcendence on our hearts.

A religion that does not recognize science to have a legitimate autonomy prevents it from growing; while a science that posits itself as absolute, with a total autonomy that denies all possibility of transcendence, is suicide.

FIGUEROA: Man is not only a spiritual being, nor is he only physical matter, he is a conjunction, a harmony. There is no dichotomy or division.

It would seem that there is currently a sort of gnostic viewpoint on the whole question, but in reverse. In gnostic thinking, the spiritual part was the good part, and the carnal or human was the bad part that had to be hidden, cast off, or punished. Today we are seeing a reverse gnosticism* that seems to equate faith with a kind of darkness, while seeing materialism and carnality as luminous.

SKORKA: I would change one word when talking about science. I would not restrict it to the word "matter," because science, or the sciences, are evidently concerned with a very broad spectrum of subjects, and often become involved with questions of the spirit and other very profound philosophical themes.

How can we avoid this false dichotomy, this unnecessary antagonism or confrontation? I think that there is only one way, and it has to do with a word that we must capitalize: Humility. We have lost our intellectual honor; many people hold forth on certain subjects without really having a deep knowledge of them.

---

* **Gnosticism:** A philosophical-religious tradition that interacted with Christian thinking in the first three centuries of our era, although Gnostics were quickly catalogued as syncretists or heretics.

Each one is a public informer about something. Sadly, we live in a very narrow-minded and superficial time, and even great scientists often are guilty of a lack of humility.

Let's not forget that in the book of the prophet Micah, when he talks about how one must honor God, he says three things: *"Act justly, love mercy, and walk humbly with your God."* Humility is a basic part of that moment when the scientist realizes that science only corresponds to the "how" and not to the "why;" that there are limits to knowledge and what I know barely scratches the surface of the subject. On the other hand, the man of faith partially perceives "a something" of God, not seeing the whole spiritual reality, otherwise he would be like God. In that moment when we enter the field of humility, this pseudo-antagonism ends, and only then do we begin to have a dialogue.

BERGOGLIO: What you said, that there is no need to overly restrict the concept of science, is true, because when one restricts it, he falls into the imprecision or the error of reducing everything exclusively to the hard sciences.

Pope Benedict XVI told a group of seminarians that when he reported for military service they asked him what he planned to study. He told them: "I'm going to enter the seminary because I want to be a Catholic priest." At that time, Nazism was already on the rise, tightening its grip, and they told Benedict: "Don't waste your time. Change your career because soon there will be no more need for priests. National Socialism will be the doctrine that will answer all questions."

In this chapter on science, I would also mention the human sciences that shape our worldview; those fields also consider it their function to move away from the idea of transcendence, not to dialogue with it, but to focus on self-sufficiency.

FIGUEROA: Men of faith, pastors, priests, and rabbis, with whom we share this world, we all find the interaction or the dialogue between faith and the life of our community has got to do with sharpening our physical and spiritual hearing to listen better, to learn to read reality by listening.

I have the feeling that the problem of antagonism that arises between faith and secularism, between faith and science, and between faith and public life, also includes the humility of knowing that I must listen and understand what is happening to someone else; and being able to say: this is what is happening in society, to people, to the community. By listening we will discover, as in no other way, the question has got to do with real problems, human problems, but also with spiritual problems. It is concerned with that emptiness that has always existed in the life of man and the life of society, and which Saint Augustine said could only be filled by the person of God. It turns out to be indispensable to consider this when we wish to discover an inclusive dialogue.

SKORKA: Long ago a wise scholar said that we all needed to carry in each pocket a paper inscribed with a verse from Scripture. When Abraham learned that God would destroy Sodom and Gomorrah, where his nephew Lot lived, he had some hard words for God: *"Will not the Judge of all the world do what is right?"* Nevertheless, he first had to present himself before God with humility: *"Lord, I know that I am nothing but dust and ashes."* Then, he had to have a paper with a verse inscribed upon it: *"We are dust and ashes."* And what's more, the verse from chapter 8 in the book of Psalms: *"You have made man only slightly less than divine, and crowned him with glory and grandeur."*

That, I believe, is the balance we have to find. It's not a question of humility which simply leads to doing nothing. No, keep in mind that God did tell us that we must dominate the Earth, but in a rabbinical interpretation this verse means: "Let us join God in the constant re-creation of this world"—of this whole cosmos, if I may speak so boldly.

Now, knowing that we have got to work with that balance, the question in itself for those of us dedicated to religion is how to make ourselves listen, and to listen well enough to hear each other.

BERGOGLIO: The very name of our discussion, "living dialogue," makes us think, almost spontaneously, of a certain idea. That in order to listen, my heart must be open to receive what the other person tells me, and have sufficient courage and candor to answer what one feels, and only there does one begin a dialogue based on respect.

Through dialogue, voices become quieter. It's curious, by talking more—and I mean "more gently"—each person says what they have to say with more respect. When someone wants to impose something they need to raise their voice a lot, and this is, for me, the most typical way people lose their authority. When the director of a company or a religious society has to say "I'm the one who's in charge here!" it is because he no longer has authority and needs to reclaim it. Through dialogue, however, the participants each gain authority; one recognizes the other's authority, while his own is also recognized.

Dialogue makes us humble. The primordial dialogue is the dialogue with that God who tells me: "Look, here you have creation at your feet, take this gift, make it grow, dominate it, make it multiply, be my partner." But man has refused dialogue with God from the very beginning. The first dialogue that the Bible mentions includes a man who hides from shame: *"Adam, where are you?"* Another early dialogue between man and God in the Bible, is the one he has with Cain: *"Where is your brother?"* In some way both frame man's position in his dialogue with God and illuminate his dialogue with others. For me, the first step is the dialogic attitude, not punishment for past crimes. We must not close any door; the greater a person's faith the fewer doors slam shut because he knows who supports him.

SKORKA: Those two verses contain some interesting things. Evidently they are rhetorical questions, but why does God ask them and for what purpose? The response from Talmudic scholars[*] is that God tried to enter into dialogue with man. God comes down to earth to speak with man; did he really not know where man was? Of course he knew. God knows absolutely everything.

I think it is difficult to reassemble that dialogue. From the biblical point of view, it is one of the greatest challenges we have. The way we can love God is by loving man. The love of God necessarily comes through the idea that "You shall love your eternal God through your love of man." And the secret for reaching that love, in a deep sense, lies in dialogue. Now, how to achieve it?

FIGUEROA: In the Bible, the text, the account, the story, and the very concept of its formation clearly shows us a God who not only engages in dialogue, but one who is fully involved in history, who becomes incarnate.

History, and contemporary history as well, offer countless examples of how dialogue between religions can build greater good in a way no other approach can. That, I believe, is a value with which our country has been especially blessed by God. For many years we have had a very fruitful experience of dialogue and religious encounter. We men and women of faith have encountered, in the richness of the design, that the other person, by thinking differently or confessing a different faith, is not my enemy, but

---

[*] **Talmud:** The work compiling the oral tradition of the principal rabbinical discussions about Judaic laws, interpretations, and traditions.

rather my friend because he helps me to improve my own faith through the understanding that we are all children of one God who engages in dialogue.

The things that can be built through faith really are transcendent. They transcend religious matters, and become introduced into social life and create changes within the life of people and their communities.

SKORKA: As the Cardinal said, we must be courageous when it comes to dialogue. There is something very important each person needs, which is to be convinced of their own truth. Who becomes too wrapped up in himself? The person who fears that the other one can destroy his identity or in some way knock it off balance; thus, he flees from dialogue.

In extreme cases, like with religious fanaticism, the fear of losing one's own identity is manifest along with the anxieties and madness that comes from wanting to dominate everything. I'm talking about fanatical manifestations of different "religions" that were created in the twentieth century, such as Nazism, fascism, and all those deviations that had a mystical conception.

This has relevance and importance for us, people of religion, to encounter the challenge to revisit and present God anew—to present him again—to show the world a living God. As the Scriptures say, he is someone who loves life and expects you to want to live a full life, because a person who does not engage in dialogue is, in a way, diminishing his own life.

BERGOGLIO: The theme of dialogue brings me back to the first issue: science and religion. They must also have a mutual and complimentary dialogue. Some things symbolize an absence of dialogue between science and religion which speak loudly to me, for example, when the religious point of view denies scientific advancements and everything new. There are still cultures that, even today, only operate according to past traditions; some which do not accept, for example, electric lights or other modern innovations. Some people do not recognize that science enjoys a healthy autonomy and does help to advance the world. On the other hand, we also encounter all the aggrandizement of science, the "Tower of Babel" syndrome, where man loses his transcendent dimension and feels so self-sufficient that he says *"I will build a tower to reach Heaven."*

SKORKA: There is a lovely midrash* with a very interesting exegesis from the late Middle Ages. The midrash says that when they built the Tower of Babel, and a man fell from it and died, nobody said a word. Nevertheless, if a block fell from the tower, they all cried out: "Oh, the time we have wasted in trying to reach heaven!"

Another rabbinical explication expresses the idea that the story begins by saying that there was only one single language and that was what led humankind to build the Tower of Babel. Then God punished them by multiplying the languages so the people could no longer understand one another. What the scholar then says, basing his thinking on the verses in Genesis, is that King Nimrod was the one who forced them to try to reach God in this way, by piling up blocks of stone. The idea is that in a tyranny there is only one single language, only one way of understanding, and only one way for people to understand one another. And therein the dimension of dialogue is lost.

BERGOGLIO: To my understanding, the best term I find to describe the "anti-dialogue" is "self-referentiality." When men, communities, civilizations, and sciences become self-referential, believing themselves self-sufficient and without the need to engage in dialogue, they find themselves alone to be enough, and they become bloated by that very self-referentiality.

FIGUEROA: It is important to have a dialogue with culture, with people, with science, with men and women, in all their different ideas, and to understand that we only represent one segment of a dialogue that comes from the past and must continue; that we are a space, a place, a milestone along a path of dialogue and meeting.

Let's not imagine that there is either dichotomy or alchemy between faith and science, but rather that the two are indispensably complementary, and there must exist between them a fertile dialogue, one that is truly and completely genuine: in its humility, in how it listens and seeks and builds, in its design, in love, in tolerating with courage, and in everything that has been mentioned.

Far from being an absolute truth, that false dichotomy of man within himself, or alone in community life, means that it is absolutely necessary to find the path of dialogue.

---

* **Midrash**: A traditional commentary on a passage in the Hebrew Bible, usually with embellishments, intended to clarify or build on its teaching.

2

Dignity

During our program dedicated to the subject of "Dignity," I witnessed a dialogue charged with emotion and profound meaning. It occurred when Cardinal Bergoglio recalled how Rabbi Skorka had invited him to come to preach in his synagogue. The cardinal said through this experience he'd found the rabbi's dignity "to be infectious." Deeply moved, Abraham thought for a few seconds and then replied that in reality he had thought his invitation had been a way of "dignifying God."

Those wonderful words define, to my understanding, the essence of Rabbi Skorka's participation in the series.

In the first place, his dignity—his own personal dignity—was contagious. In terms of faith commitment he was, you might say, outnumbered, facing two Christians at the table. Nevertheless, his comments and responses were always extremely thoughtful and precise, and it was obvious that he was considering the weight of each one of his words before pronouncing them. His contributions about the Judaic vision of the Bible, and his interpretations whether personal, Talmudic, or rabbinical were a school of wisdom for me. He showed me shades of spirituality and applications of religiosity that I will treasure for the rest of my life.

In the second place, he dignified God. Our God. Throughout the series, several times he mentioned the still-lacerating memory of the Shoah*, but he always did so without any trace of resentment or self-pity. The way he viewed those atrocities moved me, in part, because I understood how deeply they pained him, in his soul, but especially for his effort to see them through God's lenses, without simplistic shortcuts or censured questions.

We would not have been able to make the series without Rabbi Abraham Skorka. I offer my full respect and recognition to my admirable big brother, whom I consider both a friend and a teacher on the path of faith.

A man of contagious dignity and who at the same time dignifies God is not only a wise man but is, above all, a man of God. Such a man is Rabbi Abraham Skorka.

FIGUEROA: When one begins to read the Bible, what immediately emerges is the God who speaks, and with his word creates light and the heavens. However, when he creates man, he forms him, he does not merely "pronounce" him. Scripture says: *"Let there be man,"* but not only that, it also says: *"Let man be made in our image and likeness."*

Observing that we were all created, formed, in the likeness and image of the Creator, our difference from all other creatures and all of creation is essential. That profound identity, man's identification with God, gives us a unique sense of belonging. It doesn't matter how I consider another person or myself, I am essentially the image and likeness of my Creator.

This leads me to understand the dignity that we all have, men and women, given by the same Creator, something that is present in the first chapter of Scripture.

SKORKA: In the story in Genesis there are two references to the creation of man, articulating two basic elements. One, that God made man in his image and likeness, but as the learned scholars in the Talmud explain so well, there is a second, no less significant detail to consider: "Why did God make only one man when he could have made two?" The scholars respond: "Well, because if there had been two men, then a later man might have said, I am descended from man A, who is superior to man B." We are all

---

* **Shoah**: a name for the Holocaust suffered by the Jewish people at the hands of the Nazi regime during the Second World War.

descended from one man, a primordial Adam, and the Talmud goes on to say: "God created 'one' man so that you might know that who saves one man, also saves all of mankind, and when one kills another man it is as if he were destroying all humanity."

We all have a different face, but we are the same. We all descend from that primordial Adam and, for that reason, each person's dignity is important. No individuals exist who have greater or less prerogatives before God. We are all equal and each one of us is a treasure, something that we must care for and respect to the uttermost.

BERGOGLIO: I'm impressed by the fact that our dignity lies precisely in being children of God. He made us his creatures and Scripture consistently shows that he leads us as a father does his children. In the story of creation in Genesis, according to the Elohist* tradition, I'm moved by the fact that God made us by hand, in the way of an artist. The inspired biblical writer speaks of that artisanal attitude of fashioning us from the clay of the earth. Which is to say, the hands of God are involved in our existence. This is an anthropomorphism, of course, but there is an underlying message behind that artisanal task performed by God's hands. He made us not only with his word, but with something more, with his heart, with his love, with his hopes and expectations, I dare say. He placed his hopes in us.

SKORKA: The great difference between the God of the Bible and pagan gods is the matter of revelation. God reveals himself, he enters into a direct dialogue and, in the book of Exodus tells the people of Israel: *"You will be a priestly people."* A priest is one who serves God in some way. And how does one serve God? By telling everyone: "This is what God wants from man: to act justly, to work honestly, to respect the individual." I believe that in that conception is born the rationale for individual dignity, for the person in whom there is "something" of God, a breath of him, of a God that does not leave man nor abandon him, quite the contrary, God enters in a dialogue with man and gives him something celestial.

According to one midrash, the Torah existed before the creation of the cosmos. It is as if a father were to say to his son: "Here are the general instructions, but you have to interpret them, bring them to life. I am giving you the guide book. This is not an exhaustive list of instructions because you must read them and interpret

---

* **Elohist tradition:** This is one of the four sources used to write the Hebrew Bible, the Christian Old Testament. Its writers usually call their God by the name Elohim.

them. Do what you like, but within the frame of justice, dignity, and mercy."

FIGUEROA: I believe that in God's creation there is a passionate love, and that is not simply something that God was obliged to do. People are not simply objects he placed here on earth, amid nature, to amuse himself, to give them some instructions and afterwards, seated on a cloud, point out to them the things they've done wrong. Within his creation lies a deliberate passionate love, and that spiritual element of breathing his spirit into us is the most complete demonstration that he is filling us with his whole Being. He gives life, the breath of life, a full life, a life in relation to its Creator, but also in relation to other created beings. And here arises a question. Can that dignity given to us by God be blurred? Can it be diluted? Can it fade when man begins to draw away from his Creator and to live as if he had not been created by God? Can it fade when he begins to treat others as if they were objects, and not his equal brothers and sisters in creation? In what way does that essential dignity begin to blur in man and in humanity as he grows distant from his Creator and from the love of his fellow beings?

BERGOGLIO: Speaking for a moment in terms of soccer, one might say that man is capable of scoring goals against himself when he makes them at the expense of his own dignity.

We are children of God and one bastardizes that filial relationship, in some way, when he negotiates his dignity, something essentially non-negotiable, that thing to which his heart is attached, when he negotiates the mark of God placed on all of us. For me, dignity, the end of indignity, means being a child of God, a work infused with the spirit of God. And the death of dignity is the embracing of idolatry, when man makes room in his heart for idolatry. When his reference to God is increasingly distant and what takes shape is a only reference to himself, to the idol.

When the people felt bored waiting for Moses to return, tempted by the demon, they fashioned an idol for themselves. I find it significant that the idol was made from gold, or rather, the first way in which man sells his dignity is through his love of money. Man replaced God with an adherence to money.

Man's first step away from God is the adherence to measureless wealth which gives him a sense of security. But it gives a different sort of security which separates him from his initial God-given dignity. As this makes him feel strong he takes a second step, which is vanity; he feels satisfied with himself. The third step is pride, arrogance, and by that point idolatry is already well-installed in his heart, and that man has distorted the dignity of God. Nevertheless, out of pure mercy, God continues to sustain him, he does not cut him loose. It is the individual who refuses this dignity and says to God: "I do not want to be your child, I do not want this dignity, I prefer the dignity of money, my vanity, my pride, my 'self-referentiality,' etc." That's how I would define the human process of distorting dignity and moving to the side of idolatry.

SKORKA: This reminds me of a midrash that I enjoy citing which explains the Ten Commandments. It says that they are written on two stone tablets, five on one, five on the other, facing one another. The first four deal exclusively with God: *"I am the Lord your God, who brought you out of Egypt, out of the land of slavery. You shall have no other gods before me. You shall not take the name of the Lord your God in vain,"* etc. This includes the idea that when the Sabbath is mentioned, it is meant to remember God. Those first five commandments also speak of the honor one must show to their mother and father, who, along with God, give us life. And on the other tablet the commandments speak about the relationship of the Ten Commandments and the summary of faith and ethics: *"You shall not kill. You shall not steal. You shall not commit adultery. You shall not bear false witness."*

The midrash discusses the relationship of some commandments with others. Thus, *"I am the Lord, your God"* lines up with *"Thou shalt not kill"* because those that kill are essentially diminishing the image of God on the face of the Earth.

The human being is an individual; there is no idea that is worth the death of even one single man. Think carefully, even in extreme situations we must not forget that armies, wars, etc. are something harmful. We have got to seek paths of peace where each person is cared for by his neighbor. There can be no more wars. That is the ideal of the prophets: *"Beat your swords into plowshares."*

Everyone knows that the Hebrew greeting is *shalom*, which means peace, integrity. The biblical vision that we are analyzing must lead us towards that, which is common for us all. Even from a humanist perspective, because they received it through our tradition and adopted it into their humanism, beyond their agnosticism, and even beyond atheism. But this has to be what unites all those with whom we share the human condition. Without this, our human condition is depressed and does not exist as such.

BERGOGLIO: An expression of man's dignity is that God knows us by our name, he gives us a name; we are not a mass, we are not just a collection of beings, we are individuals. The word "individual" can sound badly to some because of matters about individualism, which can be a defect, a degeneration. But "individual" is not, in itself, a bad word, rather, it is the person with a name and with fundamental qualities that constitute them and their tendency towards truth, kindness, and beauty, that, in turn, forms a unity. That is the individual, it is to speak of a person with those tendencies, who is one and who bears a name. In the Christian tradition, in the Apocalypse, the book of Revelation written by Saint John, the Lord says: *"To whomever conquers I will give a new name."* This means your name will be renewed because it is what, in some way, differentiates people; it is unique. God says to us: *"I have called you by name because you are mine."*

In the story in the Gospel of Luke, when John the Baptist is named, the mother says: "Let him be called John." And they consult the father: *"But there is no one in your family named John! How can you give him a strange name?"* The name must have been very important, and his mother had to defend the reason why. In the Bible, the changing of a name always goes along with an increase in the mission that God gives to a person. The same thing happened to Abraham.

SKORKA: The name "Abram" etymologically would mean "Father of Aram," the place where he had been born; and "Abraham" signifies that he was going to be the father of many tribes, of many people.

Jacob's story also offers a very interesting example of changing a name. After they wrestle, the angel says to him: *"Your name will no longer be Jacob, but instead Israel because you have struggled with God and with the people, and you prevailed."* But, perhaps, we might see the name "Israel" in a different way. Jacob's name was explained because when he was born he was clutching his twin brother Esau's heel; nevertheless, the same word in its idiomatic root designates a person who does not act in a correct manner, a person who sometimes deceives. As Esau says, referring to his brother: "This one has now deceived me twice." But also we can understand his name as "he who was right in the eyes of God," because that name is given to him after he wrestles with the angel and after he faced his brother Esau. Talmudic scholars say that it was an angel from heaven that defended Isaac's interests. In a word, this is a profound self-criticism: "You will no longer call yourself by a name that can be interpreted as incorrect, you will call yourself the one who fights." The literal meaning of "Israel" is "he that strives with God" because after struggling with his brother they resolved their differences in an embrace. As it says in the book of Psalms: *"He did right in the eyes of God."* The name, biblically speaking, is very important. A person is not a number, something the Nazis tried to impose on their prisoners; each person has his or her own name.

BERGOGLIO: Unique and unrepeatable in the eyes of God, because there will be many named "Abraham," like you, or many named Jorge, like me, or many named "Marcelo" like Dr. Figueroa, but for God each person is unique and unrepeatable.

FIGUEROA: As you said, the name, from a biblical point of view, has a missiological focus. According to the biblical account, meaning was embedded in the mission that a person had in that moment in the history of the people of Israel. Also, each one of us has a mission in life and in the economy of God's time. And that makes our existence both dignified and passionate, because it takes us to a sphere in which there is no end to the fact of understanding that we bear the Creator's dignity. In the DNA of the Creator there is a creative vocation—a valid redundancy—of life, of development, and of vitality.

Living in agreement with the dignity of our Creator means understanding that we have to show his image in all the things that we do on our mission in life, without worrying if they are going to make a difference or not in the public sphere.

I am unique and unrepeatable, in the image of God who made me. I have a mission. What is it? How do I understand it?

SKORKA: That question is very difficult, and complex. We must ask ourselves, in what way do I dignify life; in what way do I respond to that dignity that life is giving me? In a word, this is also a question of education. In the measure which I receive, it is preparing me so that I can fully repay my fellow human beings that dignity with which they have honored me.

Now, the question is, knowing that I have to dignify life, how do I do it? The fact that someone asks this question is already very important. What do I do to dignify life? I am here for a reason, in the moment when we reach this conclusion we are already on our way, so to speak. This is the constant dialogue that each one of us must have at daybreak. What am I going to do today? Think ahead to however many years of full life with which God may wish to bless me: where am I going to place my emphasis? The essence is to ask oneself that question sincerely. I am here for a reason; God is going to help me. That is faith. God helps us to find that "something" for the sake of which we must dedicate our best efforts.

BERGOGLIO: Upon reformulating that question, one assumes the inherited dignity that the Lord gave him. God gave me this dignity of being his son. When I assume it, how do I transmit it? I'm going to phrase this a little more crudely, but it helps to make the point clear: how can I make this dignity contagious to others? What can I do to make another person feel worthy? By bearing it in mind in a dignified way.

It is worth the trouble to make dignity contagious, to treat people with the dignity that they have, even though they might be living in marginal situations that make them feel despised in the eyes of ordinary people.

Each morning, I can think about how to assume my dignity and make it contagious to others, and how to treat people with the dignity that is so often lost due to previous, unconscious, or now computerized discriminations in our daily conduct. It's about continuously thinking of those whom I am not dignifying.

SKORKA: We were educated with the idea of transcendence, of understanding that life does not end with our passing; and that existence, our own and that of all the cosmos, does not culminate in the moment in which our soul is separated from our body.

With the same religion there are distinct ways of seeing God, of approaching him, of feeling him and of expressing it; but the idea of moving forward together, walking and noting that our faces are not the same, just as our ideas are not. Nevertheless, there has to be something that is equal in us, an ethic, a respect. Here there is no room for doubt that we have to show ourselves to be in favor of the dignity of each individual, even those who, for different reasons, are found to be socially marginalized.

FIGUEROA: One can understand what we were talking about at first, that I am created by God, with living passion, and that he does not create me like other things, but rather that he shapes me and breathes his own spirit into me, making me an unrepeatable individual, with a name and a mission in life. But this human dignity, given by God, can be distorted when I draw away from my Creator or my fellow human beings. From an individual point of view, I can stain my dignity, and others', if I discriminate against, disqualify or devalue them. But, on the contrary, I can transmit it if I validate, dignify and look at the other person, as the Bible says, *"as greater than myself."*

If I seek to recognize the dignity of the other person and to see in him not only the image of my likeness or my fellow human beings, but rather the face of God: that act of love as I approach the other is contagious. And it returns to me, and it restores my dignity and the image of God within me.

3

Solidarity

Cardinal Bergoglio coined a phrase that he now uses to such a degree that it has become a trademark of his lifestyle: "Self-referentiality." He always uses it as an expression contrary to the humility that his sayings, signs, and actions proclaim.

Nevertheless, when he made a self-reference to a personal experience with a homeless woman, a person whom he referred to as one of "these everyday prophets that the Lord always sends us so that they impact us," all of us in the recording studio were deeply moved.

I believe that especially stirring incident allowed us to enter a unique climate of spirituality. After that moment neither the program, nor our personal vision of solidarity, was the same.

The Cardinal showed himself abundantly to be a shaper of theological opinion and, in this case, also a shaper of the spiritual environment. This is a gift few people have.

FIGUEROA: There is a great word, "solidarity." When one looks for its etymological root, one realizes that it comes from a Latin expression that means "something solid." In that way we understand that solidarity has to do with the collective construction of a solid cause, of something solid for the greater good.

Solidarity has many dimensions, some of which we're going to try to discuss, but it occurs to me that the discussion really begins with the idea of solidarity "within the home." In the first passages in the Bible we read about the rupture of family solidarity, with the fall of Adam and Eve, where God appears and questions Adam about what happened, and Adam answers: *"This is because of the woman you gave me."* And in the second place, the family solidarity between brothers is ruptured when the Lord asks Cain about Abel, and Cain replies: *"Am I my brother's keeper?"*

Solidarity is like a valuable family resource, but when it is broken it has consequences for all of society.

SKORKA: When I project the theme of solidarity into classic Hebraic terminology, two concepts come to mind: The concept of *tzedaka* and the Hebrew concept of mercy or pity. *Tzedaka* derives from the Hebrew word that means "justice." There are different ways to interpret the famous verse in the book of Proverbs [12:28] that says that *tzedaka* offers salvation from death. A personal way is when someone performs an act of kindness for their neighbor. That work transcends their life. Someone who saw that work surely will be inspired in other generations to realize additional works of kindness. But *tzedaka* also has to do with a rule of Talmudic law, a type of tax which is collected to help a person in need. In the Bible it says: *"You will have to help your brother who finds himself in a situation of indigence."*

Now, there is another concept, and that is mercy or pity. In one of its passages, the Talmud teaches us to distinguish between pity and *tzedaka*. The difference is that the latter must be performed with poor people, while pity or mercy with all people, with rich and poor alike; because the rich man can need the vital mercy that we are able to offer: patience, a listening ear, affection.

Solidarity, in general, begins in the family and must be projected outward towards all. It is an attitude that transcends these two concepts, that of the man who must learn to leave his egocentrism, his selfishness, aside. It is the attitude of the man who has become aware that God has placed him alongside his parents, upon the face of the Earth, for a specific mission: to plant goodness and try to be positive in each and every one of his actions. And he will never achieve that if he ignores his neighbor, as we read so well in Isaiah, one of the books of the prophets: *"You must not ignore your neighbor."*

BERGOGLIO: Yes, do not ignore your neighbor, do not be ashamed of your own flesh. These are words from Scripture that point to this line of solidarity. To give your heart to your brother, do not live inside your own "little world."

I believe, and sometimes I've said, that the man that does not have solidarity, who says, "I—me—mine—with me—for me," is thoroughly unevolved.

It's curious, but the lack of solidarity is also unaesthetic. When a person grows sleepy regarding the needs of others, he becomes closed off within himself. The others do not touch him and this goes on crystallizing. He simply does not take the other person into account, does not see him, and then begins to ignore and become ashamed of his own flesh. He lives as if he were an angelic flesh, different from the others. This is not a problem of social classes or sectors, but rather one of conscience and of opening the heart to the fraternity with which God created us. That is why, not ignoring your brother means not being ashamed of your brother's flesh, looking out for your brother's flesh.

I find myself very moved when Jesus describes what will occur in the final judgment: *"Because I was hungry and you gave me to eat, I was thirsty and you gave me to drink, I was sick and you came to comfort me, I was in prison, and you came to visit me, I was naked, and you gave me clothes,"* etc. And they ask him: *"When did we do this?"* And he answers: *"When you did so for the least of my brothers, so you did this for me."* This means that solidarity is a road towards human perfection and an approach to God. Behind this, obviously, was the concept that we are brothers, children of the same father. When we renounce solidarity in conduct, in some way we are renouncing that common lineage from the same Father. We are of another lineage, and that is something found within the first pages of the Bible, when we offer assistance to the orphan and the widow. In ancient times they did not have the systems of social assistance that the most developed societies have today. Back then, when a woman was widowed and had no one to take care of her, some brother or relative of the deceased, she lived outdoors, cast out, in the elements, at the mercy of public charity, and the orphan was helpless, too. The Lord points to the orphan and the widow, and says "Be compassionate! Take care of them!"

FIGUEROA: Joseph comes to mind: horribly abandoned by his brothers, who also commit the cruelty of saying to their father that Joseph had been killed by a wild animal. Joseph arrives in Egypt and we already know the story. There he holds a very important position until famine affects his family, and they come to see him without knowing that he is Joseph. There are two lines of solidarity, at least, in Joseph's attitude. First, he had a very important notion of public solidarity, because he thought about the people, about saving food for times when there would be none, and that is what saved Egypt from famine. But when he finds himself among his brothers who so cruelly abandoned him and sold him into slavery, he feeds them, he is compassionate toward them. There is something very profound in this solidarity that has to do with what the Cardinal mentioned to us about seeing the other as oneself, and of putting ourselves in his place. At the end of the book of Genesis, Joseph's brothers approach him and say to him: "Now that our father has died, you have all the right in the world to do with us what you like." And he answers them: "But how am I to take the place of God? The role of judge does not belong to me." And he pardons them. He is compassionate with regard to material things, but he is also compassionate with regard to spiritual matters, in the depth of his being, by offering his forgiveness. This is the second line of solidarity, and it has to do with the way the Cardinal mentioned, of seeing the other, of seeing the face of God in the other, of putting oneself in their place. In that moment, Joseph's brothers were in an extremely vulnerable position and Joseph, with all the possibilities of exercising power or vengeance, opted for a compassionate attitude.

SKORKA: With respect to the Bible stories about families, they are marvelous because they describe life in all its complexity, they hold nothing back. The authenticity that arises from the stories in the Bible is what transforms it into something so wondrous and valuable.

The cruelty that Joseph's brothers first showed was owing to his arrogance. There are no two ways about it, he was arrogant in and of himself and also because his father showed him special signs of favoritism since Joseph was the son of his beloved wife Rachel. That caused a certain problem which resulted in Joseph's being sold into slavery. What's interesting is when Joseph says to his brothers—I'll say it the way we would in Buenos Aires—"Boys, you did nothing to me. God sent me here so that I could help to satisfy the hunger and need for food that you were going to suffer during the famine. Don't worry, don't be afraid, we're brothers." And then he cries over Benjamin. However, this occurred after all of his suffering in the land of Egypt, before becoming the king's chief minister. At first he was very proud, but in Egypt they took away practically all his arrogance with what he had to suffer as a slave and, afterwards, while he was in prison. His brothers also learned their lesson. They were already in another stage of life, in that moment when one begins to understand what it means to be compassionate.

And those that already know what it means to be compassionate have got to have sufficient strength, intelligence and integrity to transmit that lesson to their children and grandchildren. This is basic.

BERGOGLIO: When I begin to care for my brother and stop letting him take care of me, I am permitting God to create a harmony between the two of us.

I worry when the harmony of solidarity between people is broken by any slogan or excuse, and what takes root are slogans like "with me or against me" or "one side or another." These words distort compassionate unity and cause anarchic decisions to spring up in men's hearts. Solidarity is a law that we carry imprinted in our vocation as children of God, in our flesh, and when we enter into that division it breaks that law. There is anarchy when one needs to position oneself as a man or as a woman attacking the other, and that causes solidarity to be broken.

And if in a nation we see people identifying themselves as individuals against others, what comes from this is the very essence of "anti-solidarity" which is anarchy, a position incapable of creating unity and enabling people to move forward together on the path of life. Factors outside our human nature, whether they be called ideology, rancor, or hatred, limit and define our behavior and do not allow room for that meeting between people.

I like to speak of that, I often repeat that idea about the culture of the encounter, because it is fundamentally compassionate in response to an anarchic culture of creating distances, abysms, and of devaluing the other. Creating a culture of bridges, with an outstretched hand, of seeking ties from philosophies and distinct points of view, but respectable ones. That's why I like the passage in Isaiah: *"Your brother's flesh"* is referred to as the most essential thing about us, about the person.

FIGUEROA: Some of our idiomatic expressions here in Argentina are so often repeated that we take them for granted, and assume that the words automatically impart the meaning they bear, but that's not true. We have always said that we Argentines are caring, compassionate people, and I believe that this is, in large part, true, but I have some questions about this.

Why do our people react generously and extraordinarily when there is a sudden, timely motivation, such as a flood, or an earthquake, etc., but we so quickly lose solidarity in the midst of daily life, like when we drive or when someone needs a helping hand? How do we take that occasional, *ad hoc* solidarity, and transform it into an everyday solidarity, that is lived out through small actions and events, in the things no one notices, in ways that are not going to appear in the newspapers nor in the media, but which make us brothers and sisters in the flesh, which bring us together and create an encounter, cure us, makes us believe and make us solid and whole?

SKORKA: The secret lies in what the Cardinal just said: there must be some type of harmony within our society.

It's true, there are sudden, occasional, temporary reactions that show an enormous feeling of solidarity, that prove that we have very important reserves of values of sensibility at an individual level, in a large part of the Argentine population. The problem that we suffer from is that we have not managed to establish a greater respect for rules that would demonstrate a greater harmony.

We've got to achieve a change in our culture, because all this that we're discussing is really a cultural question. Sometimes, as a society we don't know how to engage in dialogue. In order to be able to be caring and compassionate, the first thing we have to achieve is to establish a profound dialogue with our neighbor. We are beings composed of weak matter, flesh and blood, and only through education can we overcome this deficit. We have very great values, very good seeds, but what is needed is to water them so that they germinate in all their magnificence, and that we can become really that grand and glorious nation that our national anthem speaks of, putting aside all kinds of prejudices that sometimes make us demonize other people.

We have to learn to recreate our culture because, if not, we're not going to be able to be compassionate in the sense of helping our neighbor who needs to eat and get dressed, much less help him when what he needs is our warmth and affection.

BERGOGLIO: To teach solidarity! It's curious, the young people of our community are responsive to compassion; they are very sensitive. It seems to me that one of the doors to enter into a young person's heart is to offer a proposal of service, of solidarity. And I wonder: What is it that destroys that impulse in a young person? Precisely that which gives him an egocentric alternative, one centered on himself.

For me, what most destroys solidarity is ideology: it's what denies man in his complete being, flesh, soul and spirit. Ideological proposals always divide, they are "abyssal" (gaping holes) in human conduct. So then, to a young person who comes to us with a great internal uneasiness, we can present to him the path of service and solidarity, and make him believe in that, even without any religious content, because then the Lord will take charge of illuminating him. But I also have the other alternative, to give him an ideological proposal.

There are many ways of enclosing him within an intellectual ghetto that has all the explanations for the phenomena in the universe, but which lacks for him the base of solidarity, fraternity, the human part. It also gives the repetitive phenomenon of positions like gnostic ones, which are ideological, where the idea attempts to replace or supply the missing humanity. An idea, in and of itself, is not solidarity. One can talk about solidarity, but the meaning of solidarity is "putting all the cards on the table." Then, do you put your cards on the table, do you commit your life to service? You might, but what's needed is that the idea be incarnate in you.

Ideologies are gnostic in their manner, and in Christianity the first heresy that we confront is Gnosticism. Something that the Apostle John denounces directly because it is like the most cozy private refuge, a security fence that supposedly leads me to a type of abstract truth, and from that truth to an illumination. And the truth is flesh and blood, abstract truth does not exist. You discover the truth in the man that is the image of God, and from there one arrives at the truth. If one denies those things he remains alone with ideas, and then ideologies arrive and they create disasters.

SKORKA: I like the idea that exacerbated ideology acts like a brake in a man's relationship with others, because it makes me see my neighbor as "other" or "different," and not as someone like myself. What the Bible proposes is that we see the others as "others," as individuals with their own peculiarities, not absolutely similar to oneself but with the image of God that we all carry.

Historical examples show that when one ideology is transformed into an absolute truth it carries with it the antithesis of the compassionate proposition. That was true with Nazism, or fascism in general, and all the ideologies that create a false need to fight against someone that they demonize. Ultimately they both permit crime and justify it.

From the Judaic point of view, only God knows the one and only truth. The only one that is whole and complete is the one that knows about all things that are whole and complete: God himself. We can only know a part of existence. All those declarations or positions claiming: "This is the absolute truth and the one that does not believe in it is found to be in error!" give way to justified crime. The base of political or religious fanaticism, or fanaticism of any kind is: "This is the truth. I possess it. Those who think differently are infidels!"

The one who has an answer for everything and declares "I know it all" shows a lack of humility. The one who really knows science, knows how limited science is; the one who really speaks about religion, knows the very limited knowledge that we have about spiritual things and religious concepts. In general, the little that we know about our limited humanity is that we can reach another person, and the other can reach us.

FIGUEROA: Another element that worries me is the concept of delegated solidarity. We live in the culture of channel surfing, everything is television. One can see a horrifying image of what is happening in the world and simply say: "Poor people!" then change the channel and see something else totally trivial. We become hardened to suffering.

What I'm going to say in no way contradicts the NGOs, quite the contrary. I've worked for many years in an NGO, I've promoted social assistance, and I'll continue doing so. Nevertheless, there is something that can lead to not being compassionate, for example, when I provide supplies and in doing so transfer to another person the responsibility of helping. In that case, one doesn't really learn about solidarity, nor is solidarity built in my life, nor do I give an example of it. I can donate to an organization that is prepared and organized to offer help in a professional manner, but in no way do I exempt myself from the responsibility, from the benefits—I would add—of a compassionate action, and very much less from my responsibility of teaching about solidarity. Do we have, then, in some way, a scrawny, anesthetized, and impersonal form of solidarity?

SKORKA: It's a characteristic of the society we live in, and as much as possible, as educators, each person must do his part to change this situation. For example, to take kids to restore schools in underprivileged neighborhoods or to organize groups of women to help assemble clothing care packages; to make it possible that some of them travel to the interior of the country to see the extremely miserable living conditions in Pampa del Infierno, in Chaco Province, and in many other places where the living conditions are really painful. We set up our own network so that those supplies reach the ones who need them. We try to break that reality and we make the packets with our own hands. You have got to see the women, some of them elderly and, nevertheless, there they are and they're an example for the young people in my community, in the Belgrano neighborhood. Through many activities of this type we try, in a just way, to break away from that outsourcing of solidarity and compassion.

BERGOGLIO: When I have a spiritual dialogue with a person, I usually ask him if he gives alms. If he tells me he does, I ask him two questions, and it's curious how at that point most people hesitate: "When you give someone alms, do you look them in the eye?" After thinking a moment, most people generally respond: "No." And the second question is: "Have you ever touched the hand of the person to whom you give these alms?" And the answer is always: "No, I've never touched their hand." If I give someone a handout but do not touch them or look into their eyes, because I am doubtful in my giving, I fail to see the flesh and blood, the real person.

I want to relate a personal anecdote from around 1980, when I was the rector of the Máximo de San Miguel Theological School. One Saturday in the winter, in the afternoon, they called me from the front desk to tell me there was a woman who wanted to speak with me. I went to see her and she told me she had seven children, that she lived in a hovel, in a kind of shanty town that was about five blocks away, and that her children were cold and hungry. This really touched me, and I said to her: "Well, ma'am, let's do something about this, come on Monday when the Charities office is open and we'll give you something." That woman looked at me with sorrowful eyes, not aggressive, and with a mother's courage, she said to me: "Father, my children are hungry today, not Monday." I was filled with shame … And of course, I said to her: "Wait just a moment, ma'am," and I went to the pantry inside and I grabbed everything I could carry, including some blankets, and I took them to her and I said: "Come back on Monday." And it's curious, that woman kept coming to see me, and for me that memory signified a visit from the Lord who "slapped me awake."

We have to be careful that we don't get sleepy. The Lord always sends us these everyday prophets to "slap us awake" with a word.

FIGUEROA: I think that the Cardinal's story is sufficiently vivid and profound so as to leave us all thinking about solidarity, education, and inclusion. And about these prophets that God sends us to show us how we can build greater solidarity among families and societies.

4

Prayer

Those of us who participated in inter-religious dialogue took notice of the fact that Pope Francis mentioned Cardinal Walter Kasper in his first Angelus in St. Peter's Square. While the Pope's reference was to a book Cardinal Kasper had written, one concerned with mercy and forgiveness, it was one more sign that the encounter between different religious faiths was going to be, for the new Bishop of Rome, one of his apostolic pillars.

Cardinal Kasper is well known for his fruitful and valiant work as President of the Pontifical Council for Christian Unity, which he was personally responsible for extending towards the inter-religious universe.

On his stop in Buenos Aires, in September 2007, I happened to meet him at a barbecue at the Loyola Center in the suburban town of San Miguel. We had an extremely enriching and enlightening conversation about his current thinking, which until that moment I had only known through his books and lectures. I recall that I asked him directly what were, to his thinking, the paths which the ecumenical encounter should follow. He did not hesitate for a second; for him there were two things: prayer and the Bible.

Now I think that, thanks to his response, I did not hesitate in proposing that, for the third program in the series, we reflect together, through the Scriptures, on the subject of prayer.

FIGUEROA: The image of a person praying, even in a temple, with all that signifies, has a certain quality of mystery. For some, someone that seems to be talking to himself can appear ridiculous. But in terms of faith, that same mystery corresponds to one who is, in reality, undertaking a dialogue with God himself.

When one enters the Cathedral in Buenos Aires, he can read a sign in four different languages that says: "Silence." This reminds me of the meaning of the prayer of Mother Teresa. She said: "The fruit of silence is prayer. The fruit of prayer is faith. The fruit of faith is love. The fruit of love is service. The fruit of service is peace."

Individual prayer or the prayer of a community of people is not a photograph, it is an extraordinarily deep reality and, in some way, it is the genesis of a complete life that forges the links in a chain that leads to peace.

SKORKA: Various things you've mentioned appear in biblical literature. You said that speaking and moving the lips in a way that the voice cannot be heard is like speaking with oneself. This is exactly the painting that appears in the first chapter of the first book of Samuel when Anna, Samuel's mother, is praying in the temple so that she can have a son. The high priest that was there, Eli, confuses her with a woman who has drunk too deeply from the spiritual well.

Biblically speaking, prayer is central in the life of each individual. In Hebrew, there is a verbal form of the word "prayer" which refers to the realization of an action that is made, in a reflexive manner, about oneself. The form in Hebrew has, as a verbal root, three letters that signify "enter into judgment." There is also a place in the book of 1 Samuel, in which this verse appears: *"May the Lord be our judge and arbiter."* What does it mean to enter into judgment? It means "to judge oneself."

In order to be able to enter into judgment with God, one first must enter into judgment with oneself. Judging oneself, seeing the good that one does, is a very profound act of introspection through which one tries to feel God.

BERGOGLIO: It's true, because God also prays. Prayer is dialogical, a dialogue, not a monologue that one recites and which afterwards leaves no place for a response from the Lord. The response can be in that moment or afterwards, but fundamentally the attitude of praying consists of being open to a response. Whether I ask for something, or comment, or open my heart, but always I must be awaiting a response.

And if praying is, etymologically, "entering into judgment" with God, as you said so well, his response also enters into judgment with me. It is a dialogue of friendship, as Saint Teresa said, that consists of speaking of friendship within a frame of benevolence and mutual listening.

The prayer that does not listen is not prayer, it is a recitation, a meaningless formula. Prayer has got to have a space of silence in which sometimes nothing is understood, and at other times it seems that something happens, that the Lord says something.

Therefore, prayer does not begin and end with a rite that can be the cult of one's own making, a cultic ceremony, nor any of the ceremonies of Jews or Catholics or Evangelicals. Those are communal ways of opening up to the Lord, and he sometimes responds. But when one prays in a personal way and remains with an open heart in silence in the presence of God, he looks at me. I know that he looks at me, and I look at him and I expect a response to what my heart is saying. It is true, we pray and he also prays, because it is a dialogue.

FIGUEROA: In the dialogue between Abraham and God about Sodom, in chapter 18 of Genesis, there is a "bargaining" from Abraham when he realizes that God is going to destroy Sodom. Then, he converses with him and he asks him to spare the lives of the just ones, decreasing his unpersuasive arguments from fifty to ten people. This fascinating "negotiation" between Abraham and God is, in reality, a search, trying to understanding the one with whom he is speaking and what might be the character of his interlocutor. It seems to me that prayer also contains that intention; it is a search to understand God.

SKORKA: Speaking of "bargaining," I want to give a much stronger biblical example, in the figure of the third patriarch, Jacob. He is a very special personality because he had to struggle greatly with himself. That fight that he had with the angel, before being reunited with his brother Esau, was a fight, I would say, with the shadows of his past. He had to overcome himself so that the angel would at last say to him: *"From now on your name will be Israel."*

He was a man who was worried about his inheritance and his possessions. In a given moment he escapes from his brother Esau because he is scared that Esau is going to injure him or kill him. Then, having said goodbye to his mother and father, he leaves by himself and in solitude reaches a place that, according to tradition, is the Temple Mount in Jerusalem. There he dreams of a ladder that rests upon the earth and reaches up to touch the heavens. It is a tremendous dream. He sees angels ascending and descending; I think that it is the projection of his life. And suddenly, God speaks to him. Then, comes a direct "bargaining": *"ten percent of what I have will belong to you, God."*

I think that this is the challenge. The one who prays wants to discover himself and, sometimes, he feels the necessity of giving something in order to feel the presence of God close at hand. It is about the greatest motivation for prayer; to give meaning to daily existence and to try to feel God's presence.

BERGOGLIO: In the "negotiation" there is a placing of oneself—to force the expression—on almost equal terms with God: "Here we are, two people talking." I'm always impressed by the "haggling" between Moses and God, when the Lord, who is indignant, wants to destroy his people for idolatry and Moses convinces him otherwise; he tells him: *"'Look what the Egyptians are going to say: He led them out of Egypt only to deceive them and murder them in the desert.' You can't do that!"* In another part, when he says: *"If you do not pardon these people, erase me, too, from the book of life."* It is a "negotiation." The word that comes to my mind is *parrhesia*, the courage about which Saint Paul speaks so much.

To begin to do good works, apostolic works of evangelization, courage is needed. To pray one needs courage. If one doesn't have it, he doesn't pray well. The principal thing about courage is combining the expression, "I am dust and ashes," with the "negotiation": "I ask you, I put this problem to you." Courage in prayer consists of feeling that we are children speaking with our Father. It's the courage that comes from that relationship. Let's be clear about things. I remember once—I hope no one is shocked by this—that a woman was going through a very hard time because she had suffered a lot in life and had recently become a widow. And she said to me: "Father, there came a moment when I got angry with God and I gave him a piece of my mind." And I looked at her and she looked at me and she told me: "That's bad, right?" I answered her: "It's one way of praying, ma'am." Sometimes, like with our own dad, we get carried away and we say "exactly what's on our mind," and afterwards we say, "Well, I got carried away, dad." But there is a father's heart that understands what is behind that "piece of mind," that is not an insult, but an act of desperation that is looking for trust, to find out if the father will give him a hand. It's the courage of the son's prayer directed to the father.

SKORKA: You know that makes me remember when we first began to learn about the Shoah and I was starting my year of studies in Israel at the Hebrew University. At that time the British Mandate about Palestine was still in effect; it must have been in 1945. Everyone was rocked by the news of the Shoah, that a large part of the European Jewry, who were the heart of the Jewish people, had been totally exterminated. The president of the Commission that helped in the development of the University told an Hassidic* story: Once, after some Jews were massacred, a rabbi looked at the sky and shouted to God: "I'm not asking you why we suffer, the only thing I want to know is if we're suffering because of you, for your sake? And if all this serves you in some way." The only thing that can remain to us, the Jewish people, from those terrible times is the question: "Was this done for your sake?"

The act of praying, with its silences and its profound introspection, needs courage. I think that praying and seeking God with sincerity is an act that, in itself, indicates courage.

FIGUEROA: I find Solomon's speech at the dedication of the Temple, with all the people gathered round him, to be very moving. After several generations of building, they were going to dedicate nothing less than the extraordinary Temple, and Solomon begins by saying to God: *"This is in fulfillment of the promises that you gave to my father David, and now with all your people we are here prepared to dedicate this Temple."* And in one moment of the prayer it seems that Solomon realizes to whom it is that he's speaking, and suddenly it seems that "he is diminished" and he asks God, in front of all the people: *"Is it true that you are going to live here? All the heavens within the heavens cannot contain you, is this house that I have built for you with my hands possibly going to contain you?"* I think that there the prayer enters into a place where the attitude of the worshiper, in recognition of God with whom he is speaking, becomes extremely important. It can begin with a complaint or with a demand, but at some moment there must be some identification between the one who prays (the prayer) and

---

* **Hassidic:** Jewish religious movement of the seventeenth century that, from an epicenter in Ukraine, spread throughout all of Eastern Europe.

the one with whom he is speaking. I think that it's then that the prayer acquires a much more profound dimension.

SKORKA: The person who prays knows in every moment with whom he is speaking. But when he enters into a time of intimacy, suddenly he becomes aware and says: "Well, be careful, I have confidence but I have to step back because you are the Lord of the universe."

The blessings in Hebrew have a variation when they begin in the second person and end in the third person, for example: *"Blessed are you, God of the universe, you who have made all things ..."* and then it continues in the third person.

Someone developed a work showing that the God of the Bible has two characteristics. On one side, we say that he "Is," we speak of his sanctity, and on the other side we speak of his magnificence. These two things constantly play a dynamic role in the relationship of God with the people of Israel.

The same thing happens with Job in the middle of all his suffering. At first, he did not feel the terrible drama that he was going through, but afterwards he began to speak to God and he felt his presence in a way that was tremendously close. That dynamic relationship between man and God is one of the basic characteristics of the biblical God to whom we must pray.

BERGOGLIO: Prayer is also the way one surrenders oneself. One looks to the Father with courage, but deep inside is saying: "You are the Father, you are the one who rules, and I surrender." He finds the place where he needs to be. The two things go together, courage on one side, and surrender on the other. Saint Paul joins these two attitudes in action, in that healthy tolerance of the place that corresponds to a person when they stand in the presence of God. It is like a dialectic.

FIGUEROA: This happens to me when I tell a brother: "Pray for me" and afterwards he tells me, "You know, I remembered to pray for you," and then I feel that I don't bear this burden alone. The invitation from the Bible for people to pray for one another is a very important tool that we have as a community. Not only individual, vertical prayer (directed straight up towards God), but the prayer we make to God on behalf of others. Moreover, the liberating effect of praying for someone with whom I have problems, or with whom I do not get along, is extremely important.

SKORKA: What I would like to add to all this is the following. In Judaism the ideal of prayer is that it is realized in community. On one hand, the preparation that one has to make with oneself in the moment that he goes to the temple is extremely important. There, in the morning, we should not even greet one another effusively because we are going there for God; afterwards, yes.

When sometimes I'm asked why the ideal is that we pray in community, I respond that one sees the presence of the other, he feels it. The question is that it is not merely a selfish prayer; it begins with me but it must immediately continue with my neighbor, with the one I have next to me. Prayers have a singular, solitary moment, but the greater part must be plural. Prayer must lead us to feel brotherhood with our neighbor.

BERGOGLIO: I had a spiritual father who helped me very much in my prayer life. He recommended that each time I had problems with someone, with whom I had fought or who had done something bad to me, that I pray for that person. "Pray for him," he told me.

Prayer "cures" the bad feelings that we can have toward other people. It helps me cure myself of being a victim of those feelings, because when one harbors negative feelings in his heart, prayer goes about curing them and, in some way, also brings me closer to a brotherhood that is beyond the errors that might be inside me, or in the other. Healing prayer for the one who prays, and intercessory prayer for others.

I think of these words from Jesus: *"If you then, being evil, know how to give good gifts to your children, how much more will your heavenly Father give the Holy Spirit to those who ask him?"* Because God's abundant, overflowing goodness is such that we can ask of him as brothers, in community, and with insistence. In that aspect prayer is intercessory.

FIGUEROA: I think that a good exercise is to begin to pray for others and leave yourself for last.

Our petition takes on a more realistic dimension by including the vertical line toward God and the horizontal line toward my neighbor. In that contact with God, he makes me see in the prayer the true dimension of him and of my problems.

SKORKA: The very end itself of human history, in accord with the great prophetic mission, is that all people will go to Jerusalem, specifically, the idea is the Temple. And in that moment, God will judge the nations: *"And they will beat their swords into plowshares, and no one will train for war anymore."* A universal peace!

There are many who pray and, nevertheless, they cannot escape from their vicious circle; that means that sometimes there are errors in the prayer, instead of placing the neighbor first, one constantly puts oneself first with all ones needs, and even so thinks that they are praying with sincerity. I believe that the challenge is showing what it means to pray profoundly.

BERGOGLIO: Prayer is an encounter between man and God. From there comes the importance of showing and initiating other people in prayer. We were taught to pray by our grandmothers and our mothers. Today this custom has been somewhat lost, perhaps thanks to an exaggerated secularism or something that goes beyond the curative secularism, and which deprives young people from learning that language which is the doorway to transcendence.

I notice that our culture, our civilization is lacking this dimension of the human heart. We must initiate young people in prayer and teach them that there is a Father in heaven to whom they must turn, that he loves them and joins us all together as brothers. Teaching others to pray is one of the most important things that challenges us in this time, because it opens for them the path to an encounter with God, so that they can seek him and find him; that they allow themselves to be searched for and allow themselves to be found. I would conclude with an open question: "Am I worried about teaching prayer?" I think that when it comes to teaching prayer we are lacking.

SKORKA: It is something much more profound than the meditative action of praying. As it says in the book of Psalms: *"All my organs will speak to you, God, about the grandiloquence of all your being."* That is why, also, there are those who move their whole body when they pray, so that each one of their members that form the human body is vibrating for God.

FIGUEROA: I want to keep in mind that image that you have both described here at the conclusion. The need that we have of learning to pray, to teach others to do so, and of sharing the transcendent importance that praying to God has, not only for the individual person but also as a people, as a community.

5

Sexuality

This was our first filming session in 2011. It was very hot that afternoon, January 19, in Buenos Aires. The slow days of vacation time had inspired us to "step on the gas," and for that reason we came up with the idea of taping two different programs each time we met. At least for a time until, of course by mutual consent, we went back to one program per date.

Even though the chapters were recorded and then edited, we never filmed more than five or ten minutes of extra time, just enough to give ourselves a bit of extra margin in the editing. This meant that, in reality, our recorded efforts were similar to those televised live. It was a risk that we enjoyed taking because we were then assured of maintaining our freshness and the adrenaline of being filmed "without a net," without directorial cuts, or a broad margin for editorial correction.

In this first experience of double taping, the agreed-on themes were "Sexuality" and "Hope." We decided to take these up in that order. We knew that the theme of sexuality would not be easy, but it was inevitable that we take it up and treat it like any other, without self-censure or easy shortcuts. The feeling in the studio was perceptibly different, perhaps because of facing the expectation that we were ready to discuss a subject with certain taboo aspects. Among the three of us it was entirely the opposite. During the discussion we breathed a relaxed and empathetic atmosphere. I trust that the reader can perceive it throughout the following pages.

FIGUEROA: Independently of how we interpret the biblical text, the story of the creation of man is central. There we read that God creates man in his image and likeness, with an identity as a person and with a sexual identity. Then, God considers his creation and concludes that it is not good for man to be alone. So he makes him sleep and, according to the Bible story, extracts—and I emphasize the term "extracts"—from the man's own flesh, from his own being, what he is going to use to create his companion, his equal, woman.

When man awakens from his dream, God introduces him to the woman—I think that the creation of the companion that God gives to the man surpasses any dream that he could have had. The Bible story narrates what the man said: *"The truth is that this is indeed flesh of my flesh and bone of my bones, she is the companion that I need."* And God tells them: *"Well, you will be united and you will be one single flesh."* Once again the term "flesh" appears as both identity and union of body; and immediately, the biblical text clarifies that they were unclothed, but they had no shame whatsoever. Their sexuality was perfectly fine.

I permit myself to make this clarification promoting, in some way, my point of view, that the sexuality of men and women is something beautiful, a precious invention of God. Sexuality is a gift from God to the human being and, far from what many believe, that original sin consisted of something that had to do with sex, is not so. Original sin came later and had to do with their disobedience of eating from the tree which God had forbidden them to eat. That fall, that has nothing to do with sex, causes man to be degraded in all his identity and image. He is degraded in his identity as a person, as an individual, as a man in the image of God, and also in things related to sex.

SKORKA: The problem of sexuality is complex. Undoubtedly, from the Judaic point of view it is good and wonderful, so much so that it is used as a paradigm of the relationship of love that there must be between God and the people of Israel or, generalizing, the relationship of love between God and man. An example of this is found in the Song of Songs.

But it is a complex subject because in the Bible story, after mentioning that they were naked and that they were not ashamed of it, a very special element enters the picture: the serpent. Many exegetes interpret that as the instinct towards evil, something that is, at the same time, tied to sexuality.

In a paragraph of Talmudic literature, where it is defined what a man is, it says that he has three angelic characteristics and three animalistic characteristics. Like the animals, we feed, we reproduce, and we realize our necessities. In a word, in those ways, we cease to be a superior mammal. But from the angels we have the capacity of analyzing and of having knowledge or understanding. And the third point of similarity between angels and men is that man speaks the language of holiness. From a literal point of view this can be understood as Hebrew, but I prefer to interpret it in a totally broad sense. Man finds himself between two poles and from that place he has got to work. On one hand, he has animal instincts and on the other hand, he has the possibility of greatness. He must work ardently so that his instincts are in an equilibrium that permits us to discover a dimension of spirituality.

Sexuality is a beautiful thing, it is something wondrous, but we must be careful, while we learn to make use of it, in linking it to a very profound sentiment. In the moment in which I utilize sexuality, or any other instinct, only for the pleasure of satisfaction, I am pushing aside the three angelic conditions and I am only clinging to the animal characteristics that I possess.

BERGOGLIO: Each time a married couple love one another and express their love through sexuality, they sanctify one another. It signifies giving oneself freely to one another before the God that sanctifies; and here the word "sanctity" is key.

In the creation story, when man and woman have got to come together sexually, they are the image and likeness of God. It is not man who projects the image of God, but both the man and the woman equally. And there, in the same cell of the conjugal union is the image of God. This is like a mystical dart thrown at us from the start of the creation story. Humanity must always remember the fact that the woman as much as the man, both of them, are made in the image of God.

What I like very much from the story in the Bible is that Adam first dreams her and then meets her. The relationship between the man and the woman who are going to arrive at the consummation of their love in the sexual act, follows a path of dreams—speaking poetically, using the words of the Bible. Or rather, they seek to know one another, they dream about how the other will be and by dreaming they manage to discover themselves.

Once, having a conversation with you, Rabbi Skorka, you spoke to me about the adventure of the man trying to decipher the woman and vice-versa, that adventure that they begin in marriage and that consists of understanding each other every day. For that reason, the presence of the serpent in the biblical text is, perhaps, one of the most hotly contested points throughout the course of civilizations. To degrade sexuality one always attacks the most important thing: the image of God, the union between the man and the woman in marriage.

SKORKA: The idea of "deciphering" is a modern concept, but in essence what I did was to modernize a biblical term. The literal translation of the sentence: "And Adam had relations with Eve, his wife" is "And Adam knew Eve, his wife." One really only manages to know another person in the moment in which they love them.

When the scholars of the Talmud tried to find a term for "marriage," they used the terms "sanctity" and "consecration." To consecrate is also to choose; when someone consecrates to God something that they have, they choose the best. It is an act with projection and transcendence; this also happens in the union of the man with the woman.

FIGUEROA: When God says to the man and the woman: "You must be holy because I am holy," this is a mirror of the creation of man as an image of the Lord. The word "holy" also has to do with something set apart, something that is different, not in order to live outside of reality, but rather in order to live in a beautiful way, a very special way.

There is a conjunction of elements upon which it is very important for us to reflect, that has got to do with sexuality from the biblical point of view and with our conception of faith that, far from negating sexuality, exalts it and sanctifies it as God wishes it to be and as man needs; so much so it is that the sexual part is something complete and complex. It involves our whole being, including our soul. Saint Paul says clearly that the soul is involved in the sexual act along with our mind and our body. The sexual union of man and woman carries with it a great many forms beyond just the genital act. I think that one of the great frustrations, in terms of current human sexuality, is produced when we reduce it simply to a genital instinct.

SKORKA: If we transform what is sexual into a purely and exclusively genital question, what happens is that two people find each other, but it becomes a completely and absolutely individual act where each person wants to satisfy his own imaginary sexual self; this is not a loving dialogue.

There should be a dialogue of love which will be expressed with caresses, kisses, and in the union of the bodies, but that union should be the result of a profound encounter between a man and a woman. When everything is reduced to a purely genital question, there really is no encounter; each person will seek their own satisfaction in a tremendously selfish reality.

In the moment when I objectify someone, I am using them for my own advantage, to satisfy my need for what is purely and exclusively instinctual. In some way, our instinct is also nourished by all types of experiences in order to manifest a profound sentiment, a "something" that elevates me in my human condition through the love that I offer, through the care that I have for the other person, through the affection that I give them and by following the same path together in life. It is reductionism to think that as long as the two partners or individuals satisfy their libido they will be together and, on the contrary, they will separate.

BERGOGLIO: I think that one of the serious crises of civilization, and I don't mean of the current civilization because in one way or another this has occurred in various historical periods, is the objectification of sexuality; the sexual nature as one more object of consumption.

I remember that when I studied in Germany, once a week there was a newspaper with an enormous supplement for tourism, and there were various companies that advertised sexual tourism, including with minors. Sexuality as an object of consumption.

Throughout history, this has been seen when women have been used as an object of pleasure in harems or in chains of brothels. When we see some advertisement that show a scantily clad woman striking suggestive poses to sell toothpaste, one thinks that behind this is the idea of exploitation; the use of the human body for the purpose of marketing. The word "sexy," which is used a lot today, is one of the most "successful" expressions in what is referred to as the exploitation of sexuality.

SKORKA: The biblical proposition is very strong and poses an enormous challenge.

The book of the prophet Hosea shows the life of a man betrayed by his wife. God takes that drama from the man, or perhaps it's nothing more than a metaphor, to compare it with his sorrow with respect to the prostitution of the people of Israel, in the sense that they are not faithful to him. And in Hosea there appears a very strong verse that goes like this: *"I will betroth me to you forever."* This is what God says to the people of Israel through the voice of the prophet. And what are the conditions of this marriage? To practice piety, justice, mercy and rectitude. When Maimonides speaks about the laws of contrition and considers the highest, most excellent form of reaching God, he says: "Seek God with the same zeal as you have sought the woman with whom you have fallen in love."

One of the basic things of any culture consists of finding a precise definition of sexuality. I totally agree it is something marvelous that we have got to express in the highest manner, and it has got to involve not only the instinctual part of us, but also something more that in that moment permits me to know that I really am in the presence of God.

FIGUEROA: Rabbi Skorka mentioned the Song of Songs, of which I accept the allegorical interpretation that it has to do with the relationship between God and his people. Nevertheless, I allow myself to think that it is a beautiful poem about nuptial love. Someone that has never read the biblical text can be surprised and ask: "How is it that this is in the Bible?" Because the text talks about an amorous relationship, including the relations before sex, of the longing for the encounter with the other. The Song of Songs ends with a very beautiful poetic phrase—it is all written in poetry—that sums up, in a way, the whole book: *"The rivers cannot quench this love, nor can all the sea extinguish this love; and if someone offered me all the gold in the world to buy this love, they would only receive laughter in return."* Then that book turns out to be a song of nuptial love that exalts married sexuality in a way that is very beautiful, very poetic, very careful, and it culminates all this within love. Changing the axis of the subject, and outside of this sphere of love, it is common that sexuality is interpreted as an experimental search where the sense of sex is found in the measure in which people try out different types of sexual experiences. Then, on the one side, is the love that we mentioned, and on the other is found this concept in which the search for things sexual follows the path of experimentation.

SKORKA: With respect to the Song of Songs, I totally agree: they were canticles of love from a man for his beloved and vice-versa. In a given moment, the Talmud tells us, when the sages were analyzing how to form the biblical canon, there was a wish to exclude the Song of Songs. And the greatest scholar, the Rabbi Akiva, said to them: "God makes us free from having to hide the Song of Songs, because if all the hagiographies, all the writings, are sanctity, the Song of Songs is the sanctity of sanctities."

The Song of Songs reflects the love between God and the people of Israel, but it is offered as a paradigm of total, absolute love. In Judaism, in the Bible, and in what is learned from the Song of Songs, there is no division between the soul and the body, and man and woman are one.

Now, I'm going to the last question. Do we have free will? Yes, of course we have free will, because it would make no sense for us to be given laws and rules if everything were already determined, stipulated, and programmed as if we were all machines.

Our belief, to continue citing Maimonides, is that we have a free will and rules that appear in the Bible. In such a way that we are always faced with a dilemma: How do I want to live? Do I want to live and dignify existence? Then I am not going to steal, or kill, or destroy, nor am I going to test the idea that hurting another person is evil. There are things that I cannot try "just to see if I like them or not." There are sexual attitudes that our culture—I do not restrict myself to the Bible, I speak of culture in general—tells us are not correct. If someone prefers it, he can refer to certain sexual attitudes with the term "abhorrent," questions that have to do with sadism, with masochism, with death, with playing tremendously dangerous games to achieve some superlative sexual satisfaction. That is terrible, it is something that degrades the human being. In the moment when there is no love in a sexual relationship, and the other person becomes a thing, I am degrading them and I am degrading myself. Putting the Bible aside, let's consider what Levi Strauss or Freud say: that all culture is born in the moment when certain sexual rules are put into place. In the moment when I can experiment and do whatever I feel like, well, I am engaged in expressing a totally anti-cultural attitude.

BERGOGLIO: The phrase "whatever I feel like doing" implies a core attitude of self-satisfaction, precisely because it is self-referential. It has a selfish reference, completely contrary to love which is otherness and is a search for the other person.

I usually say to the bride and groom, during the wedding ceremony, that God made us so that we need each other and also that we "knead" each other. What do I mean by that? That the man has to help his wife become more of a woman each day and she has to help him become more of a man each day. And I highlight for them the idea of otherness, the personal sacrifice of always taking into account the other person. If the two of them have this sense of otherness, that love is wonderful.

To nourish new forms of satisfaction is self-referential, pure narcissism. Hedonism is a form of narcissism. Experimenting is a caricature. It is curious because evil—in the case of Catholic faith, the demon—always proposes to us transgression with a caricature of divinity: *"If you eat from that tree, you will become like God."* It makes a caricature, but in a selfish way.

The word "experience" is a caricature of the biblical word "to know." The biblical "knowing" goes much farther than mere experiment. Experimenting consists of a departure and a return; by contrast, knowing implies a departure and searching, searching, searching ... Experimentation brings immediately the harvest of satisfaction, self-reference. But knowing launches us forth into an adventure—in the rich sense of the word—life's grand adventure. In marriage, knowing one another mutually is the great adventure of the life that ends in the other, it is not a selfish harvest.

The headlong, unrestrained permissiveness that consists in making the genitalia the focus of the sexual life, or that menu of options to experience new things in a profoundly selfish, narcissistic, and self-referential way, has nothing in common with biblical notions of love or "knowing."

FIGUEROA: Man was created in the image and likeness of God in order to have a full, complete life in which sex is lovely within that conception and love has a fundamental role, as a guide, and where commitment is also involved. There is no place there for selfishness because I have to give myself fully to the other person, nor is there place for the banal experience of experimentation, because it would be like buying worthless trinkets.

In God's purpose, the search for full happiness, for men and women today, consists simply and fully in searching for what the Creator did in order for us to be happy, including in our sexuality.

6

Hope

"Why should I despair? Why should I worry? I have placed my hope with God, whom I shall continue to praise. He is my God and my Savior!"

Psalm 43:5

"Even if I knew that the world should crumble tomorrow, I would still plant my apple tree."

Martin Luther

"Never deprive someone of hope; it might be the only thing they have."

Mother Teresa of Calcutta

FIGUEROA: The biblical prophet Habakkuk, having lived through a very anguishing situation, both in his personal life as well as politically and religiously, culminates his account with a hopeful reflection. Without quoting exactly, he says, more or less: *"I am going to place my hope in the Lord. Although the fig tree may not flower, although the vine may not give fruit, although no olives come from the tree, although we may have no cows, although there may be no sheep, I will still delight in God. I am going to place my hope in him, I have hope."*

In some way, he is framing a very important element of hope that does not reside so much in what I see or in what I possess. Instead, I find its plenitude when I place my hope and trust in God. As the tango says: "Even though I don't even have yesterday's hay, drying in the sun," I'm still going to place my hope in the Lord.

The theme of hope is a great subject, because there are many people without hope, probably because we have become accustomed to place our hope in things that are unworthy of our expectations, and we have not placed our hope in something that is worthy of our expectations.

SKORKA: The prophet Habakkuk, at the beginning of chapter 2, along with the attitude of having hope and faith, ends a paragraph saying: "*The righteous man will live by faith.*" This text is considered by Talmudic scholars as one of the best definitions of the meaning of faith in Bible.

Having faith means fighting for an ideal, and all fighting for an ideal means following it and working to achieve it. Further, the very fact it being an ideal means that it will surely always be unreachable.

In Hebrew, the word "hope" means waiting for something to happen, hoping that something will occur, that it will materialize and be transformed into reality. This brings to mind chapter 37 of Ezekiel. After the destruction of the Temple in Jerusalem, Nebuchadnezzar seized many Israelites, and took them away into Babylonian Captivity. Before a valley strewn with bones, God says to the prophet: "*Do you know what these bleached bones are that you see in this valley? The whole house of Israel. Tell the people of Israel that to these bones and remains of dried corpses, I am going to attach tendons, I am going to stretch skin and I am going to transform them into living beings. I will call them forth from their graves and I will take them to the land of Israel.*"

Hope, evidently, has to be grounded in an idea, and in our case it has got to do with God. The expectation of God's manifestation in human reality is, in one way or another, something we have in common. For Christianity it is the Second Coming, the revelation of the Son of God, and for us it is about a king of flesh and blood, because the Messiah is nothing more than a descendant of King David. That is what differentiates us from Christianity, but the interesting thing about the question is that from a simple, straightforward point of view, what unites us is a hope that tells us that a world with a much stronger, more significant presence of God is really possible, and is not merely a dream.

The return to Zion and the reconstruction of the Second Temple in Jerusalem realized by Ezra and Nehemiah shows us that hope does not mean standing around with our arms folded without doing anything. We must act, work, and be committed so that we move closer to all those hopes we're awaiting. It means having a great ideal and working towards it, not thinking that all those things will simply happen by themselves. There is a Hebrew saying: "We cannot base ourselves on a miracle." This means that someone that needs something cannot say: "God help me" and then sit there waiting for it to happen. Hope consists of working for something while trusting that God is also going to help us.

If we want to transmit that hope, we also have to work with our children and tell them: "I don't know if I'm going to manage to realize such a dimension of spirituality, but at least take the challenge upon yourselves, know that it was a challenge for me in my life. And if I failed, it doesn't matter, you should accept this challenge."

BERGOGLIO: Recently, I don't remember where, I read something that went more or less like this: "The present moment is not the only thing our parents gave us, but also what they lent to us so that we can return it to our children." Living with hope consists of looking to our parents, who give us a whole tradition, a trajectory, and to look to the children of the next generation, to whom you have got to give that same trajectory.

But also, hope is a human attitude that ranges between inheritance and utopia, because it is something both beheld and launched into the future. It has a utopian dimension. What kind of utopia? One that is merely nominalist or ideological? No, an historic utopia. In our Judeo-Christian concept, hope has an historic utopia that is rooted in God's sworn promise. *"And Abraham believed,"* and because he believed in that promise, even in the moment when God asked him to sacrifice his promised son, as Saint Paul says: *"And because of Abraham's faith, God counted him as righteous."* He believed and stayed hopeful against all expectation.

God's oath and promise frame our utopia. It's not a typical gnostic or new age kind of utopia, it's an historic utopia that launches us forward, bearing an inheritance that we must make flourish and give to our children in a better condition than we received it.

A hopeful utopia that is seen in the slavery which we experienced in the past century, with men and women of faith who, when faced with an atheistic statism, transmitted their faith to their grandchildren and saved it, because they hoped that the Lord would change their situation. Or harder and more sorrowful still, those men and women who, when they entered the gas chambers in the Nazi death camps, were reciting the Shema Israel Adonai.*

Believing, in spite of everything, including knowing what is going to happen to us; believing that the sworn promise will be fulfilled.

The Judeo-Christian hope consists of launching towards the future from an unmovable base that has historically proven to be well and deeply rooted.

FIGUEROA: Through my contact with the biblical ministry I learned the story of a Russian bishop. Already very old, and after decades of silence, he was permitted to officiate at a Christian service, and so they invited him to give a sermon. To the surprise of those present he preached with the fluidity and clarity of someone for whom no time had passed since his last homily. When they asked him about his secret, he answered: "All these years, each Sunday, I prepared my sermon as usual, even knowing that I wouldn't deliver it, but with the hope that the day would come when I would finally be able to offer it. Now I have sermons enough to last until the day I die."

Hope is a fundamental catalyst. It is one of the three primary theological virtues that Saint Paul mentions, along with faith and love. The Bible says that Hezekiah was the greatest king, and that there was none greater, neither before nor after. Perhaps due to the historic circumstance that it was his lot to live through, his reign shows evidence of great hope. As a leader of his people, he had the courage to destroy the bronze serpent, which was an historic element from the time of Moses, and a fundamental symbol of the popular faith. Nevertheless, he realized that this symbol also presented an obstacle to real hope, because instead of worshiping God, the people began to worship the serpent. So, this brave act of his provides two very strong messages of hope. One is that we can have a hope that appears convincing but in reality is not, like the serpent. The other message is that a genuine hope, which leads us to the realization of utopias, must be based on fulfilling the law of the Lord.

---

* **Shema Israel Adonai:** Reference to Deuteronomy 6:4: "Listen, Israel, the Lord is our God, the Lord is One." Later, with the inclusion of other fragments from the same book (4–9 and 13–21) and Numbers (37–41) it became one of the principal Jewish liturgical prayers.

SKORKA: The Talmud asks: "Can a serpent give life? Can a serpent resolve questions about life and death, or even distinguish between them? No, when they raised their eyes they remembered God, and then there they overcame the venom of the serpents."

The same thing happens in the war against Amalek related in the book of Exodus. As long as Moses raised his hands, the people of Israel prevailed on the battlefield. For that reason Aaron and Hur held up his hands. And the Talmud asks: "Are the hands of Moses capable of resolving what happens on the battlefield? No, when they raised their eyes they did not see his hands, they saw God."

Our hope does not have to consist solely in saying, "We are going to succeed … from the technological point of view," but rather in, "We are going to reach what is spiritual, and technology is going to help us." It has to be a hope rooted in two aspects: on the one hand, in matters technological, the current state of affairs; and on the other hand,—and this is the most important one—in my commitment to the human condition. What destination do I want to reach? What am I working towards?

On the other side, we see individual hope, in overcoming an illness, for example. Something that occurs at another level, of course, and in which the concept of hope is supremely important. The human being is a psycho-physical unity. We recognize how we privilege the psychic over the physical, but the goal must always consist in the hope that God will help me. Returning to the general concept, you have always got to see what that goal is. The Bible gives us the goal; a world of peace, of understanding and integrity; a world where man works from day to day, establishing, within the imperfection of the human being, a certain ideal.

BERGOGLIO: I would venture to say that today our world, in general, finds itself disenchanted and at a loss for hope. For that reason men fabricate "hopes," temporary enchantments, utopias of some kind, nominalist, gnostic or some other type. When one lacks a consistent utopia, one becomes disenchanted and seeks a thousand and one enchantments and diversions for the purpose of distraction, and this leads to madness. One seeks—we can say—things that amuse him along the way, to pass the time, temporary "amusements" that are here today and gone tomorrow, but which are endlessly replaced by others, in endless succession.

It's sad to see when the human heart is not open to receive real hope, founded in a sworn promise from someone whose word is irrevocable. When this happens, man resorts to those idolatrous forms of enchantment, small idols that one creates, sets up, and later abandons, because they do not satisfy us or fill us up inside, they only entertain us for a short while.

One must know how to distinguish between what is an enchantment, and what is the enchantment of a great hope that leads you to overcome the present moment, to take what you already received and hand it over to your children.

FIGUEROA: I also think that utopia is lost once a person falls into immediacy. Nevertheless, faith can contribute to escaping from this immediacy, from this desperation.

SKORKA: From a cultural point of view, immediacy is a wonder, but if we don't know how to regulate certain things well, it can become tremendously harmful. On the other hand, what's the source of desperation? This is linked not only to this question of immediacy, but also to the subject of frustration.

BERGOGLIO: Hope is, in this last instance, a gift from God. On our own we can only realize small hopes, but God made us creatures of expectation, we are constitutively expectant.

Rabbi Skorka spoke of frustration. Frustrations test man's expectant and hopeful dimension. The author of the biblical letter to the Hebrews tells us: *"Cling to the hope that is proposed to you. Cling to it because hope is an anchor that we already have grounded on the other shore."* That dimension must not be lost. The anchor is already fixed on the other shore, so cling to the rope! It is a hope that does not deceive; it never deceives.

I recall the passage in Job 19 when he, covered in sores, having lost everything, in his utter dispossession says: "I know that my redeemer lives and that on the final day I will see him, with my own eyes I will see him." Amid the greatest despair, he does not lose hope; it consists of knowing that God lives; in having memory and seeing the anchor we have fixed on the shore of hope. Because hope does not deceive.

7

Suffering

One afternoon, a few blocks from the train station near my house, a man stopped me in the street and, respectfully said to me: "You don't know me, but I do know you, and I need to thank you for something very important." I didn't have time to ask him what it was about and thank him in return, because he continued: "I lost my wife to a serious illness ten years ago. All this time I was angry with God, and I couldn't understand the reason for so much suffering until I saw the television program you did with the Rabbi and the Cardinal. Since then I've been at peace. Thank you so much!" I forgot the words I said to him, but I remember that I embraced him, and because of this man's personal story I felt a deep connection to him.

Not long afterwards, I shared this story around the table with Cardinal Bergoglio and Rabbi Skorka. All three of us were quite moved, and we agreed that this man who had found peace in his soul more than made up for the challenge of creating this program and, perhaps, the whole series.

The program in question is the one presented in the following transcription: "Suffering." God is good!

FIGUEROA: Unless you see life from a masochistic point of view, nobody desires suffering, nobody wants to suffer. Nevertheless, suffering does form part of life. Just as life cannot be understood without death, well-being cannot be understood without suffering.

From the biblical point of view, suffering for its own sake is not a virtue. At the same time, one cannot expect life without suffering. One cannot expect that it will suddenly vanish forever, and that God is going to do something magical to transform us and eliminate that basic aspect of life. Conceiving of life without suffering denotes a false biblical theology.

When we accept that suffering forms part of life, we see that the heart of the matter lies in determining the right attitude to take when facing it. I can become depressed or angry or, on the contrary, see the suffering as something instructive for my life, a teaching that leads me to grow as an individual and raises me up a few steps higher in my spiritual life, steps I would not have climbed before or without that experience of suffering.

BERGOGLIO: If we consider life from an ascetic perspective, the negation of suffering can lead us to think about a life without suffering, but life is not ascetic.

Life is a path that presents us with situations, junctures, risks, sufferings, fatigue and all the eventualities of a journey, but also offers its own share of lovely moments. If one conceives of life as a path, the suffering is already there as a part of it, lying in wait; although I'd prefer to not conceive of it as a "bogeyman" or as some punishment prepared for us, because that would be a static vision of life.

Suffering occurs because we are moving through history and there, amid the diverse occurrences, arise situations of suffering, illness, death, and war; the thousand and one situations of suffering that one endures at times, without having to go beyond their own awareness.

SKORKA: Suffering is a very broad subject that covers the whole spectrum of life. We cannot talk about a specific kind of suffering. Many years ago, when I studied the book of Job and I came to the verse that says: *"Man was born to travail."* "Travail," of course, means painful labor, and in this verse it can be interpreted as meaning "suffering."

Suffering is not only when we suffers from a specific illness or something that prevents us from living a normal life, there is also enormous spiritual suffering; there are people whose suffering increases the more they have of everything, from the material point of view.

To speak about suffering is to speak of something that accompanies us throughout life, something inherent to and indissoluble from existence, precisely because its forms part of existence.

I'd like to mention some characteristic Judaic perspectives on suffering. The greatest of the Talmudic scholars—Rabbi Akiva—used to say that everything that God does, he does for good; thus, it's important to face suffering from the point of view of faith. In Aramaic the phrase would be: "The Merciful One does all that he does for the sake of good."

Rabbi Akiva tells how one night, in search of an inn to spend the night, he arrived at a town on horseback, carrying a lantern. However, he did not find the inn, so he settled down to camp out in a field. Then, his horse ran away into the darkness, and his lantern went out. And while all this was happening to him, he was thinking: "God knows. Everything he is doing is for the good." This was during the time of the Roman occupation and persecution, so there was a Roman garrison stationed there in that town. If the soldiers had seen or heard the animal, or if they had seen this scholar's light, he would have been arrested.

Another teaching from the Talmud says that in the same way that we must bless God for some good news, and say "Blessed are you, God, you who do what is good for the sake of greater goodness," we must bless God when things do not go well. As when, in the cemetery, the kindred of the deceased tear their clothes and say: "Blessed are you, God, who judge in truth."

This is a question of the fact of suffering and still having faith to keep moving forward; of knowing that suffering is an inherent part of our existence and that we cannot separate ourselves from it in any way. Life is not always a bed of roses.

BERGOGLIO: When Rabbi Skorka talks about accepting the blessing of suffering and the blessing of all things that come with life, he's not talking about blessing what is bad or evil, it is a question of blessing the Lord who permitted all these things to come to pass.

The two men in the Bible who are prototypes of suffering are Job and Tobias. At one point, Job's wife says to him: *"Bless God and die."* But in this case, "bless" is a revision of some translations, because what she's really saying is *"Curse God for these things he sends you."* Nevertheless, Job does not curse God.

And Tobias, after going blind became "half-crazy," because he was an active man who took care of his people and who buried the dead Jews killed by the Babylonians. His wife also reproached him: "*What good do all these good deeds do for you? Curse God and be done with it.*"

Through the figures of those two women we see the human temptation of rejecting the importance of suffering, of refusing to understand it in a positive way, of giving into frustration and the desire to curse life in the midst of sorrow rather than to bless it. "Blessed are you, Lord, even for this, for you know why this is my lot in life." The first temptation in the midst of suffering is to not offer thanks and praises, but instead to reject and curse.

I remember when I was young, I must have been about thirteen years old, during a very special, festive situation there was a sudden death in a family that was very close friends with my own. When we went to their house to express our condolences—only an hour or so after this had happened—one of the family who met us at the door, complained: "How can people say there really is a God!" In the face of some truly momentous suffering, because it had destroyed a moment of happiness, a family holiday, the first temptation was to curse God for what had happened.

Many people have this experience, and it leads to these common responses: "Why does God allow this to happen?" or "If there really were a God, this would never happen!" Or what Dostoevsky wrote: "Why do the children suffer?" Personally, that question, especially, touches my soul.

FIGUEROA: In some way, what underlies these thoughts we're sharing is God's role amid the suffering, and the real meaning of his sovereignty in the face of a person's suffering.

In general, when experiencing suffering we tend to question God: "*Why is this happening to me?*" But there are those who express the question this way: "What's the purpose for me to have to suffer in this way?" They are simply logical questions. Allow me to add a third, but this time for the person suffering to ask himself: "And why not?" Or, "Whoever guaranteed that this would not happen to me?" On the other hand, I think that although something bad happens to me, the sovereignty of God exceeds and transcends my circumstances.

Continuing with the example of Job, if one compares the Job we see at first with the Job of the end of the story, from the material point of view, he is much better off at the end. But, to my judgment, the most important difference is presented in the break that is produced in his life. At the end of his suffering he is no longer the same as he was before. At the beginning of the tale

Job was a just person, and after his suffering he became, moreover, a wise man, because he had that final dialogue with his Lord in which he was able to find himself and understand his place when God asked him: *"But where were you when I created the heavens and the Earth?"* After that Job no longer judged, and in spite of his suffering he recognized that God sits on his throne and reigns supreme.

In other figures from the Bible we also see the before and the after of a difficult situation involving suffering. For example, Abraham is not the same person when he goes up the mountain with his son for the tremendous test of the sacrifice, as he is later when he comes back down. Because he was obeying God, and although he did not understand anything about what was happening, surely he was never again the same after what happened.

The apostle Paul says that suffering and trials are productive. There is something like a scale of productivity: *"First it produces patience, then patience produces hope, and finally hope produces faith."*

SKORKA: I think that the great lesson we have from the book of Job is that one can be angry with God. Job was, and that's why at the end of the book God says to him: *"You were right when you said to your friends that you were going to have to offer sacrifices to expiate the sin that they committed by telling you that you had been wrong, that you went astray and you sinned, and that is why God punished you. Tell those friends: 'You cannot tell a man who is suffering'—and especially a just man, a good man—'that the bad thing happening to him is because of one thing or another that he did.'"* God does not act like a machine: you sin and now, here comes the punishment. Sometimes, sufferings come and, in all honesty, one does not understand them. Job's expression was: *"God gives, God takes away, blessed be his name."*

It's logical that someone feels angry towards God, but what I interpret from the Judaic message is that what someone should not do is be indifferent towards God, be apathetic, and live as if God did not exist. Job gets into a strong argument with God, and in that dispute he tries to obtain some response to return, to create that link of intimacy with him.

I often repeat a reflection from an article by Martin Buber that made a strong impact on me, about the people who survived the concentration camps. Confronted with this terrible horror on the face of the earth, how is it possible that a man can say, as it says in the book of Psalms: *"Praise God who is good, because his mercy is eternal.*" Buber's response is very interesting. He analyzes the book of Job and says: "*What do we see at the end of Job's story? There is no response. God says nothing to him about why he suffered!*" Buber uses a term that appears in Deuteronomy: "*God hid his face.*" And with respect to the Second World War, where was God? He hid his face.

Each morning, we pray to God that he would not test us the way he tested Abraham. We don't know if we're going to be capable of enduring such suffering! That's why we ask him to let us suffer as little as possible.

I'm afraid that when the sufferings come now, in some way we must try to understand them, because we know that they are inherent to life. Life consists of confronting them constantly, and the only way of doing so is by being a positive person and responding with faith. And when I say this, I mean it in the broadest possible sense of the word.

So, to sum things up: Don't let yourself be poisoned by suffering, as do many that suffer and then later strike out at others for having suffered. They are lacerated by life and later injure others. They become people totally embittered who do not respond when their neighbors greet them because of everything they've suffered. But that's not the way. The challenge is to continue loving life and respecting God even after what happened to us, and that is not an easy challenge. Like everything related to faith, it is a struggle with oneself.

BERGOGLIO: It's a question of struggling, and that's why there is that possibility which is very common in the life of men, that consists of getting angry with God, having a certain wrath towards God, like in the case of Job.

And sometimes you hear echoes of Job in the confidential remarks of faithful people, who tell us: "*I can't pray, I'm angry with God.*" And you ask them: "*Do you tell God about that anger that you feel, do you have a good argument with God?*" Because that is also a way of praying when you can't do it any other way.

In a parent-child relationship, anger is a form of communication, and in that moment even with their anger, the father or mother is praying. Sometimes people answer me: "*Well, but I'm treating God badly.*" And I say: "*Well, according to you, he's treating you badly, and so in that moment speak to him in his own language.*"

Others say: "*I'm not going to go to church anymore because I got angry with God.*" And when I counsel them to say this to God, and they tell me that they do it, I tell them: *"Ah, that's good, at least pray, then we'll see what's next."*

I share these examples to try to get people to stop imagining that getting mad at God, or having a good argument with him, or getting on his bad side, is a sin. No! It is a person's human, filial, and natural relationship with God. Sinning would be if you harbor that anger, if you keep it like a touchstone and make it a nucleus of resentment. That is definitely bad, but the spontaneous expression of anger is not.

FIGUEROA: In the prologue to his book, *Man's Search for Meaning*, Viktor Frankl relates how when he entered Auschwitz they took away his clothes and gave him the clothes of a person who had been murdered in the camp. When he put on those clothes of slavery, that horrible striped suit, he put his hand in the pocket and found a little paper on which was written the prayer from the Shema Yisrael. It was a sign from heaven which inspired him throughout his whole time in Auschwitz, to begin to reflect on what later became the third psychoanalytical current (Third Viennese School of Psychotherapy), logotherapy. Later, when one reads one of Viktor Frankl's books, they are reading the words of someone of profound faith who has grown through suffering. And who, in that growth, shows a proactive posture towards life, in which hope is always focused towards the future.

So far we have approached the theme of suffering from a personal aspect; now I propose doing so from a perspective of human history.

When we refer to the Shoah, we're not talking about an exclusively Jewish problem, but also a crime against humanity, the genocide of human beings. So, when these horrifying things occur in history we've got to analyze what happened and learn from it so that it does not happen again. The question is: "Have we learned the lessons of suffering that human history has left for us? Can we say that we have turned to our advantage the cruel pedagogy of human suffering?

SKORKA: Sometimes I wonder if humanity today is substantially different from what it was five hundred years ago. I cannot give a profoundly positive answer and think that we are really advancing. From the point of view of knowledge and technology, we certainly have. But from the human point of view, I can't see that we've learned from everything that has occurred, or that we've formulated or created a substantially different human being.

The great lessons of the massacres and of the suffering of the past were, in a certain measure, documented, but I don't know if they were spiritually documented. Suffering provoked directly by man's selfishness and by his destructive capacity is a matter that still demands greater understanding.

BERGOGLIO: Yes, especially because it produces in us a spontaneous negative attitude that, perhaps not in the moment but later most certainly, anesthetizes our memory so that we do not have to suffer from the memory. And we immediately assign everything to an historical orbit and render it inconsequential; but the truth is that history has consequences. That negative attitude has its root in something that the Egyptian monks discovered, above all Dorotheus of Gaza, who mediated deeply on the individual's incapacity for self-accusation.

We have a very natural tendency to excuse ourselves from the bad things that happen to us; even in the example of war, we do not own it, we separate ourselves from it in order to be able to live in peace. There is a phrase that says, *"A person cannot find peace in their heart, if they do not learn the science of self-accusation."* Not accusing ourselves means not taking responsibility for things that we have caused to happen. And we have caused wars to happen.

To anyone who now says: *"Well, yes, what happened yesterday or today will not happen again,"* I would ask: *"If you'd been there in that moment, what would you have said?"* And they can tell me, *"I would've done this, this, this, and that."* No! They would have done whatever occurred to them in that moment. And perhaps, whatever occurred to them would have been an act of cowardice. So, you've got to take for granted humanity's sinful, defective, unhealthy character, one that consists of denying that we might have done the same thing. In fact, now we also do the same with regards to daily injustices that we commit against our neighbors, in our own family, and in raising our children, in any area.

We cannot forget that those social calamities that affect us so closely, as in the case of the Shoah, for example. Moreover, if today there were a regime similar to the Nazi party from the 1930s and 40s, which, at bottom, claims that "God does not 'dwell' or that he 'dwells' in name only," accompanied by a process of deifying cultural projects and people, and it turns out to be economically more convenient for you to look the other way and pretend not to see, what would you do? Would you be consistent with your truth and would you speak out? Would you save people or cover for them? If a person is honest then he's got to say: "I don't know what I would do." Well, then make yourself responsible for what our elders did there. Because today, through that worldwide community that is humanity, we are also responsible for the sins of our elders. Taking charge of the sins of history consists of offering the same prayer as the exiles in the book of Baruch: *"Have mercy, Lord, listen and forgive."*

This attitude allows the soul to be very open to how God acts, and it changes me to not repeat the same things that others have done.

FIGUEROA: I think that there does exist a tendency to say: "That happened before, those things were done by others to other people." And the truth is that, throughout history, as humanity, we are all, at the same time, victims and aggressors in what happened. On the other hand, it's unjust to read history the way we read the newspaper today. Not only is it unjust, it's also hypocritical. It's a way of washing our hands, of not taking responsibility for what happened in the past, as the good Cardinal said so well.

I believe that this thought is also present in the Bible. Jesus himself says to some Jews of his time: *"You are just like your forefathers who stoned the prophets,"*—although four hundred years had passed—*"your hands, too, are stained with blood."*

SKORKA: With respect to the suffering that man causes man, perhaps the most sincere response that we can give is that we have still not overcome the problem of Cain.

The history of humanity, biblically speaking, begins with a crime. There are different verses that speak to us about Cain's inner malice, and for which he kills his brother, but God says to him at a certain moment: "You can dominate your destructive instinct." And the question, for us, is: "In what measure do we generate those antibodies to eliminate those destructive factors that we have in our human condition?

When we deeply analyze in what measure a society, a community, builds protective barriers to contain those evil outbursts that lead to the suffering produced by man, the first question one must answer is: "What needs to be done to make men become whole human beings?"

FIGUEROA: To conclude this discussion, I'd like to return to the initial concept. Suffering exists, and what matters is the attitude that we take towards it, as individuals and as people. As we confront it, we can make of it an anchor, a fountain of resentment, or a stepping stone, sometimes sorrowful, but one that leads us to grow and to elevate ourselves a little more in what is human and what is spiritual, both as people and as a society.

May almighty God help us to achieve this!

8

Justice

"Justice you shall follow, and only justice ..."

Deuteronomy 16:20

FIGUEROA: When we think about the word "justice" two concepts come to mind: one that is moral or philosophical, which has got to do with equity, reason, and balance; and a concept with a normative component which leads me to understand that there exists a law that provides rewards and punishments according to how I comport myself in society.

From the point of view of the Bible, there is also a fundamental theological component, through which we understand a just God who invites us to practice justice. But also a normative element, of course, with the Ten Commandments or the Tables of the Law, as the element of the rule of law. Additionally, for Christians, the discourse of the Sermon on the Mount has a normative element that teaches us how to practice that justice.

When we considers the theme of justice, we are walking between two streets; between philosophical and theological concepts on one side, and formal laws and spiritual norms on the other.

SKORKA: I think that justice and its sources can be broadly seen from distinct angles, as they already appear at the start of the digest attributed to Ulpian, the famous Roman jurist. On one side, he says that you must give to each person their fair share, approaching divine and cardinal matters with the idea of correctly answering the questions that they ask about the distinct aspects of life.

One can speak about justice in terms of a social contract: "Let us act, let us work in this way where all of us can live without devouring one another." Ulpian also says something similar, and we cannot forget Gallus. Let me consider Roman law for a moment because it is the basis for the development of justice in the Western world, really everything that we know.

From the beginning, the Romans had divine justice and human justice, but later these were increasingly separated, until the concept was created of a justice structured in a way that did not include God. In the Judaic conception justice is not like this, one speaks of a justice that emanates from God. The biblical position, from the Hebrew Bible, says thus: *"Honor God, first, and above all, by doing what is just."*

Psalm 89 says: *"Righteousness and justice"*—along with rectitude and equity—*"are the foundation of the throne of God."* When, for example, in the book of Chronicles the judges are named, they are told: *"You must judge for God."* Or rather, the judge is, in some way, a representative of God on Earth.

The foundation for honoring God is *"Believe in justice, manifest yourselves with goodness and be just"*—to use that famous verse from Deuteronomy. If someone wants to honor God he must work for justice. And what is justice? The normative aspect that appears in the Bible, as in the great juridical concepts from the Talmudic point of view.

The rabbinical right is a right that includes not only ritual aspects, as respecting Shabbat* and Passover, but also interpersonal relationships. How does one treat a thief? How does one punish a murderer? How is he to be judged? Which man is the witness whose testimony can really be taken into consideration or which testimony should be discarded? All of this forms a single, unique, and indissoluble block.

BERGOGLIO: I think that justice cannot be understood without a reference to the law maker, the one who consolidates all these things into one. There is a reference to God in the very foundation of all justice, of all equity. God is the figure of justice *par excellence*

---

* **Shabbat:** Based on the Ten Commandments received by Moses and its correlation in the Torah, the seventh day of the week (Saturday) is sacred to Jews. It must be observed with profound spirituality and abstinence from any kind of work.

and he wants us to behave just as perfectly, irreproachably, and justly as he does. The whole legislative apparatus is nothing more than a didactic manner of guiding us towards that justice that God wants from us.

In the passage from the Gospel of Saint Mark, a young man approaches Jesus and asks: *"Teacher, what must I do to gain eternal life?"* Jesus answers him: *"Fulfill the commandments: do not kill, do not commit adultery, do not steal, honor your mother and your father, love the Lord your God with all your might, with all your heart, and all your soul."* The young man says to Jesus: *"I have done all these since I was very young."* The Gospel says that Jesus looked at him and loved him. Or rather, he felt that before him was someone who was just, because he had regulated his life according to the justice that God wanted from him.

The just people, in the Bible, are those who follow the path of God, who try to be children of God. The path of God is laid out according to his commandments, through that Jewish system of laws that we Christians inherit and carry forward. Sometimes one runs the risk of considering the Commandments—I'm going to cite them directly, although analogously this is valid for all positive systems of laws—as coercive limitations because some of them are expressed in negative terms: you shall not kill, you shall not steal, you shall not take the name of the Lord in vain. But that negative manner is purely literary and it really expresses much more. For example, *"Do not take the Lord's name in vain"* means "Recognize that there is a sovereign over and above all things, that cannot be used as a wild card in any situation, but that is far more transcendent." The legislation that is a path, is a teacher like all legislation; Saint Paul says: *"The Law is a teacher"* because it is educational towards God. I think that it would be useful to properly clarify this conflict, because if I cannot do one thing or another, I must see that there is something positive and confirm that behind that mandate expressed negatively there is a greater depth that opens doors of greater plenitude, doors to a fuller life for me.

FIGUEROA: I think that there is a risk when one loses that conceptual or theological reference to God as the ultimate source of justice, like the National Constitution itself says, "the source of all reason and justice."

But that pedagogical element that the Cardinal mentioned has an element that I'd like to bring into the discussion. When the person who is living in a community, lives under the law and justice, never above it; he is neither legislator nor judge of the law.

There is, or there should be, a criterion of responsibility in the sense of recognizing and accepting that it is alright that the law not only has a proactive or positive normative, but also that it establishes the limits of what one cannot do. Because if I do not live with the responsibility of understanding that there are rewards and punishments, I end up taking only the part of the law that's convenient to me, and accepting only the rights and permissions, and not the obligations, that form part of the law.

SKORKA: Regarding the term "coercion" that you used, one contribution that's been made is that of the fathers of anthropology and psychology: Freud and Lévi-Strauss and many others. They introduced the following concept: without coercion there is no culture.

Freud explains it very clearly in *The Future of an Illusion*, the book that he wrote near the end of his life. The same thing happens with Lévi-Strauss, with the imposition "… here, these are lawful marriages, lawful unions, but these others are considered incest." This is certainly a question of coercion!

Now, speaking from a totally democratic point of view, as if I were speaking with a person and not with God present, what I would say is the following: There are things that can change, that a democratic society, if it so desires, can use its authority to change, but only through a very profound process of analysis, in order to know exactly what it is that people wish to change, and why. And that analysis should be done by experts, with people who are truly wise, or rather, people with the pertinent information who might know how to organize it and present it in a balanced manner, in order to avoid chaotic situations within the societies.

The first step for a society to function is to have respect for the law and a division of powers that works. In this sense I'm totally in agreement with Rousseau and with all the Enlightenment thinkers who set forth the foundations of the separation of social powers. There must be a profound dialogue, as the Greek philosophers indicated, and true wise men must have influence in the changes of the law. Wise men in the sense that they know how to listen; who understand and who try to comprehend society as a whole, not partially; wise men who know how to find balance.

Why be afraid to say "No"? Let's be honest: without coercion—I am practically repeating Freud, who was in no way a practicing religious man—there is no culture.

BERGOGLIO: The drama we are experiencing today in the area of education, between parents and teachers, is the result of the fact that the educational pact is broken. Parents and teachers are afraid of setting limits and the children are crying out for those limits to be imposed on them. In this I assume what you say to be true. Or rather, imposing reasonable limits, with a view towards human fulfillment, is necessary in all educational processes. An education without limits is not good; and in what we have said up to this point we were bypassing, or rather, just touching lightly on the theme of transgression. Transgression tempts our ever-present craving for sweet delight like some enormous moral bonbon, and in a special way for us *porteños* from Buenos Aires.* That's to say that we *porteños* are transgressors of the soul. I think that Buenos Aires—and I do not say this to be offensive, but rather being aware of reality—is a bent society, easily bought and corrupted; meaning, we love transgression.

FIGUEROA: Borges said that the *porteño* prefers to be immoral before being lonely. And I think that's true. He not only breaks the rule but also justifies the transgression and goes one step further, in the sense that the one who does not break the rule, who lives within the norm, ends up being lonely.

I wanted to return to the concept that the rabbi mentioned with respect to the dictionary definition of the word "justice": "The group of laws that govern a society in accordance with a specific culture and determined by the participants within that culture." In a way that is a dynamic vision of justice, in agreement with the society, the social processes, etc., something that I can also see within the Bible story.

The question is if justice contains, in a certain measure, a dynamic process enabling adaptation to culture, to peoples, to the foundation of civilization: What are those things which I cannot change? I can change a lot of things about the law, but there are things that I cannot change, because if I change them I am interfering with fundamental social elements.

BERGOGLIO: There is a basic principle, a moral and ethical principle that all humanity recognizes seriously: Doing good and avoiding evil. Around this basic principle there occurs a first explanation that is valid for our Judeo-Christian tradition, the Ten Commandments. This is the first explanation about things

---

* *Los porteños* are people from Buenos Aires. In Spanish, the term can be used as a generic designation for anyone from a port city, but it has become most widely used in reference to Buenos Aires, where Bergoglio, Figueroa, and Skorka are from *(trans.)*.

that cannot change. That is, one cannot kill, cannot steal—even with white gloves—in any situation. In accordance with those principles, found in the Ten Commandments, one cannot live by separating himself, disregarding someone else, someone beyond oneself, because one will self-destruct. The Commandments are ten prescriptions that, as the rabbi says, mark limits that safeguard human richness. I think that those great principles cannot change.

SKORKA: I agree with the term "great principles." Jewish law is also Talmudic, and rabbinical. It shows us a thorough evolution over the course of centuries. And there is a paragraph from the Jerusalem Talmud where it says that if we interpreted strictly the legal norms of the Torah—the Pentateuch—they would have no basis for support. Why? Because time has passed and things have changed. So, we have got to interpret the rules as great principles of the right that God conferred on us, principles that help us to deduce, from day to day, how to act. And for that reason, in the present they continue writing rabbinical texts about new situations that arise. But there are certain things that cannot be negotiated in any way. You cannot kill another or take away their right to live with dignity; those rights are inalienable.

Some rules are very broad, but if we are sincere we can interpret them properly, such as Ulpian said: "Know how to give to each person what is fair and what they deserve." In the moment when we do so with fairness, putting us all together on the same level, not like the Code of Hammurabi* that, unlike the Torah, says: "The king's son shall be judged differently than the son of the peasant." No. We are all together, we have the same rights and obligations and we must search for fairness and justice.

BERGOGLIO: I think that evolution comes through deepening our comprehension when faced with new cultural challenges, but always rooted in that natural law. That is, there is no qualitative change in evolution, or rather, if you like, quantitative insofar as explanation and going deeper. But what there is in that natural law, the same as in nature, flowers and bears fruit in dialogue with new cultural situations. Sometimes, conscience becomes refined in such a way that things which in other ages did not seem so unjust, now are found to be unjust because in the natural law they appear as such, always with reference to, and in dialogue with, new cultural situations.

---

* **Code of Hammurabi:** Created by Hammurabi, King of Babylon (1700 B.C.), the code contains a group of laws from that Mesopotamian age.

A qualitative evolution of justice and the law is not possible because it would change man's very nature. But a circumstantial evolution within the same quality, one that is developed over time, is gradually strengthened and becomes permanent.

Once I saw a caricature of justice—the one that we all know: blindfolded, holding the scales—that moved me. The blindfold had fallen from the eyes of Justice onto the mouth, to become a gag, so it had its eyes open but its mouth tied shut. This signaled the dimension of corruption that there can be in a judicial system that is the caretaker of justice. When one thinks about the administration of justice in the major dictatorships of the past century, where a whole juridical apparatus was set up to justify an oppressive regime in which the rights of the individual and human dignity were relegated to a lower level, one also sees there that the custodians of justice can deviate from justice and become ruled by corruption.

In one parable in the New Testament, Jesus says: *"There was a judge who did not fear God, nor did he care for men."* It presents the image of men as having the duty of being fair and impartial judges rather than violating the law due to their self-interest.

SKORKA: There are two factors in what you just said that I would like to comment on. In Deuteronomy, where it says: *"Judges and police must keep watch over the doors of all your cities,"* it talks about the judges and says: *"You shall not honor"*—meaning, you will not take into consideration—*"the faces of the people."* If someone is an important person, you are going to judge them in the same way as you would the lowest of the poor, that is, with dignity: *"You shall not take bribes, because the bribe is meant to falsify the words of the just."*

Every judge has to have two qualities: to be absolutely incorruptible, and to be a person of courage. At the beginning it talks about a judge's function, and it says: *"Every judge must be seated on his bench thinking as if he had a sword hanging over his head, because he is representing God."* When someone steals or kills they are destroying God's work, and the judge is the one who must impart justice, safeguarding that work of God.

FIGUEROA: I think that we have explored here some very profound concepts. We started out talking about the law as something that has a philosophical, conceptual, theological, and normative component. We talked about man's transgressive will, especially that of the Argentine; of those norms and laws that can change as cultures evolve, and those which are firmly set and must remain so, not only because they are in the biblical text, but also, as Saint Paul expresses, because those who do not have the law written have the law visible when they contemplate God's creation. That transgression can be not only at an individual level, but the greater danger happens when that transgressive violation of the law, believing oneself above the law, finds its way into the hearts and minds of those that have the obligation of exercising the authority of the law. That is where society finds itself in trouble and where we need those people who are in positions of power to be not like the unjust judge in Jesus' parable, but to be men who fear God and respect people.

9

Forgiveness

"For my own sake I must forgive you. One cannot always keep an adder in one's breast to feed on one, nor rise up every night to sow thorns in the garden of one's soul ... My forgiveness should mean a great deal to you now.... I cannot allow you to go through life bearing in your heart the burden of having ruined a man like me."

Oscar Wilde

FIGUEROA: In Psalm 130:4 there is an extraordinary phrase: *"Lord, within you lies forgiveness."* Immediately, the question one should ask oneself is: "And does forgiveness lie within me?"

One of the first images that come to my mind about this is Jesus' parable about the servant who went to settle accounts with the king, to whom he owed a lot of money. The interesting thing is that he owed the king far more than he could pay. So, when he appears before the king with this enormous debt hanging over his head, he begins to cry disconsolately and beg the king's mercy and forgiveness. So, the king takes pity on him and forgives his debt. But when this man leaves the palace, he runs into a man who owes him money, but a sum far less than what he owed the king. In fact, his own debt to the king was 600 times more than what this man owed him. Nevertheless, he demands that the man pay up the minuscule debt he owes. Unmoved by the man's pleas, he refuses to reduce the amount by even a single penny. This reaches the ears of the king, who instantly summons before him the man whose debt he had so recently forgiven and condemns him for his pitiless and miserly attitude.

Given that Jesus' teaching is a reference to how the Kingdom of God functions, it's clear that forgiveness is a central action of its laws. This parable gives us a model about the importance of forgiveness. If God forgives us a debt that we find impossible to pay, who are we then to not forgive a brother who owes us something? And, of course, this is not only about money, but also about things having to do with life and with situations that have harmed us along the way.

So, when we talk about the Bible, forgiveness is a referential forgiveness and the reference is to God's person.

SKORKA: The concept of the *imitatio dei** that appears in Christianity develops in rabbinical literature, in the Talmudic era, and it emerges from the simple reading of the Bible: "If God is merciful, so then you must be too." In many respects, God is the paradigm of what man's conduct must be.

God has a day, the Day of Forgiveness, which appears in the book of Leviticus. When a person deeply wrongs his neighbor, Judaism teaches that he must make amends for it according to the law. Or rather, if he has struck or injured someone, he must pay him—literally, it says so in the Talmud—for example, for lost income and for the medical expenses.

Now, what does it mean to forgive? When someone is harmed, and the other, after repairing the damages and injuries caused, says: "Alright, I already paid what the law says I must; forgive me," that in the end means: "I made a mistake, I scarred you. I beg you not to harbor hatred for me."

Forgiving does not necessarily mean erasing what the other did, but rather making a mental effort to not see the other person as if he were the enemy. Neither is it about taking vengeance, as mentioned in Leviticus 19, an attitude that demonstrates a lack of forgiveness.

Forgiveness is a very profound process. It implies my changing something inside of me so that my relationship with the person who harmed me becomes different, and I do not respond to them in anger.

With respect to the relationship between a man and his neighbor, the Jewish people had a great problem with the Ger-

---

* *Imitatio dei:* A religious concept through which man finds virtue in trying to imitate God. It is derived, in part, from the biblical concept that man is made in God's image.

man people after the Shoah. There was enormous resentment. For many, the simple fact of hearing the German language spoken was an offense that caused them pain, because it was the language in which they had received orders in the concentration camps. The suffering endured for a very long time. In a masterful move, David Ben-Gurion said—in spite of terrible criticism of him from within Israel: "We accept the reparations that the government of Germany is offering us, and we shall begin to speak with the German people. We cannot harbor hatred towards an entire people; we have got to try to turn this around."

BERGOGLIO: Forgiveness supposes a change of heart, a conversion of the heart towards one's neighbor. One might say—perhaps with some exaggeration—transforming a rancorous, sorrowful, wounded heart into a benevolent one.

It's true that there are things that cannot be erased, but forgiving means looking at them through a different lens. In looking with a new perspective, there are two expressions that I often think of, one from Isaiah: *"You, who have put all our sins behind your back"*; and another, from the Psalms, even more beautiful, more "playful": *"Lord you know how to hide our sins so that we change our hearts."* They speak of a process in which God awaits us.

For me, the foundation of all forgiveness is imitating God and not resolving things immediately. Although we cannot conceal or overlook an offense, as he does in his perfection and infinite holiness, what we can do is let a bit of time pass by, holding onto our sorrow, suffering patiently the offense, the injury, the injustice, whatever it may be; until the moment arrives to forgive and resettle our heart.

Forgiveness is a very difficult process. God reveals to us his example in the book of Isaiah, when he says: *"Although your sins be scarlet red, I will turn them white as snow."* If he does that it's because forgiveness is a path that, in some way, can lead us to a fraternal harmony. As was said earlier, we cannot speak of forgiveness without referring to God; without that reference, which provides us with the model for our forgiveness, we are lost.

FIGUEROA: It is very difficult to forgive because there is a grievance, a pain, a weight, an injury and one has to accept that as it is. And on the other side, forgiving is not simply saying "It's alright, nothing wrong happened. Let's just start fresh." No! That is not the correct way to forgive. One cannot treat such a profound subject in such a simplistic way. It's not true that nothing wrong happened.

Yes it happened, and it happened often. "You injured me, you hurt me, but in spite of that I'm making the effort to forgive you."

Forgiving does not mean simply erasing everything. One must remember, not so that the other person is forever reminded of what he did, but so that he will have the memory of the fact that I forgave him. I forgave him thanks to the grace of God, with God's help. I forgave him, and that is something that I do not recall with rancor, but rather with the lens of the Lord's love and remembering from what he liberated me.

SKORKA: It's true, forgiveness is a process. It is something much deeper than merely saying: "I forgive you."

When I referred to the Jews' relationship to the German people after World War II, I did not mean the Jewish people's forgiveness. Among the German people, especially among the younger generations, some began to acknowledge the disaster of the Shoah, to accept their own sin for taking part in that horror, and this helped to form a distinct human relationship.

Forgiveness is a trial, a very long road. I would say that it's a "descending" process that has various stages and ranges. Evidently, no Jew can speak for our ancestors who were massacred in the Shoah, as if to say to those who perpetrated the massacre: "You are forgiven." But at the same time he does not need to blame the children of the perpetrators.

With this clarification made, let's go to the profound meaning of forgiveness, taking God as a reference. The concept of contrition, of returning to God, that is manifested especially in the first ten days of the year—during Rosh Hashanah and on Yom Kippur—refers to the following: the first nine days I have got to ask forgiveness from all those whom I have offended, and only then do I have the right to ask God for forgiveness for the ways in which I have offended him.

Now then, what does it mean to ask forgiveness? Here comes the point. According to various sources, it means that I have a change of heart. Taking Maimonides as the basis of the rabbinical sources, we see that he explains this in his great encyclopedic work. He says that the man that forgives is that one who, if he finds himself facing the same situation that caused the sin in the first place, is going to have sufficient inner resources to overcome his instincts and not commit the same transgression again. In a word, he is a new man, and in the literature of the Midrash the exact same thing appears. In those first ten days of the Jewish year the man has to change himself in order to become a new human being. Or rather, that man who asks both his neighbor and God for forgiveness is someone who first recognized that something very profound took place inside of himself. He does not just say these words: "God, I ask you for forgiveness," but rather "I ask your forgiveness because I am different." I'll end this thought with a verse from the book of Leviticus which describes all the sacrifices one must make after Yom Kippur. This is the heart of the matter: When someone commits a transgression against a man or against God, in essence he is not only causing harm, but he is also polluting himself. In the moment in which God forgives me because I made an effort and I asked him for forgiveness, he is returning me to a state of purity.

BERGOGLIO: Using the words of Ezekiel, it is about changing a heart of stone into a beating heart of human flesh, as God wishes. It is a job that only God can do to the extent that one "willingly makes himself vulnerable" with that ascetic effort of asking forgiveness. It is difficult to recognize my own faults. One tends to excuse oneself continuously. We are masters at excusing ourselves for the things we have done. We search for words and phrases that will put us at ease, like: "Well, but everyone does the same thing." Or "If you'd been in my place, you would've done the same thing." Excuses lead us to the lethargy of impenitence or not knowing how to ask for forgiveness. What we must do to "become a target" for God is recognize that we have failed in something.

At the end of Ezekiel 16, when he narrates the entire story of Israel in terms of being unfaithful to God's love, the Lord says through the prophet: *"But I will forgive you and I will place you above your sisters, so that you are ashamed,"* referring to that shame which dignifies. That is the conversion that comes from a heart of flesh.

Sometimes I think that when it is our turn to forgive, the only one who knows how to do it is that person who has at some time felt the necessity of asking forgiveness, the one who has experienced sin. If some person has never had the need of asking forgiveness, whether from his brother or from God, it's because his heart is closed to transcendence; it costs him a great effort to forgive others.

FIGUEROA: I was thinking about a passage from the Gospels, when a woman is brought to Jesus so that she can be stoned to death for having been caught in the act of adultery. Naturally this is an act requiring another's involvement; nevertheless, no one accuses the man in front of Jesus. In the story, Jesus listens and says almost nothing but as he writes in the dust he says: *"Let him who is without sin cast the first stone."* There is an interesting detail. The Bible says that the people began to leave the place, first the oldest people, then the youngest ones. I think that the older ones, unlike the impetuous younger ones, still remembered all that they had done, and for that reason carried a heart more punished by their own sins, but also more open to forgive.

Cardinal Bergoglio spoke about the importance of shame. Saint Paul says: *"If your enemy is hungry, feed him; if he is thirsty, give him water; and thus you will make his face burn with shame."* For what reason? To give him the opportunity to repent and for the relationship to be restored. And, in this case, the offended person must abandon his pride and personal interests and mend the damage he suffered.

SKORKA: After the first man ate of the forbidden fruit he did not go looking for God; man hid himself and God went to find him, to ask him: *"Man, where are you?"* This could not be clearer. The question is: To what extent does the world, the society of which we form a part, really know how to handle itself regarding forgiveness? If the act of forgiveness is so profound and depends on the two sides involved, it means that there must be a fully formed, very profound, cultural question. To what degree, really, does forgiveness exist in our Argentine culture? This is a very difficult, very complex question.

BERGOGLIO: We love to keep track of what people do to us. That is very much how we are, keeping account of the things that they do to us, an attitude that does not permit forgiveness. We stop looking at the good that someone has done and instead we start making a list of their all their faults and transgressions. And who does not have some page full of misdeeds in their life? Everyone does, and I'm at the top of the list. We are experts at turning resumes into rap sheets; we like to "charge people with crimes," and that doesn't help.

On the other hand, it's true that there are ways of getting around the attitude of having a forgiving heart. Loopholes that excuse and justify such a lapse: "Well, he did something wrong, he has to make up for it." Meaning it is one thing to forgive in the heart and it's another thing for the other person to accept the forgiveness. I can pardon you if you offend me, but if you have no interest in ceasing to offend me, then you are incapable of receiving my forgiveness.

The same thing happens with God. He forgives us, he never tires of forgiving us, but we get tired of asking for forgiveness, of having that opening to receive forgiveness and forgiving.

Thus forgiveness involves two sides, the one who gives it and the one who is capable of receiving it. One gives it, but there are those who do not want to accept forgiveness, who prefer what the tango calls "that sweet rancor" which is really just a slow poison. That rancor prevents us from restoring the harmony after a conflict that happens between two persons or two peoples.

Closeness to God is what, in some way, gives us that sensation of protection and of tenderness that he offers as father, and which assures us that he can get us out of the trap into which we have fallen by our own mistakes, error, or sin.

And the closeness between us humanizes us. Distance always distorts, it erases the face of the other, it sees an enemy that no longer has a name, but has only epithets. By contrast, in closeness, one sees the true face of the person and it makes understanding and exchanging opinions easier; and if there is offense, the recognition of the offense and the request for forgiveness also come more easily. Distance never helps when we need to ask for forgiveness or when we need to forgive.

SKORKA: There is a verse in Deuteronomy that I often cite, when God says: *"If the people of Israel goes astray and does not follow the path of justice and rectitude, on that day I will hide my face from you."*

When Martin Buber wanted to talk about the Shoah and he wondered what had happened to God in that moment, he spoke about the "eclipse of God." There is a book published in Argentina with his articles, taking this phrase that he used in such a special way. That expression about the concealment of God, as if he removed himself from humanity, indicates God covered his face because of the barbarities that were being committed.

What we want, one way or another, is to be able to see that face of God, as it says in the book of Psalms: *"I, with justice and mercy, will be able to see your face."* One part of justice consists of speaking with and drawing closer to see the face of one's neighbor. In that approach, in the dynamic of the offense or injury, of the error that is committed, it is important to keep this goal in mind: that there must always be a reparation, a change in direction.

Since we're talking about how God is so patient with us, my father—blessed be his memory—used to say to me: "Look, I'm more afraid of men than of God. He's going to understand me; the ones who usually have their minds already made up and fail to understand are men." Over time I've come to realize just how right he was.

10

Love

"Teacher, which is the greatest commandment in the Law?"
Jesus replied: "'Love the Lord your God with all your heart
and with all your soul and with all your mind.' This is the
first and greatest commandment. And the second is like it:
'Love your neighbor as yourself.' All the Law and the Proph-
ets hang on these two commandments."

Matthew 22:36–40

FIGUEROA: There is a central verse in the Bible: *"Love the Lord*
your God with all your heart, and with all your soul, and with all
your mind; and love your neighbor as yourself."

Even though love involves feelings, there is a commandment
about love and this means that it is not only a question of feelings.
Because feelings vary according to one's mood, today I love you,
tomorrow no; today I accept you, tomorrow no; today I like you,
tomorrow no.

Love is, from the biblical point of view, a volitional action,
proactive, provoking well-being in the other and acting in a loving
manner. It is not only about feelings.

SKORKA: We find this discussion among the sages of antiquity.
What do these words mean: *"Love the Lord your God"* and *"Love*
your neighbor as yourself"? Are these commandments or a question
of feelings? Is there some mystical path for finding our way to God?

These are two very difficult verses. Why? What happens if a person does not love himself? Does he have the right, then, to expect the same standard from his neighbor?

Rabbi Akiva—the greatest of the Talmudic scholars—said: "This is the basic biblical verse, the verse of the Torah." And there was also a colleague of his that added: "For me, the great rule is found in chapter 5 of the book of Genesis, where it says: *"This is the text of the histories of man, the day that God created man in his own likeness."* What does this mean? One said: "You've got to approach your neighbor with the very best things that you offer yourself and in the way that you love yourself, and this has to be the rule of the relationship." Another said: "When you approach your neighbor you've got to do so knowing that God is present, in some way, in your neighbor's face." Finally, one Gentile asked another scholar: "Define for me what Judaism is while I balance on one foot." The scholar answered him: "Do not treat your neighbor as you would not wish to be treated."

And that is one of the Aramaic translations of that verse; in place of: *"Love your neighbor as yourself,"* the verse is cast in a cautionary form.

But the problem arises again: if someone happily accepts suffering, and that is the standard by which he judges himself, does he have the right to make another suffer?

Now, with respect to what that verse says about the love of God: *"Love the Lord, your God, with all your heart, all your soul"*— I'm going to contextualize this in terms of the Talmud—it follows that although life is not a bed of roses, because it has some very hard things, even so, one must retain some special feeling with respect to God. Because *"with all your soul"* also means "Although he take your soul, although he take away your soul, you've got to keep loving him."

I think that is the basic issue. Love, in the deepest sense, means having a committed relationship.

BERGOGLIO: Love always supposes a nearness, an encounter; one can come to love God if he happened to meet with him. And it is God who goes out in search of man. He is the great seeker! He is constantly searching for us. What matters is that the encounter actually happens, meaning, I allow God to find me.

On the other hand, we have inside us a seed of eternity, an uneasiness in our hearts that is only satisfied by an encounter with God. It is as if both God and man are searching for each other. Therefore, love supposes an encounter with God.

I like the expression in Jeremiah 20:7: *"You have seduced me, Lord, and I allowed myself be seduced."* Or rather, love always supposes a seduction that has to do with the approaching of the beings that love each other, between us and with God, too. He approaches us, he reveals himself and places in our heart that desire to find him.

One of the first steps needed for the meeting with God to happen is the capacity that we must have for allowing ourselves to be seduced by him—in the noble sense of the word—allowing him to reveal himself to us and to fall in love with us in a way that touches our heart, whether that be from his mercy or his majesty. God has many ways of doing this.

The path of Elijah touches me deeply. God had prepared a very difficult moment for him so that Elijah could experience a profound encounter with him. After a long road, Elijah reached the mountain and then the storm came, and God was not within the storm. Then Elijah hoped to find him in the earthquake, but God wasn't there either. And then, as the Bible tells it, Elijah heard *"a very soft voice from out of the silence"* which was indeed God. He manifests himself as he chooses. In one way to some; and in other ways to others, but the realization is that God is manifesting himself and I manage to find a way to meet him. Elijah, through his fear, walked, believed, and found himself with God.

FIGUEROA: The Bible also says that we love God, but that it was he who loved us first. The apostle John says: *"God is love,"* or rather that he is the essence and language of love. And Dostoevsky wrote that he conceived of hell as the place where one can no longer love.

The biblical example of Jonah comes to mind. God sends him to Nineveh to speak about love and God's mercy to a people who were his enemy, but Jonah disobeyed God and fled to Tarshish. Then from the well-known episode of being swallowed by the whale, Jonah is finally "convinced" to go to Nineveh. There he speaks about the love of God and, to his surprise, those people convert and turn to the Lord. Far from being happy, he gets depressed, he gets angry and tries to flee again. God searches for him and protects him with a castor-oil plant with broad leaves that shelter him from the sun like a parasol. But when the leaves of that plant dry out, Jonah gets angry again. Then God speaks to him and asks him: *"You have pity for the plant that protected you from the sun, but you didn't have pity for all the people of Nineveh who did not know me, nor my love and mercy?"*

As was so well said, you have got to let yourself be loved by God, but we must also be vehicles so that God can love others through us, including those whom we ourselves do not love.

SKORKA: The thing is, believing in the existence of God is not only believing in him, but also believing in a God that really is aware of each and every individual. This is one of the cornerstones of Judaic belief and, I think, of Christianity, too. If one lives with that conviction that God, in some way, is with me and near me in the drama of my existence; if one is really convinced of this and knows that he has that same relationship with his neighbor, this is evidently a requirement in order to complete the triangle.

There is also a verse that is very difficult to put into practice, and it speaks about love: *"Love a stranger, because you were strangers in the land of Egypt."* It is about a more extended love, because "love your neighbor" means loving someone with whom we have the same scale of values, the same code. But "love a stranger" refers to someone with whom we do not share all the same codes and rules, it is a great biblical challenge that consists of extending a bridge to every person who is sincerely searching for justice, spirituality, and for the basic values that we share. I have got to try to have a special relationship with him, based on love.

Love is a circle that opens ever wider. It begins with the most intimate thing, which is love between a couple, and then it includes love of parents, of children, of the neighbor. By means of that loving relationship with others one can really reach God. The one who wants to "skip" the relationship with his fellow human beings and go straight to God, doesn't get anywhere. Believing in God, seeking him and feeling him must bring with it, necessarily, the love for man in order to, through man, close the circle once again and reach God.

BERGOGLIO: With respect to that triangle that you traced: God, man, and the return to God, I'd like to highlight two things. First, the necessity that my encounter with God also leads to an encounter with man, with my neighbor. And second, sometimes my neighbor is not someone from my own people or place, he does not share my blood, he is a stranger, a foreigner, one who is alien to my culture, to my language, to my way of thinking. Let's take the stranger as a symbol.

I'm drawn to chapter 25 from the Gospel of St. Matthew, when Jesus talks about the last judgment. There are some on the left side and some on the right side. God is going to say to some:

"Come with me blessed of my Father, I was hungry and you gave me to eat, I was thirsty and you gave me to drink, I was in prison and you came to visit me, I was sick and you cared for me" meaning those on the periphery, as an example—to force the expression—, those foreigners in my life, those that are on the periphery of my existence, from my natural habitat, those that are at the margin of life. St. John said: *"If you don't love the neighbor whom you see, you don't love God whom you don't see."* Or rather, by showing love to your neighbor, you show love to God. And by loving that neighbor who is most marginalized, the one who has given up hope, those of whom the prophets spoke: the orphan, the widow and the stranger, in some way, one denies oneself, and selfishness is lessened.

For that reason, love is so challenging. Sometimes it is trivialized into what can be superficial experiences. The love that the Bible asks of us is a love where we put "the flesh in the fire." Meaning, we bet our life for this God with whom we find ourselves and we demonstrate that we find ourselves with the living God, serving our brothers, our neighbors, loving them, caring for them and going to the margins of "neighborliness," reaching out to the stranger, the widow, and the orphan.

For that reason, the love of God is something that you've got to demonstrate through good works. I think about Mother Teresa in Calcutta. That woman prayed a great deal, but then she went out to save dying beggars from the street, she took care of them, she treated them with tenderness, she helped them to die. And she did not proselytize, she did not worry about saying: "Come, let's baptize this man so that he might die a Christian." No! That person was the "flesh" of God, and in that flesh she was loving God. When one carries the love of God to those limits, one realizes how immense and difficult it is.

FIGUEROA: The love we have is shaped and formed by, or rather, it has a model: God. For that reason, as the time of Jesus' ministry drew to a close, he spoke very intimately to the apostles, and he told them: *"I'm going to give you a new commandment, love your neighbor."* And what is new about that? Jesus added: *"Love them as I have loved you."* Jesus is referring to himself, and the love he means is loving in the way that God understands love.

Now, making a turn in the debate, as a society we always talk about love, but there is a great absence of love all around us. As a society, we do not manage to create a culture of love. In the city of Buenos Aires, for example, there is a great deal of pain, loneliness, anguish, and selfishness, and there is a great lack of love. We need to form part of a society that knows how to love itself, that knows how to look after itself. We have a large number of foreigners in the city of Buenos Aires, and very distressing problems of xenophobia, like women forced into sex trafficking and slave labor. A host of problems we did not have before and that show us that very often love ends up being an empty word if we do not incorporate it as a society.

SKORKA: Before talking about the subject of Buenos Aires, or a large part of what we know as the culture of the Western world, I would like to trace another line with respect to the concept of love at the individual level. Very often, when I interview the couples that I am going to marry, I tell them: "For us, in this moment, the two of you represent a paradigm of the faith." Why? Because one of them has confidence in the other one, because they are betting their life together, they are going to build a home and to carry on God's work.

Now, when we talk about the level of the people, in the flight from or exodus from Egypt, the people's greatness did not lie in the fact of breaking the chains of slavery, because it was God who did all that work. So, then, wherein lay the people's greatness? As Jeremiah says in the name of God: their greatness lay in their going out to pursue God in the desert—that was an enormous act of faith.

What is it that's going on in the city of Buenos Aires? What is happening with culture, the culture in which we are immersed? Zygmunt Bauman, the famous sociologist, defines it as "the culture of liquidity." Everything is liquid, and so too is love, in order to differentiate it, in some way, from concrete reality. Everything is liquid when there is no solid bridge and an iron hand that clutches the other and says: "We will argue, we have different points of view, but we will always try to find a middle way. In some cases, I will see that you are right, other times you will see that I'm right, but we will always go hand in hand, because we are convinced that we want to be together. This is a lifelong pact!" It happens in marriage, where there is a lifelong pact, the same as the lifelong pact with my parents. For me, this is love.

BERGOGLIO: I like the fact that you have placed love in the image of matrimony, because that reality is what God uses in the Bible to express to us his love.

In chapter 13 of his first letter to the Corinthians, the apostle Paul wrote a hymn of love. He says: *"If I spoke all the languages in the world and I had no love, I would be like a bell that is silenced; if I had all the riches but had no love, they would serve me no purpose at all; if I gave my life for all others, but without love, it would do me no good."* Or rather, love is what helps to make sense of everything that I might do in life.

And it's curious, when Paul ends that hymn, he defines love by saying: *"Love is patient, it is forgiving, it is tolerant, it listens, it does not attack, it does not shout."* All those characteristics of love are referring to a climate of tenderness. We've lost, sometimes, the notion of respect and of tenderness in the way that we treat others, through aggressions, insults, personal attacks, defamations, and slanders. We must not stop focusing on the characteristics of love: *"It always trusts, always hopes, always perseveres."*

1 1

Violence

We were wrapping up the program on violence when Cardinal Bergoglio said on air something that he had shared with us several times in private, which encouraged me to keep going forward with this television project. He talked about why he enjoys participating in these round-table discussions: "It does me good every time we meet. We come from three different faiths and we realize that we do not need to insult one another, nor quarrel, but simply come together around what we have in common, the fact of being children of God."

In that same session he presented us with one of his many touchstones on the theme: "The paths against violence are meekness and dialogue."

FIGUEROA: A few days ago, everyone was moved by the tragedy that happened in Brazil, caused by a 23-year-old young man who went into his former school and killed a dozen children in cold blood. Sometime later, investigators learned about this young man's background, and it was discovered that while there, being a student, he had suffered for years from bullying; to call it by another name, permanent psychophysical harassment. Of course, that does not in any way justify the violence it caused; but the point is that we are looking at a person who suffered violence in his life.

In a country as rich as ours, when we learn that around 250,000 children under the age of five suffer serious problems of malnutrition, that is another kind of violence. Similarly, there is violence in the heart of the family, towards children, the elderly, and gender-based violence towards women, both physical and emotional. The lack of justice is also a form of violence.

One perceives that our society lives with such a scenario of violence, that violence can break out at any moment and without reason between two people that don't even know one another. It would seem to be that violence surrounds us, encloses us, invades us, and penetrates us.

What's happening to us? Are we intrinsically violent? Do we live in a violent society? Have we become accustomed to living in a climate of violence?

SKORKA: I think there's a verse that can serve as a response to those questions, from Genesis 4:6, where God gives some instructions for knowing what is happening with human comportment, how to manage the theme of violence and life in general.

We know that Cain and Abel each made an offering to God, but he accepted Abel's offering and rejected Cain's. I understand that many people interpret this superficially; the one to do this most recently was José Saramago in his book about Cain, because the Bible stories—if they sometimes seem simple and obvious—have within them a very deep layer which we must reach.

Returning to the Bible, there exists a reality where one is seen as more blessed than the other, in some way, and this is what engendered Cain's jealous discontent. Then we read in verse 4 where God says to Cain: *"Why does all this make you so angry? Why are you so downcast?"* And here, God speaks in words that are difficult to interpret, but I think they mean the following: If you do what is correct, you're going to be able to endure and get through things, and if you do what's wrong, then sin and transgression will live crouched on your doorstep, but you can manage to overcome them.

In the first place, we've got to learn to bring a dimension of resignation to life, to understand that we cannot have it all and that we are completely limited. In the second place, in life there are going to be some things that make us angry whether they come from men or from God, things that we're not going to understand, and they're going to make us confused and feel turbulent inside. But we've got to try to find the dimension of goodness and faith, something that permits us to work out, or as the psychologists would say, to "sublimate" our destructive instincts. And here is the last part of the verse: *"And you must be able to overcome it,"* which I interpret to mean that we are capable of doing so. But, of course, when the society where we live constantly gives us an antagonistic message, we must hope to overcome all of man's violence and aggressive attitudes. What we see is what we get.

BERGOGLIO: Cain's envy and jealousy is the first act of violence we read about in Scripture. It reminds me of a verse from the book of Wisdom that in a wise "rereading" says: *"Jealousy led the way for sin to enter the world."* The invidious dimension creates an imbalance that, in this case, leads the way to violence.

Any sin that leads to violence is an injustice, and something destructive. The sin against justice destroys the equity among people. The sin of ambition can lead us to realize spurious business enterprises that can also mean human trafficking.

The substrate reality is the underworld of violence that exists in the world today that emerges in situations such as the one that Dr. Figueroa related at the start of our conversation. The text that Rabbi Skorka mentioned about Cain and Abel reminds me of another one from Deuteronomy: *"Today I place before you life and death."* This means, that our freedom, ultimately, is at stake due to the problem of violence. Either we're on the side of meekness which makes us brothers and sisters, as God created us, or we're on the side of confrontation.

FIGUEROA: This inclusive idea about the subject of violence is very interesting. Because there is always the temptation of following Jean-Paul Sartre's line of thinking: "Hell is other people," and in that way we conceive of violence as something that happens to others and to which we are mere spectators, like one who sees a violent movie.

I think that a realistic approach to violence is for us to realize that we can be factors that deepen the conflict or protagonists for peace.

I recall the hard and penetrating words of Jesus when he says that within the heart of man good and evil live side by side, a thought that also is present in the apostle Paul, when he says: *"I find that the law is good, but there is something in me that revolts against the law of God and that leads me, precisely, to do what I do not want to do."*

Once, speaking with Ernesto Sabato at his home, I asked him about the "Report on the Blind" (from his novel *On Heroes and*

Tombs) and what that had to do with his own personal introspection and the search in his heart. There, like one who enters into different rooms, some light, others dark, he penetrates his own being and he discovers that sharing those spaces are the most supreme good and the most terrible of evils.

SKORKA: That is the very description found in the Bible, and raised by the Talmudic scholars, that both instincts live side by side within man. The concept of envy, that it is something evil when exacerbated, is also necessary. When someone says: "That other person achieved such and such a thing," and then thinks: "Well, I'll steal it from him, I'll kill him and take it from him," then envy is transformed into the instinct for evil. But when I say: "If he can do something like that, then so can I," then I can come to be an engine for my own improvement, in order to be able to reach a goal, because man has a challenge to grow closer to God. There is a verse, at the end of the first paragraph of chapter 2 in the book of Genesis, where it says: *"And on the sixth day, God finished his great creation and he took the seventh day, the day of Shabbat, and he made it holy."* And at the end it says: *"And God created all things with a purpose."* This can be interpreted to mean that God's work is not yet finished; God hopes that man will continue his work, always recreating. And to do so one needs a certain aggressive energy. Then, good and evil are a reality, they're within us like a constant challenge which the Bible proposes to us in that verse: *"Life and death, blessing and curse."*

On the other side, even while pretending to pursue what is good, one cannot follow incorrect paths. Justice means working with truth, to be incorruptible. When the truth is applied well it is one of the many safeguards against violence. But what happens is that the world is also emptied of justice. There are some people in certain positions of leadership who are not really involved with truth and do not work to make peace, but just the contrary. Often what such people do is "add fuel to the fire," stir up people's feelings and justify violence.

One must always seek a path of peace because nothing has more value than a human being's life. Nothing justifies crime or death, absolutely nothing. When people incite violence, we are swept into the vortex that so characterizes our society and the reality of the world we live in.

BERGOGLIO: The Rabbi has said some things that pique my interest. First, the difference between envy and emulation. Envy is destructive, but emulation, by contrast, leads me to do the same, and even to surpass what someone else did. A scene from the life of St. Ignatius of Loyola comes to my mind. When, after the mundane life of being a soldier, he read the lives of the saints and was in the process of experiencing a religious conversion and turning towards God, he said: "If St. Francis did it, I must do it; if St. Dominic did it, I must do it," as if saying: "Yes, so can I!"

Second, the rabbi spoke about when violence is, in some way, incited. And that is a most serious point that we're not very aware of. Today it's very common for people to carry an insult on the tip of their tongue; and we don't realize that this is also something contagious.

I think about that daily manner that we Argentines have of provoking violence by degrading the other person. It consists of three things: slander, defamation, and misinformation. With slander we invent a story about someone, and then that person is no longer "John Smith," or whomever; he becomes "that guy who did such and such a thing." When slander enters the picture, it's very difficult to get rid of it. One thinker said that it's like casting a bag of feathers into the wind, that you can never gather them up again. Once you blacken someone's good name you can't undo that, some trace always remains. Remember that French thinker who cautioned against it because: "Slander, slander, hangs around forever."

Second, defamation. It can be that some person has done something reproachful but it's not widely known. Who has the right to spread that about or publicize it? People publish reproachful deeds on the slightest pretext, and this can destroy a person's reputation. Smearing a person's reputation is a form of violence.

And the third is very subtle, but toady it happens everywhere: misinformation. I say something true about a person, but I don't tell the full truth. I don't explain it in its full context. So, by telling a partial truth, I'm distorting the truth. I lie, and sowing the seeds of a lie is also a form of violence.

Slander, defamation, and misinformation are three bastardly ways that violence is generated, instead of generating unity.

As Dr. Figueroa said, the teachings of Jesus contain a very great truth: "There is no need to consummate an act for you to have done it. If you hate your brother, you have already killed him in your heart." This means that hatred and inner-violence are something criminal. Jesus taught that, and from there he urges us toward meekness in search of understanding, justice, and rapprochement towards others in order to extend a bridge to counteract violence that essentially "burns bridges" between people.

FIGUEROA: I think that those of us who are involved in some means of communication, thinking about the fight against violence and establishing peace, we have got to be conscious of the fact that by sowing the good word, the firm anchor can sustain us. At the same time, we also need to be conscious of the fact that a bad word can destroy much more rapidly than the time it takes to build a good word.

Changing the angle of analysis, I wonder: why the need to create antagonism? Why so many times, instead of creating a bridge of encounter it is much easier to create divisions and schisms? You're either a fan of one team or another. It's black and white. You're for the left or the right. And soon a person is labeled for the rest of their life: "That's what you're like." However, in the middle there is a whole range of different shades and possibilities that help me to construct an encounter because, in the end, dialogue means approaching, through that whole range of shades of difference, until finding a meeting point. And I think that we men and women of faith have the responsibility of making that contribution, of facilitating dialogue that helps to build a bridge of understanding.

BERGOGLIO: That's where you find the root of the division. Life is not a matter of "either/or," but rather it's "this *and* that *and* that." In some way, within the field of good, one always seeks the position of the other so I might approach them little by little. The spirit that guides us must always be that of meekness and not of aggression; one of dialogue, not insult. I think that those are the paths against violence: meekness and dialogue.

It does me good each time that we three meet together, we come from three distinct religious traditions, and we realize that we do not need to insult each other, nor quarrel, but simply come together around those things we have in common, the fact of being children of God.

SKORKA: The reason for the increase in violence is a subject for psychologists, sociologists, and many other specialists. I merely look at that which is developing around us and I try to interpret it, as Ortega y Gasset wrote in his famous book about the masses and their awakening.

What I notice is that it is based on the concept of human excitation; things are promoted and sold to people for excitement, in one way or another. It would seem that people have got to live like they've consumed or must consume the elixir of life itself and be constantly excited; and violence is something that, for some, evidently, is a means of excitation.

Now then, I think that we have to seek a change of attitude; that things can be exciting, but for the spirit. That excitement should not be centered on that which pulls us down, but on that which elevates us. An excitation for approaching God, for doing something to help elevate our neighbor, centered on something positive, not in tearing down another person.

FIGUEROA: It would be naive to imagine that we are not in a violent environment and that we are not, either, part of a violent society. But it would be unrealistic, from the human point of view of faith, to not think that we can be builders of peace and creators of an encounter between people. Therefore it's good to get angry about violence, because that is an anger in favor of what is good.

For my part, I'm going to keep betting for good news, for the dignity of the other person. I'm not going to defame nor attack; I'm going to try to understand the other person and to perceive information in a realistic way, while always looking toward what is good. I think that if we all propose to ourselves to do that, even in little ways, those seeds that are more difficult to plant and cultivate are going to bear fruit sooner or later. Let us trust in that. I think that God is much more interested in that cultivation than we are.

12

Ecology

"And God saw that all that he had made was very good."
Genesis 1:31

FIGUEROA: Probably the most serious ecological disaster in recent history was the one that occurred in 1989 off the coast of Alaska, where more than 11,000,000 gallons of crude oil spilled into the sea. But we must also remember that every day they clear cut almost 5,000,000 acres of trees in the Amazon, that region being the most important ecological reserve we have on the planet, and that 200,000 tons of trash are dumped into the sea.

The planet where we live is our house. Nevertheless we are not good housekeepers. We treat the earth as if she were someone else's house, or with the selfishness of thinking that it's just other generations who are going to suffer these ecological problems, without thinking that this means our children, grandchildren, great-grandchildren, great-great-grandchildren, and great-great-great-grandchildren.

There are some who say that the problem starts in the Bible, when in Genesis 1, God tells man that he should dominate the earth, take possession of her. Of course, I don't share that point of view, given that the text doesn't really mean those things. The context is one initiating the idea of God's care for the earth, a care that we must imitate.

SKORKA: When we read about how God placed man in Eden, Scripture says that he put him in a fruitful place *"so that he might care for it and work it."* The image of man seated in the shade of a tree and the fruit dropping right into his mouth was not really the idea of Eden. The heart of the idea is *"that he might work the land."* When does man receive God's blessing? When he can achieve and enjoy the fruit of his labor.

A careful reading of the Pentateuch reveals to us how God teaches the people of Israel—although it's a universal message and for that reason is later adopted by Christianity—how they must care for the world, the planet, their habitat. *"The land is to be worked for six years, and in the seventh year the land must rest."* For example, in Deuteronomy 22 we read that when someone finds a nest, they may not take the mother with the chicks, they have got to leave the mother alone. They can make use of her offspring, but without extinguishing the species. Also, when one sees an animal that is stumbling beneath the burden it carries, even if it be the animal of one's enemy, their duty is to run and remove the weight to relieve the animal's suffering. There is a concept discovered by the Talmudic scholars that teaches we should try to avoid the suffering of all living things. They cite the book of Deuteronomy: *"When plowing the earth, you cannot yoke together an ass and a bull, because the ass will have to pull harder than the bull, and so will suffer for the sake of the other."*

The Pentateuch teaches us to show great respect and care for the habitat where we live. This is also caring for God's work. The long and short of it is—to speak plainly—that here we live a borrowed life, we're not the masters of anything.

Man's selfishness, his desire for convenience, his extreme utilitarianism—and we can also cite Isaiah: *"Eat and drink for tomorrow we die"*—is a lifestyle resulting from the technological developments of the twentieth century, the idea of "use it and discard it." And now what do we do with the things we discard? We're filling the world with garbage.

BERGOGLIO: At the start, Figueroa spoke about the Amazon. In the Fifth General Conference of Latin American Bishops, in Aparecida, the care of the Amazon region was a strongly recurrent theme, because this region represents the largest reserve of water, air and oxygen anywhere on Earth.

One very grave problem that we're experiencing today in Argentina is deforestation. Currently our lands are being killed. Forests are being clear cut with the idea of making them more productive by planting them with cereal crops, most soy beans. And the earth is subjected to this, planted and replanted, one harvest after another, without rest. This makes me think of the biblical counsel to let the field lie fallow every seven years.

I remember that fifty years ago, when we were studying soil chemistry, they explained to us that if you plant corn three years running, then in the fourth year you've got to plant alfalfa or something similar to replenish the nitrogen in the soil. Today they're annually harvesting two crops of soy beans, from the same fields, one after the other. What we're left with, then, is a totally impoverished land, which needs to be "enriched" with chemical fertilizers. It's no longer a noble land, but a land that is manufactured or produced, which in the long run brings us problems. There is an aphorism that says: "God always forgives, man sometimes forgives, and nature never forgives."

On the other side, we've got global warming. The fact that the North Pole—a place with no arable land—is melting faster; makes the seas rise and causes important animal species that keep the earth in an ecological balance to disappear.

All this is very serious and indicates a neglect for God's first commandment: take care of the earth!

FIGUEROA: With respect to deforestation in northern Argentina, from having visited, for many years, the indigenous communities in Salta and Formosa, I remember how sad it is to see areas of the mountain clear cut so they can be planted with soybeans. There are two terrible effects, one is the climatic change, all that ecological balance created by God in the environment that, when disrupted, produces flooding along the Pilcomayo and Bermejo rivers. The other is a very serious change in the culture of the original peoples. For our indigenous brothers and sisters, their contact with nature is not like what we experience; they interact with nature in a very profound way. So then, if we strip them of those elements from nature with which they have developed that relationship over the course of centuries, we are robbing them of a fundamental part of their culture and cosmological vision.

But let's speak without euphemisms! The ecological problem is due to selfishness, neglect or apathy, and most of the time enormous economic forces are behind this. They are exploiting the earth and deforesting it to plant soybeans in northern Argentina. They do this for purely economic interests, and they care nothing about ecology.

One needs to have a loving concept of the earth and of everything created by God, to recognize it as a gift or, as the rabbi said so well, as a loan, knowing that we are simply the stewards, circumstantial administrators of an earth that continues to belong to God and God alone. Although we may not see that, although we might be myopic and not see it in that way, at least we must have the instinct to preserve the species. Contrary to all this, I think that there is a concept of destruction that goes beyond the ecological, and that is the destruction of humanity. The ecological drama is always going to lead to the destruction of humankind.

With ecological care, God has a compromise or personal pact, because after the Flood, when he makes a pact with man, he himself signs it with the rainbow, and he is very clear when he expresses it: "*I am going to make a pact with Noah, with his children and their descendants; but I am also making a pact with all of creation.*" There is a covenant of God. Are we living up to this covenant? How can we be collaborators with God in that pact that he himself made?

SKORKA: When I read the biblical text about the Flood, year after year—because as part of our liturgy, we read the Pentateuch every Saturday morning, and afterwards we gather together and we analyze the reading—the idea always comes to my mind that that verse has a part that is not specified. It is as if God was telling us: "I'm not going to bring any more natural destruction. But consider, if there is going to be any natural destruction, it is going to come from man, this is going to be the responsibility of humanity."

If we think about nuclear power plants, when they are designed to what extent are questions of safety overlooked for the sake of small profits? Are they really made, in line with all the safety measures necessary so that we do not have another disaster like Chernobyl or what recently happened in Japan? We're playing with fire! We're risking the lives of millions of people. What do I really know about how many people are going to suffer from cancer or genetic problems? And what do I really know about the genetic transmutations that radiation can cause?

Sometimes man takes a risk. We were born to play and to take risks, but when it comes to nature we must be careful, because every game has its rules.

BERGOGLIO: When man exceeds that dominion he has over the earth, he ceases to be a lord of the earth and becomes its tyrant instead. He begins to perform experiments that go beyond the respect for the gift received from God, and that can lead him to create things that later escape his control. In that way, man, who has got to be the creator of culture through God's mandate, ends up being the creator of ignorance. Man can dominate culture and make scientific advances grow, but when it slips through his fingers and beyond his control, because he exceeded the limits that a respect for nature presupposes, then he can no longer dominate it. This form of ignorance is an idol fabricated by man through the misuse of God's gift, similar to the pride seen in the story of the Tower of Babel: *"I'm going to climb to the heights of heaven and we're going to show who we are."* Generally, in that zeal for discovery which lacks respect for the gift received, there is at least a trace of idolatry.

FIGUEROA: I'm not going to construct an apology for God because he doesn't need me to defend him, he defends himself just fine. But it's curious, because when man ignores God's rules for creation and then, as a consequence, enormous ecological problems arise, the first thing man says is: "So where's God when you need him?" What we should be wondering is what did man do, because God already saw what man needs to do. In reality, God has nothing to do with the damages caused, they're signals or signs from nature that he created that tell us: "Respect me!"

There are two people who, in some way, pulled us forward beyond a Platonic vision: one is St. Francis of Assisi and the other is Albert Schweitzer. Both revived the theme of man's relationship with nature. Some accused them of being pantheists, but I think that they helped us to see the necessity of living in partnership with God's creation.

The apostle Paul expressed this in a very vivid way in chapter 8 of his letter to the Romans: *"Creation groans and suffers waiting to be liberated from the slavery which man has imposed upon it."* Creation is not some silent, unwanted guest; its life is given by God, something that we must respect, care for, protect, and work with.

My question, then, points to thinking about how each person, from their particular place (home, school, faith community), can help to create a healthy ecological culture.

SKORKA: I think that we must work with the different authorities as much at the neighborhood level as the provincial and national one, to deal with certain norms and speak about them from our various pulpits. On the other hand, and in reference to everything we've already said, I thought about a great Jewish thinker from the first half of the twentieth century named Franz Rosenzweig. In his magnum opus, *The Star of Redemption*, he raises the following idea: In the Greek world there are three concepts that are inter-related: God, nature, and man. In the world of the Bible there is another overlapping triangle, that's why we have the star of redemption: God—man—nature.

Between God and man is the Bible, and there is a revelation in the pact of Sinai because man matters to God. They are not two things completely unconnected between themselves; there is "a something" that is manifest through revelation. On the other hand, between God and nature, which has got to do with God, is creation. And what is there between nature and man? Redemption. In order to be able to redeem, one must be a caretaker and a liberator. To redeem is to take something to its primary state, to the perfect state in which it was created. It's not true that between nature and man there is nothing more than a mere usufruct; not at all, there is a challenge: redemption.

BERGOGLIO: What you're saying is very interesting, because all redemption means accepting and coming to terms. So then God, on giving us nature, creation, is asking us that we accept it as it is, not how we would like it to be. In the moment when one ceases to accept creation as it is, and treats it as something it is not, he begins to attack it and to give way to all the deviations that lead to catastrophe, to ignorance.

Redemption means always accepting things the way they come. We see that in the love of a father and a mother for their child. If you want your child to grow up well, accept him as he came and help him to progress in order that he might be able to give the most of himself. Accepting nature implies tenderness and affection. Accepting something implies doing so with sympathy, in the Greek sense of the word, with empathy. Without this we are bound to use nature as something that is given to us, but we're not going to be able to experience it beyond the framework of experimentation.

I want to talk about something that Figueroa said about the indigenous peoples, who have a dialogue with nature that is totally different from the one we have. The dialogue that we have with nature is through cement, while the indigenous peoples are suffering an aggression because of the misuse of nature. Here, only a few blocks away, at the intersection of the Avenida de Mayo and Avenida 9 de Julio, there is an encampment of Qom people from the northern part of the state of Formosa, who have been there for months. The Qom are a people that have been cornered and everything has been taken from them. They have come to reclaim at least what belongs to them, which is their land. They have no electric lights in their villages, but they do have a dialogue with nature. We don't understand that those peoples maintain that living dialogue and that it is going to do us good if we listen to them and respect the spaces where they live. Instead, we've taken away their lands to clear cut them and plant soy beans.

Without going very far from this point, when I was very young my grandmother took us to fish in the Reconquista River, which in those days was called Rio de las Conchas, or Shell River, because in the river bed there were fresh water mussels. You could see them! You could just reach down and pull them out. But today we see what the Reconquista River has become, because the industries that are all throughout the area dump their raw, unprocessed waste products there, illegally. It wouldn't cost them hardly anything to clean and process the waste first and thereby keep the river clean; nevertheless today the river is just a sewer. A particular kind of sewer, but a sewer nonetheless.

And the same thing is happening with our Riachuelo River. As a boy, one of my favorite things to do was to go and swim in Olivos. Today it's impossible to swim in the River Plate because it's polluted with all kinds of things. Even here, in our city, we also have situations and conditions that result from this ignorant misuse of nature.

Fanaticism

"Who is a fanatic?"

"The one who gives primacy to secondary things and who relegates important things to second place."
Rabbi Abraham Skorka

"The one who makes the detail into the main point, and the main point a mere detail."
Cardinal Jorge M. Bergoglio

FIGUEROA: We want to take up a complex subject: fanaticism. According to the standard María Moliner dictionary, a fanatic is "that zealous person who is an extremist and intolerant of a belief." It can be a religious belief, something banal like a soccer team, or something much more profound, the way an ideology can be. Usually, fanaticism brings to light the worst aspects of the human being and of society.

SKORKA: I'll start with an example related to justice. When someone was prosecuted as a criminal, there was a Sanhedrin* composed of twenty-three wise men that would analyze and discuss

---

* **Sanhedrin:** An assembly, a council of wise men, elected as the only Jewish tribunal with authority to try matters of national importance.

the case. But if there was no public prosecutor or defender, even if the council of twenty-three said *"This man is guilty,"* the man was set free because it wasn't permissible for anyone to be found guilty without having had a proper defense.

In agreement with Judaic interpretation of fanaticisms, there has to be restraint, because no idea or concept should be defended by means of outbursts and accusations without consideration for one's neighbor.

Considering this definition, I want to cite Rabbi Menachem Mendel of Kotsk, who was once asked: "Rabbi, why do they say that I'm a fanatic? Why do they not say instead that I'm a pious man?" And the Rabbi answered: "Because you gave primacy to things of secondary importance, and you made what's most important secondary."

BERGOGLIO: Fanaticism is an ideological problem, a mental construction that is imposed on the whole person, to the point of leading some to deny that we are both flesh and spirit. We see it, for example, in the case of the kamikazes or suicide bombers. For these people their own life has no meaning, because for them what matters more is the idea that they derive from it. It's a form of logic where the detail becomes the center point, and the center point a mere detail. Speaking of "domestic" fanaticism, we also see it in religious legalism. For example, in Córdoba I was once asked a question: "Look, Father, we went to a wedding on Saturday afternoon, and it included Mass. The Bible readings were not the ones from Sunday but from Saturday. So, does this count for me attending Sunday Mass?" With a bit of irony, I felt like saying to this person: "Take it easy, you've been vaccinated, you're safe."

FIGUEROA: I was very impressed to read in the Gospels that the great discussions of Jesus were not with adulterers, nor with sinners, not even with the tax collectors working for the Roman Empire; his heaviest discussions were with the religious fundamentalists. When they argued about fulfilling some legal detail of secondary importance, Jesus said to them: *"It's fine, do that, but don't forget that the most important thing continues to be love the Lord your God with all your soul, all heart, all your might, and your neighbor as yourself."*

I think that in fundamentalism there is a great narrowness of mind and spirit. Fundamentalists need to construct something small that they can dominate, manage, and make their own to become possessors of an absolute truth. Then, the person who doesn't fit within their own personal version of the truth, whether because they don't practice the same religion or because they don't have the same ideology, is automatically disqualified and considered to be in a lesser category, and they are attacked as if they were an enemy.

SKORKA: Fundamentalism does not engage in discussion, it refuses to analyze its own faith, in no way does it sit down at the table to debate because it totally disdains another person's thoughts. It possesses a truth that it considers to be absolute. In their exclusive thinking about the truth, they disqualify others and form a distorted image of them, denying them and, in the worst cases, eliminating them directly.

It's a phenomenon of the kind that, lamentably, we had a fresh experience of during the past century and, so far, even now during the first decade of this century it continues to overwhelm us.

One would have to ask psychologists and sociologists: How can it be that those people have so grossly distorted the desire to be an individual? Why does the fundamentalist take an idea and then allow himself to be guided by a pernicious leader? The question is: Why doesn't that person wish to be "himself"? How is it that he goes, as the Bible verse says, *"like sheep to the slaughter"*? How is it that fundamentalists destroy the "self" so much that they're capable of considering themselves part of a political machine in the service of a single ideal?

BERGOGLIO: They're afraid of freedom, and that same fear pushes them forward until they abolish freedom, and go on to become servants of whoever brainwashed them.

In our three religious faiths—and also in Islam—there are fundamentalists. We Catholics have fundamentalists, meaning people who put aside goodness and beauty and cling to the truth and distort it. The truth, without a relationship to goodness and beauty, is not truth, it's a caricature of it. These people take the truth and they formulate it into dogmas, into concepts of historical analysis of reality, and they proceed based on that, no matter what. There is no freedom of confrontation, thinking is exclusive, and it becomes crystallized.

Now, it's curious how, generally, the great fanaticisms arise in response to a people's need. Let's think about Germany in the 1920s when the country anoints Hitler as its leader. This arises from a people's need to allow themselves to be dazzled by a leader who has a special plan of action, who begins to brainwash everyone and adjust and arrange the national institutions based on that fundamentalism.

When the people begin to realize what is really happening, they find themselves too frightened to speak up when they don't agree, and they fear being punished. In this second phase they realize that this is not so good, but the power structures by now are so strong that there is a real fear of speaking out. And the third phase occurs when there is no longer any possibility of reaction thanks to brainwashing or the sowing of fear—as happened when Nazism really showed its true face. That's how the single-mindedness at the heart of fundamentalisms are created.

FIGUEROA: My whole time at university was spent under the years of the dictatorship, and I remember that we'd be terribly frightened when we got stopped and searched. The mere fact of having a university notebook made you suspect. Of course, none of us had any idea of the dimension of horror the country was living through, nor of the thousands of abductions and everything else that we know about now, but we were afraid of speaking out freely.

You just mentioned Nazi Germany. What do we do so all that doesn't happen again? These types of things happen because, in some way, people follow certain paths, and this doesn't come out in the light of day. There is a whole process of deterioration of willpower, of thinking, of ideas, of dialogue, of openness; a deterioration of the freedom that leads to a situation like that becoming the norm.

SKORKA: In Nazi Germany, evidently, the first thing that began to be terribly destroyed was culture. Let's not forget that the books of banned authors were burned in bonfires. In Argentina there were also banned books. I remember that it was dangerous to own a copy of Marx's *Capital.* If you had one, and the police raided your house, you could have serious problems.

Every book is worth being studied and analyzed, so why constrain or prohibit culture? It's important to stimulate dialogue, to create incentives for there to be all kinds of ideological demonstrations within a society, and especially in the schools and universities, in order to help young people think for themselves.

Do you know what the Talmud is, essentially? To properly understand the law, the Mishnah,* one must try to interpret it in

---

* **Mishnah:** Along with the Torah, the Mishnah forms the basis for Judaic or rabbinical law. It is a body of thought and wisdom gathered from oral tradition around the end of the second century and now compiled in six volumes.

relation to certain cases, and for that purpose one must listen and discuss the opinions and sayings of the rabbis which are found in the Talmud.

Years ago, the University Press in Buenos Aires published a book which I was involved with, a compilation of some articles about Hebrew law. The title was *Introduction to Hebrew Law*. The article that made the biggest impression on me was the final one in the book, written by a professor from the Hebrew University, which raises this question: "Can we say that Hebrew law is structured in a philosophically similar way to positive Western rights?" He comes to the conclusion that they are not. Why not? Because when you go to talk to a rabbi you can't know if your position is really going to be the one that proves you right. He can manage to find some things that you don't see and interpretations can emerge that are specific to that moment, with distinct analyses. What do I mean by this? The best form of avoiding fundamentalism is teaching the other person by means of questions, especially, very hard questions.

BERGOGLIO: In the description of the fundamentalist, one of the things that appears most clearly is the lack of dialogue. The fundamentalist is a "monologist" who talks with himself only in order to strengthen his own position. A fundamentalist doesn't know what dialogue is. His heart is closed to everything meant to confront a point of view different from his own.

In addition to the clear, obvious figure of the fundamentalist with his narrow, exclusive way of thinking, we can also recognize the pseudo-fundamentalists, people who, without reaching quite such a crystallized position, in some way elude dialogue and confrontation because they're afraid. They hide inside their strongest ideas, which excuse them from having to seek the truth or engage in dialogue or integrate other people into their life's core beliefs.

I want to highlight the word "fear" because, in general, at the basis of a fundamentalist there is fear. Fear that someone else tells me some truth that shakes me up. Fear of life. The fundamentalist fears the richness of life—he seizes on some truths, excludes others, and objectifies them. He doesn't do it, his master does it, the one who brainwashes him. And so, we have men and women who are ruined, in our streets, in our society, attending our churches, our temples, but gazing on with detachment, looking for the fault in others, trying to spot the place where "orthodoxy" is being forsaken.

"Orthodoxy" is a gentle word; it consists of being in agreement with the "doxa," the law, and with the glory. The orthodox person is the one who adjusts himself to that law, who at the same time glorifies it and makes it grow in the widest sense of the word. But the fundamentalist conceives of orthodoxy as a secure possession, closed off from all dialogue, that admits no plurality.

14

The Capacity for Surprise

I don't know how many days had passed since that momentous March 13, 2013, when the white smoke announced the election of Cardinal Bergoglio as Pope Francis. I'm still not been able to rationally process such news. I kept remembering his voice on my telephone, a day before he traveled to Rome, saying goodbye with a simple: "I'll be back soon, and we'll keep taping the program." It was a wait for a return effectively undone by the endless images on TV of him dressed in white. My capacity for surprise, this time, had been pushed to unimaginable limits.

My birthday often falls during Holy Week. This time it was Holy Saturday. I answered my cell phone casually, expecting it to be just another birthday well-wisher. Once again, more surprise. Pope Francis had remembered me and was calling from Rome. This time, his words touched me deeply: "Have a very happy birthday, Marcelo. Please give my love and blessings to your wife and children." I was standing there alone in the street, and while I walked faster to get home, I wanted to tell this news to the first person I ran into. When I reached home, I told my wife about the Pope's call. Our eyes teared up from the emotion.

A short while later I turned on the television and there was Francis, facing millions on his first Holy Saturday as Bishop of Rome—the same man who, on such an important day in his life, had remembered and taken the time to call his Protestant friend on his birthday. Again, I was overwhelmed with surprise. And that precisely was the theme of this program that we recorded in mid-2011.

FIGUEROA: With the intention of not wanting to lose our capacity for surprise, I'll allow myself to take up this theme from two different angles or go in two completely different ways. In the first place, not losing the capacity for surprise in a relationship about what bad things produce in us because, in some way, it is resistance that helps us not accept bad outcomes as normal. Second, not losing the capacity for surprise that good things produce in us, which give us happiness and hope that everything can go much better. Or rather, on one side, resist losing our capacity for surprise due to bad things and, on the other, to retain that capacity to receive the hopeful freshness of good things.

SKORKA: The Judaic proposal with respect to this theme lies in a phrase that we say in our everyday prayers: "Because God is the one who renews, with his goodness, his creation, every day." On the other hand, in the first verses of chapter 2 of Genesis we find the description of the divine creation of the cosmos and of everything. That can be interpreted as something that was not left completely finished; that God left creation to man so that he might work with it and bring it to completion.

I think that a man begins to die the moment he passes by a rose, a mountain chain, a small hill or a lovely landscape, and none of that says anything to him; he fails to be moved by God's creation. We've got to see life continuously in a completely fresh way, like a child who sees the ocean for the first time. With respect to attitudes about life, one cannot remain indifferent either, and without at least a touch of surprise, when receives the manifestation of love and affection of a friend.

In relation to evil, we must remember history and not take for granted that certain manifestations are not important, for example, when a demagogue or a despot threatens or speaks in terms of destruction, of denying or demonizing another. It already happened once and it was a terrible surprise that cost millions of lives. No one believed that Nazism could do what it did, and what it ended up doing. There was a famous Hassidic rabbi named Menachem Mendel whose personal passion was to understand and know the truth. He said: "All truth that is imitated ceases to be true." I apply this to life every day. If one day is the imitation of another, if something doesn't turn out to be totally fresh or new, on that day you'll begin to move away from the truth. Your truth must lead you to discover things.

Life can become cyclical, but man's challenge is to not live within vicious circles. Man can and must strive for a different world, in spite of everything that happens. The moment we get used to vicious circles, and there is no longer an attitude of surprise in the face of something that fires our hope for a new world, in that moment we move away from the truth and we begin to die, even while we are still alive.

BERGOGLIO: There is a verse in the book of Lamentations that says *"Each day your mercies are reborn"* or rather, our encounter with the Lord is different each day, it's new, and he comes to our meeting dispensing mercy freely. It's good to conserve the capacity for pleasure and to be surprised with God's generosity towards us.

On the other hand, reading Genesis shows the idea that Adam was surprised by all the animals that he had named, but his surprise was greater when he found himself with Eve, and he exclaimed: *"This, yes!"*—surprised by this great wonder that God had made. Surprise in this case, opens for us the road towards love and towards receiving from the other person.

If one reads through all of Scripture, one notices that the Lord is the God of surprises.

FIGUEROA: What Cardinal Bergoglio says about surprise in the Bible is true. After the patriarchs, God establishes an ordering and a regime of justice around the judges. However, the people of Israel begin to see the neighboring peoples and miss having a king like them. And so the Israelites ask God for a king. To the surprise of many and the anguish of Samuel, the Lord agrees to grant their request, but not before clarifying that such a request is not against Samuel but because of their rejection of God and his decisions. Then they elect their first king, Saul, which turns out to be a very bad experience. From there arises, once again, the theme of God's surprise.

When the Lord sends Samuel to a house in Bethlehem, to anoint the new king who will replace Saul, the father of the family, Jesse, presents his children in the order of their favorable qualities. One by one, the seven candidates are rejected. It would seem as if the story will only end in frustration until Samuel asks Jesse: *"Do you have any other child?"* Jesse, with shame, answers him: *"Yes, I have another, a good son who is caring for the sheep in the pasture, but he's too small."* Nevertheless, the prophet orders him to call the boy and Samuel anoints him as king. And he is no less than David, the future great king of Israel.

God always surprises us, and that shows the dynamic of the biblical text. Today, the very same God keeps on giving us surprises.

SKORKA: God is life, a living God, not a static element. And life is something that we never finish understanding profoundly; he's a great mystery in all his aspects, both life itself as in the sense of the individual and even the discovery of God.

We can also talk about surprises in science. At the beginning of the twentieth century there were people who believed that physics had gone as far as it could. They had to come up with a new physics to interpret the phenomena that occur at the molecular level, of atoms and subatomic particles: quantum mechanics. We thought that time and space were absolute and then the theory of relativity appeared in 1905. These were two enormous shakeups that surprised those who said that classic physics was perfect. I relate this to the story of Samuel anointing David. There's something that God says to Samuel that should not be overlooked. When Samuel suddenly sees one of David's brothers and says: *"It's this one, tall and strong!"* Then God says to him: *"Man looks into the eyes, but God looks into the heart."* And that is the question.

One ceases to be surprised in the moment that they look only at the surface, at the external appearance, when they see only the wrapping but don't look to realize what's inside the package. For that reason, I return to a personal thought, when someone says: "Well, I know everything by now, I know it all; I know what rose petals are like. Nothing surprises me." As Florencio Sanchez said in one of his books: "The man without character is a walking corpse." Paraphrasing those words, I would say: "The man who is not surprised, who has lost that sense of freshness, is like a dead man walking."

BERGOGLIO: Such a man's heart is closed. When one has lost the capacity to be surprised it's because his heart is overburdened and confused. How does this happen to the heart? Always expecting to feel good, a lack of challenges, taking pleasure from the dullest things life has to offer, is a certain spiritual laziness.

A heart that cannot be surprised is a stagnant heart, and the same thing happens to stagnant water that doesn't flow, it becomes putrid and unhealthy. A heart without surprises, in some way, already has begun to be corrupted from within and has begun to die, to close itself off. It becomes corrupted because it's dead and no longer has any hopes and dreams.

Philosophers say that the beginning of the philosophical act lies in admiration, which is the capacity for surprise. The one who feeds that capacity for surprise, cares for it and makes sure that it is alive on the inside. He is essentially a poet, a continuous creator of new things, both internal and external.

Last Sunday, being the day of the workers, the statue of Christ of the Workers in the Parish of Cristo Obrero was inaugurated. The statue is three meters tall and is made from old railroad ties and scrap metal. It's the work of a young Argentine artist, forty years old, who is installing art in factories to stimulate the artistic dimension among the metalworkers.

The capacity for being surprised by things, and of being creative with new things, is wonderful.

FIGUEROA: I think that there are two factors. The artist who in his mind first "sees," imagines, creates, develops, and builds; but it also requires that the person who approaches that image has the capacity to be surprised and to let himself be touched by its beauty. Isn't it true that our capacity for surprise —which also has to do with the spiritual dimension—depends a lot on our looking at the same thing but daring to see it in a different way?

Sometimes, we get used to looking at something and we always see the same thing. But one can also look from another angle and find things previously unseen. For example, where there is a problem, we can find a new opportunity, or in something seen every day, we can find something new and beautiful. I can apply this to the spiritual plane, too: faced with a circumstance that happens in my life or facing something that I'm seeing, I can ask God to give me that capacity to look beyond what is merely visible.

BERGOGLIO: I would also point out the need to raise children in this manner of maintaining the capacity for surprise. At first, the child is surprised by anything, and it's nice to see how they discover the world. Later comes a moment when that capacity is diminished or closed off. Then the world becomes something utilitarian and not something to contemplate, something that permits him to have other viewpoints and to discover what beauty is.

I think that among the transcendent blessings, truth, goodness, and beauty, the one most taken for granted is the one having to do with beauty. Why? Because the habits needed to draw closer to beauty are the ones least fostered in school. Habits do not form much part of education. Children are not educated to be surprised, although this is very much a part of the early expression of children. We must cultivate the soul of a child and of the poet to maintain the capacity for surprise in the face of life, to know how to be surprised by what a grandfather or grandmother is, about the wisdom of the elderly, and of opening the heart to listen to them.

I recall a little old couple that used to come to the Luján Porteño parish—Don Pascual and Doña María—they were both around ninety years old. Every day they came to Mass together, holding hands; they'd hear Mass and then go home. When I was going to that parish it did me good to see them. I noticed them, I admired them. At every stage of life it's important to have an open heart that can discover that message.

I think that today we must discover the richness within others, in all people, and especially I mean to include people on the margins of society. One can come to have a utilitarian sense of life and consider some people to be "disposable material," for example, rejecting young people because they can cause problems and rejecting old people because they can be a bother, because it's difficult to look after them, or because they smell badly. The old person is often despised but the Bible condemns this attitude—in the book of Proverbs, I believe—it says: *"Do not shame an old man, we will all be old someday."*

SKORKA: With respect to the capacity for surprise, or new things, it's like the child who already knows the story and who still wants to hear it again. That little old couple you mentioned, how many Masses must they have heard in their 90 years? They must've known it all by heart! It's what happens in my synagogue each time we pray and we already know by heart what's going to come next. However, there is always some word, a "something" that reflects what's happening to us in that moment.

What is a ritual? It's the repetition of something. Psychological studies of religion affirm that we are repeating things in all rituals, in all religious cultures. But, be aware, when the ritual becomes mere repetition, I think that it becomes a question of schizophrenia.

When that story you've heard before still brings you certain sensations: "I'm at peace because I know how it ends, I know how the story goes, but I like listening to it again because I experience it again, or I feel surprise with one aspect or another of myself." This is precisely an experience of the sublime, like a prayer where I tremble all over again, with the weekly Torah reading that leads me to discover something new or with the annual cycle of the reading of the Pentateuch.

BERGOGLIO: The capacity for surprise has the strength of transforming a fact—sometimes a banal one—into an event. We've got to encourage ourselves to transform the good or bad occurrences into events, and we can only achieve this by maintaining our capacity for surprise. The event makes my story. It says something to me and touches my heart.

15

Power

"Service is true power." This enormously meaningful sentence was uttered by Pope Francis in the first homily of his Petrine ministry to a multitude of the faithful in St. Peter's Square in the Vatican, and in the presence of heads of state representing 132 countries.

Many were surprised by his courage and amazed at such a concept of power. Others wondered if these were only political words or a convenient speech for the time and place.

For those of us who knew him well, it was the most complete demonstration that he had not yielded a single one of his lifelong pastoral commitments. We smiled silently. He was still one hundred percent Cardinal Bergoglio, and from now on he was going to be, one hundred percent Pope Francis.

FIGUEROA: When we think about the word "power," we habitually imagine the most prominent spheres of society or the ones that have the most influence. Nevertheless, we all have a certain amount of power in the place where we live and work: the father of the family, in his house; the boss in his company, and even the clerk behind his counter. Of course, the implication or magnitude of the effects of its use corresponds to the place where that power is exercised.

The question, perhaps, is not whether we have power or not, but what do we understand through power? How do we conceive of power? Why do we want it? For what purpose?

I recall a quotation from Abraham Lincoln: "Nearly all men can stand adversity, but if you want to test a man's character, give him power."

Today's subject is complex, but it's a very important one because we are subject to people who exercise power over us and, in turn, we also have our own measure of power.

SKORKA: Power is a function that we often choose to exercise, and other times it is imposed upon us. The power that a teacher has over his students is decisive, is important, and the teacher must exercise it. Equally the father over his children, especially when they are in early stages of growth and need someone to guide them, to impose rules and limits. This applies to private, intimate matters and in public, in the loftiest hierarchies of power.

The organization of human society teaches us that structures are necessary for guidance and creating order because otherwise we would live in chaos. Power is necessary to live in a civilized way.

One of the most important themes in biblical literature is the exercise of power. In the book of Judges, chapter 9, we find the parable of Jotham, a story with enormous strength and applicability to life. It begins by saying that the trees went to anoint themselves a king. First they went to the olive tree and they said to him *"Be our king and rule over us."* And the olive said: *"I have no time; I must grow good olives to make good oil."* Then they went to see the fig tree, but he answered them: *"I've got no time for that; I've got to grow good figs."* Next they paid a visit to the grape vine, who also found an excuse for not wanting to rule, saying: *"I've got to form the most beautiful clusters of grapes I can. Who has time for anything else?"* Next they went to see a shrub, the blackberry bramble, who accepted the honor of being king, but first he warned them: *"You must know that if you go with me and stay on my side all shall be well for you, but if you go against me, I shall light a fire that will destroy everything, even the cedars of Lebanon."*

In biblical literature, this constitutes a paradigmatic example of the magnificence of nature. It is also, lamentably, something that happens in fact! Sometimes the contributing members of a society say: "I'm very busy with this, I'm really caught up in that ..." thus leaving a vacuum in the power structure. This biblical book still carries the testimony of brilliant minds from approximately 2,800 years ago. Their parable tells us: "Be careful with power!"

Power is something conferred by God. Whoever exercises power somewhere needs to know that they do so because God chooses this. They must understand that humility is a basic element in the exercise of power, the basic key for its exercise.

BERGOGLIO: What Rabbi Skorka says, that "God chooses," can be seen in the first pages of Genesis, because God creates man and immediately gives him power: *"Grow, multiply, dominate the earth!"* Or rather, there is a power, man is an *animal potens*. God anoints him for the mission he gives him, because power is a gift. It's as if God said: "I deliver power into your hands, but you've got to use it for the reason I gave it to you"—that is, to grow, to multiply, to dominate the earth, so that civilization advances—and, in relation to one's neighbor, so that the other is, increasingly, a person.

On the other hand, I think about those that grasp power in any institution and do not accept it as a gift for the service of others, but as something for their own interest and use.

The Evangelist remarks that power is meant to be used to serve. For example, when the mother of the children of Zebedee asks Jesus that her two sons, John and James, be placed, one on his left hand and one on his right, when he is in his Kingdom, Jesus answers her: *"You don't know what you're asking; that is for my Father to decide."* This is not something that someone reaches for, it is a gift. For that reason it's the symbol of the holy unction that appears in the Bible since the Old Testament. And what does this mean? That God poured out the oil upon the head of whom he chose and to whom he gave a mission to fulfill.

If one does not conceive of power as a gift, but as something of one's own that one deserves to receive, that's where one begins to go astray, just like with a detour on a road. At first the detour seems to be just a short distance but then it goes on and on and by then one's orientation is not focused on the gift but rather on their own personal profit from it.

FIGUEROA: In the Bible, in the first book of Samuel, more precisely, we read about two people who each had their own space of power and who exercised it in opposite ways. Saul was the king. He had the power to be so and he exercised it. David had been anointed by the prophet Samuel in secret, by direct order of God, in such a way that he also had power, and he used his power to defeat Goliath. The people praise him for this and Saul goes power-mad—he can't stand not having absolute power, can't delegate power or see others grow in power. He becomes ill in such a way that he wants to kill David, and there we see a perverse form of exercising power. Saul believed that the power came from himself. He had forgotten who had gifted it to him, and for that reason he feared to be overshadowed. In the scenes in chapters 24 and 26, David has two clear opportunities to kill Saul, but not only does he not take them, instead he shows Saul that he had that opportunity and he let it pass by out of the respect he had for Saul's being a king anointed by the mandate of God.

From this arise three reflections. In the first place, power is something that we do not earn by our own efforts alone. In the second place, power is something that is delimited, and thus not eternal. And third, power is limited to certain spheres or certain situations; we need to understand that it is not the same, and cannot be duplicated in every area of life. As Lord Acton said: "Power tends to corrupt, but absolute power corrupts absolutely."

SKORKA: Saul knew that he was mortal, that at some time his days would come to an end. But he imagined a possible succession of his reign through his sons, especially through his son Jonathan. The figure of Saul is also problematic because at first he didn't want to be king; he was a shy, very introverted person who did not wish power for himself. Nevertheless, Samuel, in a certain measure obliged him to accept power, and he granted him strength to exercise power as king. On the other hand, it was politically important to unite all the people to form a single army. Saul was anointed because it was necessary to do this, in a given moment, and because they'd had very bad experiences with the tribes separately. The crux of what Figueroa described is that Saul became power-mad. Someone who at first didn't desire power suddenly had it, and then did not want to relinquish it.

In a certain way, David later experienced something similar with regard to what happened with Bathsheba. David could have had many women, but he only wanted to have the wife of Uriah, the Hittite, whose only wife was Bathsheba. Nevertheless, when the prophet reprimanded him through a parable, David had the greatness to recognize his fault: "I was wrong!" And God punished him with the death of his son.

This is a syndrome: sickness for power. Evidently, power, for the sake of power itself, is terrible. One must always have a goal, and that goal must be very important.

BERGOGLIO: God wants the power he gives us to be used to serve others. When someone who exercises power forgets this command and they start to enjoy their power, as happened to Saul—and as can happen to all of us who have a certain degree of power at some point in our life—they become ill. When we forget that one is made to serve and we begin to see how we can consolidate that power and rise up in life—all the while focusing on ourselves—that constitutes a pathological syndrome of the sickness for power.

The contrast between Saul and David lies precisely in David's greatness in recognizing that he had gone mad with power, unlike Saul who, when faced with an eventual competitor, found his soul corrupted.

David "believed in himself," sent men to war, lived large, strutted on the terrace, and glowered. I think that David, whom I love greatly, and who I know is in the presence of God, behaved shamelessly. He desired Bathsheba, and later he wanted to "conceal" the child that came of his desire. He couldn't manage this because of the loyalty of that man Uriah who was fighting in the war and did not want to return home while the ark of the covenant was fighting; and then comes the crime.

But David's greatness consisted in listening with his heart to the words of Nathan, meaning that he'd not lost his religious heart. He knew that his power came from God, and he said: *"I have sinned, I have been wrong, I have taken the wrong path."* He had the practical humility of the man who makes a mistake and recognizes it. He was a man who knew how to manage power. David's repentance in the face of sickness for power is very great, and is one of the things that has got to make us reconsider ourselves when we trespass badly in how we exercise our power.

I often wonder about my service in power, and when I'm honest with myself I see that I have flaws, and that I make mistakes. And sometimes, the Lord sends some person to point them out to me. It's curious: some people wrap up their criticisms like gifts with a ribbon on top, but inside you find a bomb! Others, by contrast, tell you their criticisms directly: "I don't agree with this; you should have done things this way."

When I feel power a bit too strongly, I can get angry that others limit me in some way, but I see that God helps me through my neighbor, that the Lord himself draws near and tells me: "Careful! Be careful!" For that reason, I try to pay attention and listen to what comes from everyone, and afterwards pray and ask for guidance to better understand what they've told me, to see how I can integrate it into my actions or not.

Sometimes, the words are wrong but the tone is right. Be careful! Someone is telling you that something doesn't work—maybe they told you badly because they didn't know how to express it, but they're alerting you. Or sometimes the words are fine, they tell you exactly what's not working, but they tell you in a way that sounds off-key, with anger, and as if to injure you. There you've got to forgive how it sounds and accept the words.

But it's a grace from God and you've got to pray for it. I don't feel strong enough to fix these things by myself alone, because I know that if I don't listen, if the Lord doesn't give me the grace, I get sick from power. And then a person, without realizing it, falls into vanity, pride, and arrogance.

16

Authority

We were midway through taping the program about power. Almost inevitably, our discussion was moving along the fine lines that exist between this concept and that of authority. As was his habit, Cardinal Bergoglio seemed to be in an attitude of listening, attentive and a little bit detached from the rhythms and routines of the television studio. In some way, that was my responsibility, in my parallel role as the host of the series. Nevertheless, while I was speaking he asked me respectfully if he could interject. That was the first and only time he did so. He did this to draw our attention to the fact that we were moving off course from the theme, and he said that the concept of authority was so important and distinctive that it deserved a separate program devoted exclusively to it.

Far from bothering me, the Cardinal's intervention did me well. On one hand, I didn't feel alone in the job of "feeling the pulse" of the program. On the other, it demonstrated for me once again that the contents and the depth of this series interested him very much—so much so that, for a moment, he assumed the role of conductor and had us pick up the thread of the chosen theme.

In the next program we did discuss the theme of authority. When we recorded it, we realized that he'd been right. It deserves its own chapter.

FIGUEROA: Sometimes, when we speak about power, we put the concepts of power and authority together. Nevertheless, at some point, something can happen to the person who has power so that they cease to have authority. It can happen that although they continue to "wear the badge" or possess the title, they lose the authority to exercise their power.

The concept of authority involves many things, because it is not only about someone who has a position, an office, a task, or a symbol of power; but also seeing if such a person has sufficient backbone to exercise that power with credibility, with formative support, with appropriate character, consonant with what is communicated through the example of daily life.

From my perception, when we talk about authority we're referring to a life that completely supports, sustains, and gives a foundation to the one who exercises power. In that way, the authority is exercised in a way that is ethically legitimate, because someone could have legal power, but illegitimate authority.

BERGOGLIO: There are two anecdotes that can help me to outline the concept of authority, so that we can then define it together. A woman, a delegate of professors on the board of regents for the University of Buenos Aires, said that she knew if a new board member had moral authority by what they did during their first days on the job. She said that the first thing many of them did, on starting their position, was to place an order to have their office redecorated, thus displaying their authority through how the office was set up, the furniture chosen, how it was arranged, etc. Or rather, the concepts of power/authority fused together made them say: "I have authority to the degree in which I am present here, and I am going to make a demonstration of power and authority in my personal office environment."

The other anecdote is a personal one, from my own life. When I was around ten or twelve years old, my maternal grandparents owned one of those old houses in Almagro. There, on the back patio, in the rear part of the house, was my grandfather's carpentry shop. He was one of those carpenters who does everything himself. With a certain frequency a bearded man came to visit him who sold him aniline oil, and those two old men sat there drinking cups of tea with a little bit of wine, which my grandfather had. Everybody knew this aniline vendor as "Don Elpidio." One day, my grandmother told me that Don Elpidio had once been the vice president of Argentina but when he retired from office he had declined his government pension in order to live from his work. He was Elpidio González; this man had lost his governmental power but he had authority at the highest level.

It's curious how those two cases have stayed with me so vividly. The description of this woman, about people who base their authority on appearance, and the other example of the man who had the authority of personal integrity. This is integrity in what I think, what I feel, and what I do—or rather, the way in which I live, how I comport myself. The language of the mind, of the heart, and of the hands. In this way we can distinguish authority from power, and thus talk about "moral" authority. Ultimately, one has moral authority through the consistency of personal integrity.

SKORKA: Evidently, moral authority and power are two things that go hand in hand. The one who leads must be a paradigm in the deepest sense of the concept, because doublespeak is one of the worst sicknesses with which a leader can infect his followers. The one who has no moral authority and who does not act or live in accord with what he teaches or demands from his followers, really is infecting them.

Double messages pervert a society and lead to its destruction. It is one of the sicknesses of our time, in which one sends a message but acts in a completely different way. No leader who demands a certain attitude from his followers—or those over whom he exercises power—with which he himself is not consistent, and who does not really have his hands clean, is a paradigm of justice.

I don't believe in the grand pompous leaders. I like the simple man who operates from the basis of this concept: he has moral authority and has a position of power. Dr. Arturo Illia was someone like that, according to all the testimonies we have about him as a person. After holding office as President of Argentina—the same as Elpidio González—he went back to live in Cruz del Eje and continued working, with humility, as a doctor.

I believe in a humble leader, like Moses, who was not a leader of surpassing charisma. There were many moments when he experienced crisis, felt bad, and showed humility as he asked God for help. He does not appear in any of the Scriptures as a grand revolutionary.

People—I do believe—need a man of integrity, someone who is not crafty or dishonest, who is also perhaps a bit naive. A society, sometimes, needs a bit of naiveté.

If we want more spiritual men, we need fewer crafty rogues and more innocent folks—but innocent ones who know how to interpret, who know that sly dishonesty exists, but who say, at all cost, "I'll continue with my innocence!" And it's that innocence or naiveté, that integrity about doing things, that I think confers on these people moral authority to carry out a task or hold a position of power. I wasn't referring to innocence in the simple sense of the word; I mean that person who has certain dreams and never ever abandons them.

I like a leader who is cautious, calm, and thoughtful. We've got to see to what degree the world's societies, in general, are prepared for leaders with these characteristics.

FIGUEROA: In the book of Judges we read the story of the life of Samson, who had all the power and the authority, but who ended up a victim of his own folly. There is a terrible verse: *"Samson did not know that God was no longer with him."* It's one of the sharpest and most terrible texts there is: Samson continues living as if he had the same power and authority, but he did not realize that at some point along the way he had lost them.

The question is: How can we protect ourselves from the possibility of going astray that comes with losing our authority—authority that is forever tested by those over whom we exercise power?

SKORKA: If we want to answer from an objective criterion for those who exercise power, the loss of authority begins in the moment when people put themselves, their ego, the "I," before everything else.

There is a tale from the Hassidic world, which teaches through parables. The protagonists are a young man and a *rebbe*, which in the Hassidic world is the leader of a given congregation. This rebbe was seen as a kind of saint and he exercised a special power over his congregation. The young man comes knocking on the rebbe's door and the rebbe asks him: "Who is it?" When the young man answers "It's me," he doesn't open the door. Then the young man knocks again and hears the same question: "Who is it?" When he gives the same answer a second time, the door remains closed. Finally, he knocks again, and this time he gives his name. Only then does the rebbe open the door. Once inside, the young man asks him: "Why didn't you open the door at first? Didn't you recognize my voice?" The rebbe answers him, "No. The only one who says 'I' and who can pretend to be immediately recognized, is God; as the Ten Commandments say: *'I am the Eternal one, your God.'"*

When I place my own "I" before everyone else, when I think that things begin and end with me, that is the first syndrome of the loss of authority.

Authority is born from a very deep conviction that one can make a mistake, and the people who surround you know that one makes mistakes. When someone really accepts positive criticisms, when they don't think themselves possessed of an absolute power, nor do they put "I" before their actions, then—for however many errors they commit—they continue having moral authority. We all make mistakes in what we do; no perfect person exists, as Ecclesiastes reminds us. The question lies in having integrity.

BERGOGLIO: It's true. When one puts the "I" before the mission entrusted to him is when he loses his authority. I'll return to the two biblical personages. Moses, the most humble man, on the shore of the Red Sea. When they told him the Egyptians were coming after them, I'm sure that he felt anguish, because he was a normal man. He must have thought: "I've failed, like a fool." Perhaps he was tempted to say: "Why did I believe so easily?" or "Could I have misunderstood what God was trying to tell me?" After all, he must have been tormented by doubts.

That man had few options remaining: quickly go back to negotiate with the Egyptians and return to slavery, declare war against them, or commit suicide trying to preserve his honor. But what was his attitude? I imagine a certain thought towards God that's not in the Bible: "You got me into this, now get me out of it!" Moses showed integrity and God acted.

The other person is David. If he had said to Nathan, "Come on, let's go eat and talk things over. You know what human weakness is like—forgive me, don't take it badly. How can we fix this?" If David had "fixed things" he would have lost his authority and today he would be remembered as a tyrant. Nevertheless, he didn't strike a bargain and he humbled himself. He had integrity.

One loses authority when he begins to be complicit. Complicity is like a loophole to get away from integrity. Integrity is weakened through complicity and moral authority is lost.

FIGUEROA: At the end of the Acts of the Apostles, the Apostle Paul is imprisoned. The Roman governor Felix summons him several times to testify and, as Paul relates several times the story of their conversation, the text tells us that Felix was not very interested in listening to him; instead he hoped to receive money from him or accept a bribe to let him go. The truth is that the Apostle Paul might have been able to act with a "pseudo-spiritual complicity" and to say: "It's for the good of the mission: I'll make a deal, get out of here, and continue as a missionary." Nevertheless, he didn't give in, and he stayed there close to three years, while every day the governor asked him the same thing to see if he could get something out of him. Finally, he ended up being condemned to death in Rome.

It's important for us to be wise in the moments in life when one has to choose between the difficult road of integrity or the easy path of complicity. If I begin to negotiate my authority, it begins to degrade until I lose it.

There is an advertisement for an emergency aid organization that says: "By the time the emergency occurs, it's too late to become a member." I think that when we find ourselves facing a test or a temptation, it's too late to start thinking: "What should I do?" One must have the muscle of integrity in good shape, and the mind and character clear and clean so that when that moment of decision arrives on the path I can emerge gracefully, with the integrity that authority gives me.

SKORKA: In our daily prayers, we ask God to not lead us into temptation. But life teaches us that there are constantly situations in which we must pass just such a test.

Another of the points where authority can be lost lies in thinking: "Alright, well, nobody sees me. This is just between me, myself, and I." For that reason, in our daily prayers we say to God: "May man always be fearful of God, both in public and in private alike." Because even though others may not notice my transgression, in the moment when I become complicit with myself something in my life begins to erode.

When one commits an abject sin, something incorrect, and makes peace with oneself about that impropriety, evidently this is a kind of complicity, and when it multiplies it ends up corrupting the person in every aspect, at a private level and then in the power that he or she exercises over others.

BERGOGLIO: I was thinking about the virtues that sustain moral authority. There are many, but right now there are four that occur to me.

The first is courage. A person has to demonstrate courage in their paternal or maternal authority when the need arises to enforce limits. The courage of seeing something through, of being consistent with an ideal, of experiencing embarrassment if others mock them for an ideal they have, or for whatever reason. Courage.

The second is grit, endurance. Men and women of authority have got to endure, they've got to be people with strong backbones. Courage and grit are two virtues that St. Paul mentions often that help us overcome difficult moments in life.

The third, as has been mentioned, is integrity, and we've already said a lot about this subject.

And the fourth, which I believe is key, is meekness, humility. Authority must be both firm and meek. That meekness that makes relationships possible, helps to weave the social fabric, teaches us how to be receptive to another and how to respond in a language that's not aggressive or insulting. This is very important nowadays when it's difficult to listen to the opinions of others without insults in the middle. Men and women with moral authority tend to be meek. This does not mean that they are cowards. On the contrary, they've got the energy and the strength of meekness and humility.

FIGUEROA: It's true. But we're engaged in a fierce cultural battle. All this that we are saying goes against the current social paradigms. I remember very well a passage from the book *The Resistance* by Ernesto Sabato. In it he relates an anecdote about a labor union leader who was walking along the road and fainted. On attending to him, those helping him found a significant quantity of money in his pocket. When they asked him what had happened, he confessed that he'd not eaten for several days, and that was why he'd fainted. Then they asked him: "Why didn't you use some of that money to buy yourself some food?" He answered: "No, it belongs to the union. How could I spend it?" Sabato presents authority in idealistic terms.

How can we change a little that cultural pressure that shows us concepts of authority and power that are the exact opposite of what we're talking about?

SKORKA: By not letting ourselves be bullied, by being consistent with our faith and our hope, by continuing to be leaders through our example, and by transmitting the message. I don't know to what extent we're going to be able to achieve a better society, but at least we can transmit the message that it's possible to do something better. That justice, rectitude, kindness, mercy, and spirituality are true and valid matters and that, for us, they are the essence of our life.

Each person has got to try to make a *mea culpa*, a sincere self-criticism that puts aside selfish private interests, and reduces the ego a little. Let's try to create, truly, a different reality.

BERGOGLIO: That happens when one feels themselves to be in the service of others. When we remember the Second Commandment: *"Love your neighbor as yourself."* Or, as it says in another translation: *"Be your brother's servant."* Power is meant to serve. Authority is given to you by serving. You earn it, it's not something that can be purchased. One might be able to buy a position, power, a job, status; but the authority one has is either maintained or it's lost. It is not bought and sold.

17

Old Age

In 2008, walking through La Montonera Park in Pilar, a province of Buenos Aires, I had one of those extended conversations with Cardinal Bergoglio that I now remember, revisit and value anew, and long for.

At that time, the Cardinal told me that he often visited nursing homes and retirement communities for priests. He cited for me, with precision, the first and last names and stories of people that he used to visit just to spend time with them, listen to them, or give them a hug. And he told me something that gave me a lot to think about. He confessed that when he was with them he also experienced doubt, because it did him good to go "to challenge my beliefs, so I don't end up believing too much in myself." This was a phrase he often used. These visits helped him to understand that someday he, too, would be like them—old, forgotten, and, in some cases, neglected.

Many times I had heard him speak publicly about what he called "dump truck culture," a metaphor that describes the case of elderly people being tossed away in a place designated for things that are no longer useful, and at the same time hidden from the sight and love of their loved ones. Cardinal Bergoglio loved to go to these "dumps" and meet with the elderly, drink mate, listen to music, or celebrate Mass with them.

At that moment, I promised him that when he retired and was an elderly man I would go to visit him in his retirement home. Now I know that won't be possible. But he left me that teaching so that I would also visit the elderly, to love them, and so that I would also "challenge my beliefs and not believe too much in myself."

FIGUEROA: Reading the Bible, one encounters a clear prophetic voice about the importance that God gives to those sectors of society that are habitually—and now it seems to occur more than ever—discarded, neglected, discriminated against, and forgotten.

In the Bible, God emphasizes the care of children, the poor, widows, orphans, women, and the elderly. In that sovereign gaze of God revealed in his Word, there is a message that is a call to attention: "Let us not forget about those whom surely many are going to forget!"

The same Word establishes a first commandment with the promise: *"Honor your father and your mother, because if you do, you will have a long life."* In addition to the clear message of recognizing and honoring our ancestors until the final moment of their lives, there is a very profound thought that consists of understanding that some day we are also going to be old. It is a commandment with a promise, and a promise with a warning, which could well be expressed as follows: *"Honor your father and your mother, so that your children, when you are old, will also learn to honor you."*

SKORKA: The theme of old age can be looked at—and in fact this is what we find in the Talmud—from two different angles. On the one hand, it's about our common morality, that is, about respecting life, and it's manifested through caring that the old person has food and a dignified dwelling place. And on the other hand, if we don't honor life, we undermine one of the basic structures of all biblical thought, and the pact that the people of Israel made with God, because as we honor life we are honoring him.

In addition to the Bible verse that orders us to honor the father and the mother, the progenitors that, along with God, have given me life and for which reason deserve special consideration, there is another very important one that we find in Leviticus 19: *"Stand up in the presence of the aged, show respect for the elderly."* How is this verse to be interpreted? Because here it's not only about showing care, but that I must stand up and have special consideration for the elder. I believe, to my humble understanding, that this passage has a meta-message which is the following: we must respect all people, but we must have a special consideration for that person who has already lived longer and learned something about life. It's something, I believe, that deserves the category of an extra respect, and this is the challenge that the Talmudic discussion raises: "Prepare yourself for old age, for the moment when you reach that time and you can say a word of wisdom with much more standing than someone young." I think that is the challenge.

As the scholars observed, each elderly person deserves respect for the fact of being old—not necessarily because they've been a genius or received a Nobel Prize or something like that, but rather for their effort in showing behind their word an experience, a profound message about life. That, really, puts a crown on existence.

So, on the one hand we must honor those who are broken and give them strength and, on the other hand, show that in the same way that a young person prepares for adulthood, we also must prepare ourselves for life's final phase, the autumn and winter of life.

BERGOGLIO: The elderly person, in addition to their knowledge, the wisdom that you outlined so well—and that reminds me of Solomon's prayer for wisdom—must prepare one for the final stage in life and asking for wisdom to carry it off well, with dignity and service.

Besides that, the elderly person carries history with them. It's curious how God defines himself: *"I am the God of Abraham, of Isaac, of Jacob,"* or rather, the God of your predecessors, of your elders, of those who passed down their history to you. There is a continuous resource in the road traveled by our elders.

Today's elderly person is in that cloud, in that chain of witnesses the Bible mentions, by means of which God's salvation was revealed. It's a long chain with which God is greatly occupied, so that it doesn't get lost. Deuteronomy, chapter 26, comes to my mind: *"When you reach the land that I shall give you and dwell in houses that you did not build, and eat fruits from trees you did not plant, you will take the first harvest to the temple and you will say this: 'My father was a wandering Aramean.'"*

There is a whole history that comes before me and my parents; and the elderly person, in some way, reflects that continuous memory of the fact that history did not begin with me. For that reason, a people that does not attend to its elderly not only denies its own history, but it mortgages its future.

FIGUEROA: I wonder if everything we're talking about here isn't one of the reasons we continue to make the same foolish mistakes over and over again, generation after generation.

We can read informative and factual history in a book, but with elderly people we have the history of life, the scars that remain from having confronted the struggles of existence and learned to overcome. An old person has information and an education from life that can't be studied in any university nor read in any book.

If we discard them, hide them away, cover them up, if we are ashamed of them, and if—although it may be painful to say so—as a society we hide them under the rug, as the Cardinal said, we're mortgaging the future.

SKORKA: The serious problem that we have in our times is that certain things that previously seemed to us truths needing no proof or demonstration—self-evident truths—Western civilization no longer practices, and for that reason we commit the same mistakes as in the past.

After a great catastrophe, such as the Second World War, that should have meant a turning point for humanity, the young generations of today look with a certain scorn and disdain at their elders, and they think: "What is it exactly that you can teach me?"

Some days ago, I heard an anecdote about a young man who says to an older person: "What do you know about the computer and all the new electronic devices that are being made at such a rapid rate?" And after the young man mentions the whole list of these products, the older person says to him: "You know what it is—it was my generation that created all that."

The problem about intergenerational dialogue is not knowing how to listen. I understand that each person has a unique reality, and that the manner of thinking and being, and the historical time are totally distinct. The problems faced by people today are not the same as ten years ago, but I think that there is an essence—love, the manner of facing suffering, one's relation with their neighbor. Meaning, there are certain themes that have a common denominator and, to a certain degree, a common solution. This has been happening since biblical times, or even earlier, up until our times and so on, towards the future.

BERGOGLIO: You've got to listen to them and take them seriously because the elderly person's "wisdom" is good advice.

There is a passage in the Bible that touches me deeply, I believe it's in chapter 12 of the first book of Kings. It's when Rehoboam, the son of Solomon, assumes the throne of the kingdom. Those who were previously subjected to heavy taxes suggest to him that he lower them, and by doing so he would serve them: *"Let us make peace, do not tax us so highly."* And Rehoboam tells them: *"Return in three days."* Then he summons the elderly. They listen to him, and then they give him this advice: *"Look, lower their taxes, because then you're always going to have them as your friends."* The old people leave and Rehoboam summons the young people, and they tell him: *"No, don't be soft, double their taxes."* They make the matter much more difficult, because they have no sense of history. The result: a rupture.

The old person is aware of the importance of advice thanks to the wisdom granted him by time. The young people are more impetuous—as in this biblical example—and they cause a debacle.

I remember once, I was about twenty-four years old, and I had a problem. I went to see an old priest to ask him for advice, and I told him: "Look, I've got this problem. I had a falling out with someone; I told this guy to go to hell." This man spoke in a very low voice, and the only thing he told me was: "In life, if it's not for some very serious reason, it's not good to break off relations with anybody." To this day I've never forgotten that advice.

Also, there is the other point which is underestimating and undervaluing the elderly person, the temptation to undervalue them due to their physical decline. The elderly person sometimes has involuntary physical problems that repel others, that can make it unpleasant to get close to them.

I always remember a story my grandmother used to tell us. There was a family and the grandfather was getting older. When he tried to eat his soup he spilled it and drooled and made a mess of himself. One day, the father gathers the family together and tells them: "Look, your grandfather can't eat here anymore; we can't invite guests to our house with him here." Then the father set a table apart in a different room in the house for the grandfather to eat there. One day the father comes home from work, the children greet him, and he sees the smallest of his kids with an apple crate and some nails. He asks him: "What're you doing?" The boy answers: "I'm building a table." The father asks: "A table for what?" And his son answers him: "For when you're old, so you have someplace to eat."

The old person, although in physical decline, is still your own flesh and blood, the one who gave you life, and is still wise, although they might drool or smell like piss.

FIGUEROA: I'd like to take two examples of old married couples from the Bible. One of them is Abraham and Sarah. When God tells them that they're going to have a child in their old age they laugh themselves silly, but there the promise is born.

The other example is in the New Testament: Elizabeth and Zechariah. When the angel tells Zechariah that Elizabeth is going to have a child, although she is old and barren, Zechariah refuses to believe the heavenly news and so he is struck dumb until John the Baptist is born, the birth that was promised—the birth of the messianic prophet from the Christian point of view.

That speaks to me about the importance of recognizing the elderly person as God makes them, and of giving them opportunities appropriate to the life potential they still have, through the grace of God. I think that one of the grave problems is that the person who reaches old age would seem to be sitting there awaiting death.

I want to mention a personal aspect. By living right across the street from my parents I was able to witness the last moments of their lives. Basically, they both died at home; it wasn't nice, it wasn't pleasant. But afterwards, as years went by, I thought about the enormous privilege God had given me to care for those people who'd given me life, and to accompany them in their final moments, those people who had taken care of me during my earliest years.

In those days, I remember that, knowing that they were going to die, I felt that I had the mission of accompanying them to help them die with dignity. In the case of my mother, already a widow, I went every day to see her, even if only for a short while. What I noticed was that she was always sitting in the kitchen, at a spot at the table from which she could see the front door of the house. Every time I came in, I saw mom watching the door. She spent hours and hours watching the door, waiting for someone to come—a meeting, a visit that would brighten her last days. She wasn't waiting for death, she was waiting for some living presence in her solitude. I think that between us there are many old people who are waiting for something in life, who do not resign themselves simply to sit down and wait for the death knell to toll for them, but instead they're dreaming that there is still something or someone remaining for them in their life.

SKORKA: In our prayers, which acquire a special force at Rosh Hashanah and Yom Kippur, we make a petition to God, a very strong exclamation: "Hear our voices, our Lord, and have pity on us. Do not leave us in our old age, when we no longer have strength. Do not abandon us, do not put us aside, and do not remove from us the spirit of your holiness." My dad used to tell me that "the spirit of your holiness" means the capacity of intelligence and of discernment that we have. My way of understanding the prayer is that I'm not handing God a bill: "Please, pay this." Instead, I've got to begin to pay it along with him. What I'm asking him is: "Help me when I become old, but especially that other person, who is very old, so that they don't lose the spirit of your sanctity, so that they feel your presence in the moment of death, in the moment of their suffering. Help me so that I can also be by their side and give them strength, so that they don't feel that everything is at an end and all meaning is lost."

BERGOGLIO: There is an example in the Bible that means a lot to me, a passage I always return to because it fulfills me. It's the second chapter from St. Luke. It's curious: Luke says that Simeon and Anna *"were driven by the Spirit."* And when they encounter Jesus as a boy in the temple, this is the meeting between the generations. They make a celebratory liturgy, they praise God, they sing and want to tell everyone who that boy is—meaning, they celebrate. Sometimes we must care for and create spaces so that the elderly can enjoy that celebratory capacity.

SKORKA: There is a verse in chapter 17 of the book of Proverbs that speaks about the relationship between grandparents and grandchildren, and it says: *"Grandchildren are a crown to the aged, and parents are the pride of their children."* That is when there is a lovely family relationship, when the grandfather says: "Well, I must be good for something."

My grandfather took me to school when I was very young. And on our way there he would read to me the newspaper in Yiddish.* I remember that on holidays, like May 25 or June 20, he would give me his interpretation based on what he'd read: "Well, you've got to know that Belgrano fought for freedom." He was always telling me something between the lines; the importance of freedom, the dignity of the human being. He wanted to be useful!

FIGUEROA: I'm very pleased with how we've covered the subject of old age, from a positive perspective of life, of joy, of dignity, quite removed from pity.

---

* **Yiddish:** A language spoken by Jewish communities residing in central Europe; it has German syntax and influences from Slavic languages, Aramaic, and Hebrew.

Let's continue reflecting on old age from the dignity of its quality of being an image of God, and from a perspective removed from pride, because soon, God willing, I will also be an old man.

Let us in our families really value how important it is to have our grandparents with us, of how much they help, how they help us to see things in another way. Let's go through life with them, and if they walk slowly, well, let's walk slowly and learn that that, too, also has its charm.

Let's build a family and a society that are absolutely inclusive, where each person can shine, illuminating the other, and where the old person has a place of honor, as God in the Bible also gives them.

18

Education

It wasn't easy to find a birthday gift for Cardinal Jorge Bergoglio. Although I knew that he'd be happy with nothing more than an affectionate greeting, I preferred to take the trouble to dig around and find some novelty that would surprise and please him.

On December 17, 2011, after a modest personal investigation, I headed to the oldest, most prestigious record shop in Buenos Aires. The concert of the "Gospel According to St. Mark" featuring music from Handel had been out of print for more than a decade, but I now stood there with a recently arrived copy in my hands, a real find, with which I hoped to surprise my friend and brother, a lover of that music and genre.

When I presented myself at the Archdiocese, I was quickly summoned upstairs, something that I knew was not habitual given the occasion and the quantity of friends and acquaintances who came round to visit. He received me like always, coming down the hallway without waiting for the secretary to announce me or any other protocol. The moment he opened the package and saw what was inside, he said: "You found it! I've been looking for this forever. Thank you so much!"

The same thing might have happened if I'd given him a tango record, a book of theology, or a work of art. Cardinal Bergoglio has a surprising level of education, from the generally eclectic to the particularly exquisite.

For that reason, now that we were on to the theme of education, I knew that we could not focus exclusively on academic or curricular concepts; the discussion was going to include both a holistic wide-ranging education and a supreme profundity. I wasn't mistaken.

FIGUEROA: The etymological roots of the words "educate" or "education" have little to do with information, per se, but rather come from concepts like guidance, direction, leadership, or companionship. Education, although it includes information, is very much more than that. It has to do with the formation of the individual. In this sense, I think that if education does not shape people for the better, it can do the opposite—deform or mislead them.

We're accustomed to saying that there are well-educated and poorly educated people. Considering the words of Jaime Barylko, we can say that people are, in reality, miseducated, and a miseducated person is a person who is not free.

SKORKA: The chapter from Deuteronomy that summarizes the creed of Israel and what we must say in our daily morning prayers, culminates by saying: *"And teach these words to your children."* It doesn't mean merely to teach the words, but to transmit them with insistence. From this, I deduce that the father's role in raising his children is very important. In the Talmud there is a place where the rules are laid out for how a child must treat his parents and for how a parent must treat his children, but it specifically talks about the father.

Now then, teaching has two parts. One thing is a teaching about life. When we speak about the Torah, we refer to the study of a teaching about life. The other is the teaching that we are called to live on a daily basis, the teaching from school. Our time has privileged the development of the intellect far more than the deep formation of the human being. I refer to my own personal experience; the school was a good one, because we learned and they gave us a certain kind of discipline, but the question was teaching us to comply with things without any proper, deep conviction. Education is not an easy subject. You've got to try to shape a human being; you've got to try to help that person become himself, too.

There is a very interesting book by Paul Johnson called *Intellectuals*. Johnson writes about how, since the time of the French Revolution, intellectuals have taken the place of priests. He discusses many of the vagaries and flights of fancy of these intellectuals. Reading it, I was struck by the high percentage of people with university degrees that formed the ranks of the SS, who were the real murderers of the Nazi regime. That means that something went wrong, that educating a human being is not only teaching them how to read and write. That is basic, it's very important, but alongside that there must be teachers of the spirit. I think that's what the Bible verse is referring to when it says that the first teacher must be the father.

This coincides a little with Freud and the question that the father is the one who represents the law, the one who sets the limits; and the mother, the one who demonstrates mercy and forgiveness. Independently of all interpretations, in the heart of the family the people who gave us life have an enormous mission. The first teachers have to be the father and the mother. They are the ones who inculcate us with our values, the ones who teach us to think and to figure out what to do with our lives.

I agree that when my father wanted to transmit to me some deep message he sat down to read the Bible with me in Yiddish, although his Hebrew was not the best. And why did he do that? He was saying to me: "Here it is, here are some very profound things; it seems to be that this is the truth of life, the truth of existence. There are messages here that are like fine old wine, there are things here that for some good reason illuminate the minds of many people."

So, I began to love the Bible—in a manner of speaking— to take it seriously and to understand that it contained a truth beyond what is simply called the Word of God. It's the Word that was meant to guide other people existentially.

BERGOGLIO: I'm impressed when I read in the Bible about the Lord telling his people: *"I led you like a father leads his children."* Throughout the history of salvation, God has educated us in a paternal fashion.

Along the same lines, God teaches his people by leading them farther than they thought they were capable. The Bible speaks to us about those wonders when it appeals to the memory as an educational resource to help me follow the path of God, of the forty years in the desert. It's as if God said: "You thought that you wouldn't be able to make it, and, nevertheless, because I guided you, you were able." Meaning, God teaches us by driving us forward. Using a bit of the etymology that Figueroa mentioned at the start, to teach is to guide. But there is something more that this passage says, that in that guidance, God draws from people things that they did not expect.

"Educate," etymologically, also comes from the verb *ducere*, which means "to bring out the best in someone." Then God, to this people that is the smallest, the one that matters the least, says: "That is why I chose you, so that you see what I can bring out of you when I guide you."

Educating is just that, bringing out the best that someone has inside of them through wise guidance and not only with a bunch of knowledge. As Rabbi Skorka explained, the intellectuals and the SS agents with university degrees took over the priests' traditional task of teaching, but they simply imparted information without any knowledge of moral values.

In education, the teacher is the fundamental thing. The teacher is something more than the professor. The professor is the lecturer who teaches us things, but the teacher is the one who accompanies us along the road of life. And how do they accompany? Fundamentally by being a witness.

There is a saying from John Paul II that is very strong, very hard, and it says: "We, in this century, we do not need docents so much as we need witnesses." Or rather, the educator, fundamentally, has got to be a witness, someone who is bearing witness to the values that he is transmitting.

FIGUEROA: I was thinking about the concept of teaching on the path and I remembered that biblical proverb that says: *"Teach the child to follow the right path and even when he is an old man he will not stray from it."* An exegesis we can make of that text is that teaching or education is something that is done along the way, alongside the one who is traveling. It is not a single, delimited event in life, where one has a specific number of years or hours in the classroom; it is about teaching a companion as we walk along the path of life.

On the other hand, the word "student" also has to do with someone who is feeding. Sometimes there is food we like, and it's delicious, but other times there is food that at first we don't like, and nevertheless we still have to eat it just the same.

When I was in high school, I was assigned to the read the poem of *Martín Fierro*. At the time I hated that book. It seemed to me like literature for old people, ancient, something I didn't understand, but I was forced to read it. Many years went by and thanks to the fact that they forced me to eat a small portion of literary food I hated at first, but that I needed to eat, I later discovered its value. I have reread that book dozens of times, and I came to love it.

Sometimes it seems to me that from that very rigid education I also had, we have moved to a style that is a bit lax. Nowadays the attitude is that a student shouldn't be forced to receive an education that they don't like. But if we ask him: "Do you like to eat your vegetables?" What is he going to say? "Of course not!"

I have the feeling, but it's simply an assumption, that we're afraid—sometimes as parents and also in school—of demanding that children learn things they're not going to like, that are not going to motivate them, or that they're not interested in. The current situation in schools is in danger of going to the opposite extreme of rigidity, meaning that students will only read and study what they like or what pleases them.

SKORKA: Here I think we have two different subjects to distinguish. One has to do with intellectual content, and the other has to do with education as a spiritual question.

Socrates spoke about educating as "bringing forth an idea." For some reason he said that his mother was a midwife, as an example of his methodology of refutation and maieutics. First, to show you, to refute you; and afterwards yes, to rearm everything in order to have a perfect knowledge of the thing.

First, and before anything else, I think that you've got to teach the child the capacity for reasoning in all the areas of their life—to have the proper attitude for critical reasoning and not simply accept things at face value.

Talmudic thinking is very close to Socratic reasoning. When Alexander conquered Asia Minor, there was a meeting of cultures. Much of that is reflected in Talmudic literature. For example, in the Talmud there is a brief part about the law where it attempts to understand the different cases that branch off from it. It's full of reasoning and deductive methods. In a word, the critical attitude of digging, thinking, and of not accepting things at face value, has got to go along with sacrifice, in order to try to fix certain things that are known and understood.

On the other hand, much of this knowledge is technical, like finding a square root and techniques for multiplication and division. And, in accord with our traditional point of view, some things must be imposed—like a doctor or a lawyer not being permitted to commit errors in writing—in order to avoid accepting just anything. But I would point out a difference: one thing is the technique that I demand and that must be explained to the student who has to know it, and the other thing is to seek ways to give them incentives, to make the teaching more attractive, even with very dry subjects that make many students nervous.

BERGOGLIO: I like to conceive of the educational process as a tension between zones of security and zones of risk. One cannot only seek within the zone of security because that is going to create a fundamentalist. Or rather, the person is going to adopt closed concepts, with values, contents, and attitudes that are completely encapsulated and self-referential. On the other hand, a person cannot only be educated in areas of risk, because that can lead to a lot of scattered thinking.

There was a school in Hamburg that began to have an influence in the high schools, but it ended up closing. In it, the student was free to do what he liked: to come, to go—everything was a zone of risk in the sense that nothing was firmly marked or delimited; there was no set course.

I think there must be a tension between the two zones. The image that comes to my mind is that of flagstones; if you want to educate a young person well, you've got to try to have one foot in the safe zone while obliging them to start feeling around with the other foot in the area of risk, in order to assimilate it and convert it into a safe zone. You must demand that the student begin to move outside the security he has at present, so that later he can advance more. That tension is what makes him grow, because he faces a continuous set of new challenges, but from the support of a base where he feels safe.

Discarding this equilibrium in tension—because it is not a static equilibrium, it is a dynamic equilibrium—sometimes leads to disasters in education or such facile solutions as "Let's teach pure content." The student must be formed through a combination of content and values that create habits.

The educator, the one who brings out the best and guides, has got to know how to impart incentive not only regarding content, but also in habits and values. Education is a combination of content, habit, and value. The same is true for lifelong formation. The father who says to his son: "Look, do me a favor today by running this errand. Just head over to this place and take this for me …"—it's an incentive that propels the young person forward. Being made to feel an incentive is gratifying, because the person thinks: "Good, they have confidence in me. This opens new perspectives for me."

There is also another tension in education, which is between incentives and limits. Educating is not only pushing forward and giving incentives, it is also imposing limits. I think that here I would make a healthy criticism about current education, not only in schools, but all formation and upbringing in general. I get the impression that we don't have a desire to set limits, and the boys and girls are shouting for us to impose them. Because the limit, in some way, makes them feel that it is guiding them. Refusing to impose limits on those we are teaching how to live is leaving them to their own luck, saying "fine, let them hurt their soul, let them get mixed up and confused." That's something very serious.

Sometimes, in family situations, there are parents who let children do what they like and are incapable of setting limits because they don't want to appear unpopular. Therein lies a sin, a very serious defect that parents and teachers can fall into, which is demagogy. Meaning, in order to stay on good terms with the person I'm educating, I'll be permissive and not set limits for them.

The tension is, then, between knowing how to give incentives—always put new things ahead, and push—and knowing how to establish limits. This tension is also fundamental in education.

FIGUEROA: I agree with this last point, I think that perhaps parents also must be trained; because if the children don't have limits the parents have a conceptual problem. The father cannot put responsibility on the shoulders of his child for which the child is not prepared, leaving it up to him. This is going to have damaging consequences for the child.

I think everything we're saying here is good. Let's keep thinking about all these things—that teaching means to bring out the best, to guide, to find a balance between what's attractive and what's substantive, between things that are pleasant and unpleasant, between motivation and limits.

I don't want to forget to mention the important fact that education is an integral concept for the human being. It's about educating the human being with values and in the spirit, raising them up with things that are good for the soul.

1 9

Communication

Cardinal Bergoglio's communication resources are extraordinarily varied. They can be summed up in three semiotic ways.

First, by what he says. His discursive contents are precise, pointed, and concrete. He manages the most academic philosophical or theological analysis with surprising flexibility, and this leads him to find turns, new and unconventional viewpoints. He has a highly developed oratorical capacity and handles silences, tone of voice, and narrative velocity opportunely and with precision. In journalistic terms, he's a "machine" at providing headlines, and in television terms, he is a skillful dispenser of ideas, themes, and turns in the debate.

Second, through his gestures. His looks, smiles, hand movements, and other body language are for him indispensable tools in communication. I noticed this in one program after another. I knew him by his gestures of genuine humility as he walked like any other person along one of Buenos Aires's busiest streets or by stopping to listen, touch, and bless some beggar that he came across on his way. Today the whole world knows those gestures and is beginning to discover the enormous symbolic value in his casual, "unfettered" way of communicating the gospel of Jesus.

And finally, through his own life. What makes his communication solid and unique is the full integrity of what he says, does, and lives. This element is vital in his apostolic conception and in his dimension as a disciple of Jesus of Nazareth. He could well say, along with the Apostle Paul: *"Be imitators of me, as I imitate Christ."*

FIGUEROA: Communication is more than simply having something to say. Communicating means finding a space, a feeling, an approach, something in common. It is an encounter in which the emphasis is not on what I say, but rather on finding a place of common agreement, a communion.

Of course, for those of us who take the Bible as the inspired word of God, in the very structure and formation of the biblical text we have a living example of how God understands communication. He does not "drop a line." He doesn't make pronouncements from the skies. Instead God chooses common men and women so that, inspired by his Spirit, they write what he wants to communicate. God wants to find a common place with man—a two-way communication. For that reason, the Word of God is much more than a book, it is also a symbol of what God understands by communication.

SKORKA: The descriptive thought in the Bible, of a God that wants to communicate and to have something in common with man, is central to the religions of the Book. For those of us who have the Bible as the basis of our cosmological vision, it is really surprising to explore this concept deeply: the omnipotent God who created all things, the one who makes all things out of nothing, suddenly creates a being in whom he places a spark of his divinity and for whom he shows a personal, individual interest. Even when there was only one man, and then the first couple, God communicated with them. And that basic relationship is repeated. I can extend it to each one of us.

The Psalmist's exclamation in Psalm 8 is marvelous: *"God, what is man for you to be aware of him, for you to consider him, for you to know him?"* And later he says: *"You created him slightly less than divine."* Or rather, a duality is presented: we are a mere point in the cosmos and, nevertheless, in the biblical worldview we are important in our individuality because God spoke with individuals, the prophets, by means of whom he approached and communicated with us.

It's interesting that the Bible speaks to us about how God intends something more, something special for man. It is not simply speech: God wants to make a covenant. His covenant with the first man failed because Adam transgressed. Then he made a covenant with Noah, and when Noah emerged from the ark, God said to him: *"I will not send another flood."* Later he made a great pact with Abraham, which continued through to the people of Israel.

Now, to make the dialogue properly inter-religious, the concept of the New Testament, which we Jews do not accept as holy Scripture, derives from chapter 31 of Jeremiah: *"And I am going to make with you a new covenant."* I prefer the expression "New Alliance" over "New Testament," because God does not merely summon man, but rather he wants to be with him, profoundly, committed, and for that reason he invites him to make a covenant.

BERGOGLIO: The idea that God "needs" to bend over backwards, to communicate, to participate in his own mystery, includes a particularly impressive notion that I would define as God lowering or humbling himself. He descends to put himself at the level of man's comprehension, feeling, and language. And if for that reason man believes himself to be very important, there is that very beautiful passage that Scripture shows us through the words of the Lord to Moses: *"Look, I did not choose you because you were powerful or because you were very wise, but because you were from the smallest nation of people, the tiniest"*—that is, from pure love. I think that only through his love can we understand this "need" of God for communicating—through that love that's a mystery. He had no need to do what he did, nor to share his mystery and his greatness—and nevertheless that's the risk he takes. And he does so by making a commitment, and assuming the risk that that covenant might be broken. Therefore, he puts his destiny in man's hands.

The other day I was reading in the Bible the first chapters of Jeremiah, and then chapter 16 of Ezekiel, where it is very powerful to see how God takes the risk that his people might betray him. And there it speaks of idolatry, that God experiences idolatry like an adulterous breach of faith. There are other idols apart from those named in Scripture; they are the idols of every age, the ones we invent for ourselves nowadays—large or small, idols we prefer to adore instead of adoring the living God and surrendering our life to him.

We see that these things happen, yet God still chooses to work with them. He says, *"Well, but I'm still going to forgive you, I'm going to soften your heart of stone and I'm going to give you a new heart of flesh and blood so that you can love."* He is a God who never tires of mending the covenants we have broken. This is a sublime manner of communicating.

FIGUEROA: It's also important to consider that in God's communication with man, he reveals himself through his Word, he removes the veil, shows his countenance, his heart, his thoughts, and discloses himself to us.

This is important so that we might analyze the ways that we have of communicating with ourselves. We probably know that communicating, seeking something in common, reaching an accord with another person, opening the heart and wagering again on the other person—it has a cost, the cost of coming down off the pedestal of "my truth" and of believing that communicating is only saying what I want and nothing more. That's why there is an interesting concept that begins to arise. It says that in order to communicate one must take courage and make the decision to disclose yourself before the other just as you are.

SKORKA: Courage to break situations.

There are two very expressive examples in the first chapters of the book of Genesis. The first was when the man transgressed. God could have taken the position of: "Fine, man has transgressed, and I'll say no more." Nevertheless, he went to meet with Adam, and the man hid himself away. Did God, perhaps, not know where the man was? Nevertheless, to enter into dialogue with him, he said to him: *"Where are you?"*

The second example occurs after Cain killed Abel. Evidently, Cain became closed up within himself and his solitude. But God did not abandon him and he showed an attitude of courage—let the anthropomorphism stand—and he said to him: *"Where is Abel, your brother?"* Did God, perhaps, not know that Cain had killed him? Taking the classic explication of this verse: "He tried to speak with him, in words, in concepts." In a word, God tried to communicate with him. He did not leave him alone.

What does all this teach us as human beings? The famous concept that we Jews and Christians have is that we must imitate God—*imitatio dei*—we must act appropriately with our neighbor in the same way that God relates with man.

BERGOGLIO: I was thinking about communication disasters. It really stands out to me when I read in the Bible that a man doesn't want to answer; it's the breakdown in communication due to cowardice.

An example of this is when Elijah, after having killed almost four hundred prophets of Baal, is startled to learn the words of Jezebel: *"I shall do the same to you within twenty-four hours."* Then Elijah tells God: *"Zeal for your house has devoured me and now I must pay the price."* He fled from God's presence and felt so sad that he wished to die.

The same thing happened to Jonah. God sends him to Nineveh, but instead he escapes and goes toward Spain. He argues with God: *"I've escaped because one cannot make an alliance with you, because deep down you are so good that you fix everything and forgive."* As if saying: *"I don't want to know anything or communicate with you, because you have a style of communicating that I don't understand."* At the end of the story, when the castor-oil plant is gnawed by the worm and withers, Jonah probably feels the same sadness as Elijah. But God tells him: *"Look, you're angry because of this castor-oil plant that sprang up one day and withered the next. So, then, should I not be sad for a people that cannot distinguish between their right hand and their left, and doesn't even know where it stands?"*

That is how God helps to correct us when we reach situations where we don't understand his path by way of dialogue, when we are not at the level of responding to that manifestation or that mission that God gives us.

Elijah and Jonah find themselves with God, but only after passing the test, because the communication between us and God supposes both an encounter and the possibility of a rift, a misunderstanding. Real communication is generally buffeted by life's twists and turns, by one's own selfishness or by the idea that one has the response necessary to resolve what's happening. God, sometimes, has got to tolerate that we're not up to his level of communication.

FIGUEROA: I'll permit myself to add two concepts from opposite sides of the communication spectrum. First, hyper-communication: We live in an age in which, at least from appearances, we have all the instruments within our reach to communicate with each other in every possible way.

A few days ago, I went with my wife to a sweet shop to eat something and chat. At the table next to us were two people, but instead of having a conversation, each one was on their cell phone talking with someone else. Each one finished their phone call, then they made a few brief comments to each other, paid, and left. In some way, these new communication tools can actually lead to a communication breakdown.

On the other side is a kind of communication that we tend to be afraid of because it involves silence. Silence sometimes communicates a great deal and is preferable to saying something inopportune.

BERGOGLIO: Sometimes when we're going to visit a person who's very ill, the only thing we can do is take their hand and sit in silence. We're communicating with an enormous intensity—we're participating in that person's suffering.

I think about Job's three friends. When he's suffering terribly, each one offers their own theological explanation of what he's going through. And to make matters worse, along comes the fourth friend, "fresh out of college" you might say, the one who knew all the explanations! And he makes the whole thing worse. What they needed, instead, was silence. But the passage in the Bible says something very lovely, that before talking the first three cast ashes upon themselves and sat for a time in silence. And in that way, they did indeed communicate with each other.

SKORKA: From that image in Scripture, rabbis deduced that when someone is going to visit relatives they do not need to begin to speak, they must first wait for the relatives to begin.

There are two types of communication: one in which someone expresses to the other many things that they formulated in their mind, with precise words and well-formed arguments. And the other way is to say to someone, and I often use this phrase, "Look, I'm just thinking out loud." What do I mean saying this to them? It's: "I'm not quite sure what I'm saying, but I want to share it with you, I want you to help me think."

There is an expression in the book of Lamentations that says: *"Pour out your heart like water before God, in the presence of God."* What does this mean? That we must say it all, we must express all the sorrow that we have, because sometimes that's what we need to do.

How many times do people come to see us who are in anguish?

When I was young, I didn't understand exactly what someone was going through when they expressed their anguish and problems to me, and so I tended to respond like someone fresh out of "Job University," offering stock responses ... "God this ..." and "God that ..." I didn't realize that the only thing the other person needed was what the verse says: *"Let someone listen to their sorrow,"*—they needed to share that suffering with someone who supposedly has a special sensibility, someone who talks about God. With time I began to understand what it means when someone tells me: "Thanks for lending me your ear."

BERGOGLIO: "Lending an ear" is a ministry of love, it's a fraternal ministry, the ministry of listening. If we had to make a list of all the things that impede dialogue, the thing I'd place at the top of the list would be not knowing how to listen. And in second place, the selfish response. Meaning, you tell me something that you're going through and immediately I answer: "No, but I'm going through something even worse ..." There can be no dialogue that way—it's merely a meeting of calamities and then each person goes their separate way. Those two things are key impediments to dialogue.

FIGUEROA: Also, it's important to not use the time that the other is talking to think about how to respond, but instead to use that silent time to understand the other person, to put myself in their place, to understand them and get closer to them. It's not an easy exercise. We're always more inclined to say things and to want the other person to hear us, than in listening to them and putting ourselves in their place.

The subject is deeply moving. God would like us to be able to see in what way we can improve something so precious as this unique gift that he has given exclusively to man: the ability to communicate. Because our being able to communicate better is always going to mean living better, and living better is, in the end, living as God wants.

2 0

Truth

"The sum of your word is truth."

Psalm 119:160

FIGUEROA: Normally, when we read the Bible, it's clear that God is a God who speaks about truth, tells the truth, and intends for his children to do the same.

Now, there is an interesting event in Genesis 12, when it tells of how Abraham travels with Sarah to Egypt and decides to not tell the truth or, in nicer terms, "not tell the whole truth." As Sarah was very beautiful, he was fearful of saying that she was his wife because they would kill him, and so he introduced her as his sister. And this works well for them, because they enter Egypt without problems and they even receive some gifts. But one day, the Pharaoh discovers their deception, and he says to Abraham: *"Why have you done this to me? Imagine if I had done something with her, the punishment I would have received! Why have you done this to me?"*

What I want to highlight from this passage, and which is interesting, is that there is no clear, strong censure of Abraham by God for not telling the truth, as one would expect. So then, the concept of truth from the point of view of this biblical tale seems very complicated to me, and as I am with a rabbi and a Cardinal, it would be very helpful that we seek to shed some light on this somewhat controversial passage.

SKORKA: That whole paragraph is complex; its exegesis is difficult. Abraham is afraid, and what he says to Sarah is the first thing that comes to mind: *"Say that you're my sister."* The Talmudic scholars say that she actually was Abraham's step-sister, so he didn't lie about that detail, but he should have declared her to be his wife. After all, we see that when the Pharaoh takes her to his palace, it's God who appears in the Pharaoh's dreams and tells him: *"Be careful, she's Abraham's wife!"* One of the very many explanations of that paragraph can be that Abraham had faith in God. To himself he said: "I'm not going to reveal the full truth of the matter right away because that can endanger me—they might decide to kill me; but God will surely help me."

But the greatness of the Bible is that it tells us about the lives of men of flesh and blood, not machines that do everything perfectly. It shows us doubts, fears, and bravery. Suddenly there is an Abraham who carries out wars to rescue his nephew, among other moments of impressive bravery and courage, and then other times when he doesn't know exactly how to solve his own problems.

But, the question is: Is it possible that, in the interest of peace, one might avoid telling the whole truth? That's the point. While some Talmudic scholars say that it's all right to tell a little white lie in the interest of peace, other scholars say that one can simply not tell the whole truth. When God says to Samuel, *"Go to Bethlehem and there anoint David as king,"* Samuel answers him, *"But if I go to Bethlehem and anoint David, Saul is going to come and he is going to kill me."* Then God says to him: *"Well, go and take a few animals with you and then everyone is going to know that you're going to make a sacrifice in Bethlehem, and then you can anoint David in secret."*

There is another Talmudic concept that is called "stealing another's conscience." What does that mean? That the other person needs to know something but you don't tell them, and this causes them a dilemma. For example, this problem arises when we are faced with someone suffering from a terminal illness. Do we tell them the truth or not? It is a deep problem. Some say we must tell them, because they need to be conscious of their condition, but on the other hand, there are those who don't want to hear the truth.

I'll never forget a life lesson I received from a wise friend of mine, a rabbi, blessed be his memory, born in Jerusalem, of distinguished rabbinical lineage. We went to visit a woman suffering from lung cancer and we knew she wasn't doing well. When we said goodbye to her, he encouraged her by saying: "You're going to be fine." I left there with the feeling that she knew he was offering her a prayer and good thoughts, although her condition was very serious. And in that moment he said to me: "It's not necessary to tell the whole truth." But be careful! It's a very controversial subject. These are simply different responses to this very slippery question.

BERGOGLIO: You're right. Truth doesn't come prepackaged but instead presupposes a path towards the encounter; one finds the truth by following that path which has no end in this life.

I find the last verse of Psalm 16 to be very moving: *"You will fill me with joy in your presence."* This means that we will be completely fulfilled with the great truth in that final, definitive encounter, but meanwhile we keep on moving forward. The pedagogy of learning that we use in schools consists of encounter and companionship because that is the way truth is transmitted—because no one can tell another one hundred percent of the truth—they give what they have; they are merely following the path towards the encounter with the truth.

A person has to express what they know in the way the other person can receive it. If I go too far, if I say too much, I leave the other person bloated, so to speak, unable to digest everything I say. The truth is given bit by bit, step by step, in the same way that we also receive the way towards truth, by means of dialogue. We must always go forward so that we might receive truth, because it is all about the encounter, about small encounters.

The truth is an epiphany about Being, which consists of truth, goodness, and beauty; and one finds oneself through small epiphanies and progresses towards the final, definitive epiphany of truth, goodness, and beauty, which is that moment of becoming filled to overflowing with the countenance of God, with whom we are going to come face to face.

There are things that one only discovers at a certain age, things which, no matter how often they've been previously explained, are never understood until that time. God's words to Abraham tell us about the right conduct along the path: *"Walk in the presence of God and be irreproachable,"* meaning that pilgrimage to elicit a clear explanation of the truth, which always signifies an increasingly deeper encounter with the truth.

SKORKA: I just thought of the exact opposite case, that of a young woman, a doctor, who was discovered to be seriously ill with leukemia. She lived for something like fifteen years with that illness. She possessed several things: the desire to live and the desire to see her children grow up. Each time I called her or went to visit her she'd tell me that was all she needed: that I call her and talk to her about her soul. When things seemed gloomy to her, I would tell her: "You'll get through this," and she'd answer me, "Oh, don't talk nonsense. Look at the tests—the numbers are bad." Later she improved. She'd come to temple with her oxygen tank, and we gave her something to do, like to do the alternate readings on Yom Kippur. She bought herself a new dress for the occasion and I said to her: "You're going to wear it." So, the days and months went by, but she knew the truth—she was a doctor, she read her own test results, she knew exactly which drugs they were giving her and everything that was going on. She continued, in one way or another, to cling to life, knowing this truth, and the other truth: the truth of faith, that not even doctors understood but which was helping her to keep living. That's why, when it comes to following the path of truth you've got to know how to handle the subject according to the circumstances, because the truth has many facets. In our conception, God is the absolute truth.

FIGUEROA: There is a popular saying that goes: "Everything you say must always be true, but you don't always have to tell the whole truth."

St. Paul says something very interesting: *"Tell the truth with love."* Because the truth simply by itself can often hurt if it is not expressed with love and in the moment, in the circumstances, and to the degree to which the person can adequately receive it; love should be the conduit through which that truth is transmitted.

When I was young I considered many things to be absolutely true. Nowadays, fewer and fewer things remain that true for me; I have the existence of God, the revelation of his Word, the importance of love, and not many more. One increasingly realizes that there are ideas one used to defend "at all costs," and they weren't true, nor was it necessary to defend them, because it wasn't the right time or the circumstances didn't warrant it or it wasn't the right person with whom to discuss them.

However we are approaching the subject, none of us denies the value and supreme concept of the truth; but it can't be served up alone and cold. It must be seasoned, we might say, so that it does not become some fundamentalist truth that is spoken and repeated with neither sensibility nor humility. In trying to defend the truth we believe in, we often move rather far away from it.

What, then, is the sense of the word "truth"? How do we construct it? What are the realistic and genuine paths that we must follow in order to get closer to that concept?

SKORKA: I think that we cannot separate these three concepts: love, truth, and peace. Truth in itself does us no real good; it must lead to peace and must be linked to the concept of loving affection for one's neighbor. In general, in life, so that these elements make sense, they must be linked. This is what Judaism teaches. Life shows me that in the essence of this thought these elements are linked together. I would say that love is "a truth unto itself," that truth is "a truth unto itself," and peace is also "a truth unto itself." But they must go together so that each one can become fully developed.

A peace that is not true is no peace. A love that is not true is not love, but merely a convenience or a way to satisfy one's instincts. The truth is, or it should be, subject to those principles.

BERGOGLIO: Rabbi Skorka just spoke of love being linked to truth and beauty, and those are three transcendental elements for the human being. That creates that harmony that is peace, the harmony of conviviality; but love, truth, and beauty go together. They are being.

Dr. Figueroa mentioned fundamentalisms. A fundamentalism, for example, is the explanation of one truth separated from love and beauty. For that reason, fundamentalisms are grotesque; they are merciless and evil. They are a truth separated from love and beauty, and for that reason they are lifeless. The fundamentalist clings to an idea that has nothing to do with the truth that he wants to express. He takes it out of context, he falls in love with the idea; he is a nominalist, he wants to impose that idea and thus creates division, wars, and conflicts.

I greatly fear the sort of fundamentalist positions that occur within our congregations, because they fail to connect the truth with love and beauty. Fundamentalism is only the explication of a truth, but the truth is something more than this.

When one organizes their life around the search for the truth, they immediately enter into a relationship with goodness, beauty, and love, and as a result peace and harmony appear. By contrast, when one organizes their life in relationship to an explication of truth and then erects it as The Truth, then they become "bulletproof"—that is, impenetrable—and without having truth or beauty they do not know how to make peace, and then the arguments begin.

As long as there is an exchange of theological ideas it has to happen within that field of fraternity, as when our interdenominational or ecumenical theologians meet together. They take that for granted.

FIGUEROA: I think the problem is when people think that they can dominate the truth, or rather, that the truth does not possess them, but that they feel themselves to be its sole owner. And when people believe they possess the truth like an object they can manipulate (and think themselves superior to), they are, in reality, far from the truth.

In light of the New Testament, the problem the fundamentalists of the age had with Jesus was that he turned out to be someone whom they could not control. They could neither categorize him nor manipulate him.

So then, the truth is such that I do not consider myself master of it. When the truth possesses me, we're fine, but when I'm convinced of possessing it—that's when the warning light goes off to indicate that perhaps I'm becoming a fundamentalist, and then I begin to be dangerous.

SKORKA: The fact is that God is the only one who possesses the truth. Now, handling the truth requires parameters. How do I handle or manage what I consider to be my truth? The parameters that must serve me as a support to manage the truth have got to be the search for peace and love; if not, the truth that I have is transformed into fanaticism.

If the only goal set for some particular truth is to dominate the world, or that everyone come to think in a certain way and that everything be defined through those who believe they hold the absolute truth, then we've reached the absolute lie.

Now, insofar as the truth of faith, it's a very subtle question; each person feels God in a different way within the same religion. When we Jews begin a prayer, we say: "Our God and the God of our fathers, God of Abraham, God of Isaac, and God of Jacob." Why do we say it that way? Didn't I already say "Our God and the God of our fathers"? Why then be more explicit? Because God dealt with Abraham in one way, with Isaac in another way, and with Jacob in another. God's relationship with each one of us is so different, like that of our parents with each one of our siblings and with us; for which reason each person has "a truth," a different perception of life that they think is the truth; as many colors and shapes as there are in a kaleidoscope.

FIGUEROA: That concept is also present within inter-religious dialogue. Each person has a profound perception of their faith in God, which is the absolute truth. But if I lack the openness to engage in dialogue, as we are doing now, about our point of view of the truth or of my own intimate and extremely profound perception of faith, then I fail. Perhaps I'm afraid of showing it or I'm not so sure of what I believe in, or I want to impose my truth so that the other person thinks like me, without realizing that the other person can help me to find greater truth within my own search for truth.

I think that the truth, in itself, needs one to be generously open to it. If one is closed about what one thinks, they move further and further away from the truth. And that openness implies having, as we have said other times, the courage to seek, to debate ideas, thoughts, and concepts that lead me to enrichment.

This is something that is very clear in the Word of God, because the New Testament and the Old Testament, from the Christian point of view, are permanently engaged in dialogue and each one enriches the other. Paul says: *"Such things were written in the Scriptures long ago to teach us."* When the Apostles quote from Scripture, obviously they are talking about what we know as the Old Testament, the law and the prophets, the Torah.

So, far from fearing that search, we've got to have the openness and the courage to let our version of the truth be placed on the table for discussion, not in order to win an argument or a debate, but rather so that I might be enriched and I might enrich the other person.

SKORKA: The way in which I manage what I say and what I don't say is a dynamic question, and the same happens with respect to God. I always liked the verse from the book of Amos that says: *"Seek me and you will live."* We must seek him. God is a question of constant seeking, and the truth of that search, in the way of finding him, must be recreated again tomorrow.

The link between man and the intimacy of his being each day with God requires a re-creation. There is not just one single way of being connected. There are some forms that are preserved through time, like saying a Mass, for example, or the music or the religious service that has been performed the same way for centuries. A Passover supper, or *Pesach* as the Jews call it, has its forms, and I would say that it has an historic truth, an old thing that must be cared for and preserved. But the feeling, what one feels, cries out year after year. Faced with certain circumstances of the liturgy, I am always profoundly moved.

BERGOGLIO: Along the path of truth, of continuously going deeper, one must make a distinction regarding appearance. For example, if I take this glass and I say: "Gentlemen, there's nothing solid here," you can say: "This man is crazy." But no, there's nothing solid: there's the water, which is liquid, and the glass, which is a fluid. Or rather, appearance tells me one thing and reality is something else. That's an example of going deeper into things, and that is the path.

The second thing is the skeptical position of the one who says: "Why should I try to go forward if everything is relative?" This is an example of the pessimism that we all carry inside ourselves and which sometimes prevents us from going deeper into the truth. When we don't go deeper and we don't go forward along the path in the profound possession of the truth joined with love and beauty, we get stuck and the same thing happens to us as with all stagnant things, we become corrupted, meaning that we corrupt our own condition.

21

Testimony

I won't deny it. After recovering from my shock at seeing Cardinal Bergoglio dressed in his white papal robes,
I looked for television clips that showed especially two
different parts of his clothing and accessories. His old,
worn, but impeccably polished big black leather shoes;
and his old black wristwatch, made of plastic, practically
worthless. Those shoes and wristwatch were very familiar
to me, and I had always been surprised to see them worn
by the man who headed the largest ecclesiastical hierar-
chy in Argentina.

And there they were—unchanged, extraordinary.

As the days went by, the photographers and camera-
men discovered them and journalists described them in
a variety of symbolic terms. For me there was one word
that summed them all up: "Testimony."

FIGUEROA: Testimony has a lot to do with being a witness to
something. There are countless passages in the Old Testament
where God reminds his people that they were witnesses to the
escape from Egypt. That quality of being witnesses gives them relevance but, at the same time, it confers on them the responsibility
of continuing to give testimony about that liberating event they
experienced. It is the memory of an extraordinary fact of libera-

tion, the birth of the people of Israel, and it also implies the great responsibility of living in harmony with that testimony.

We could find the same thing in Pentecost with the formation of the Church and the descent of the Holy Spirit: *"You will be my witnesses."* From that moment not only were the apostles who were by Jesus' side going to be witnesses, but also all those present. This is about a recognition that implies a belonging, in this case, to the Christian Church, but also the responsibility of transmitting and living up to that caliber of witness. That privilege that God gives his people throughout biblical history, and it still impacts us today.

SKORKA: The most explicit verse with respect to this is Isaiah 43:10 when God says: *"You are my witnesses, and my servant whom I have chosen, so that you may know and believe me and understand that I am he. Before me no god was formed, nor will there be one after me."*

In short, the story of the liberation from slavery in Egypt serves us as an internal testimony, a pact that we as the Jewish people have with God and which must carry us, through our actions, our words and our prayers, to be witnesses of the presence of God on the face of the earth.

There is a very powerful saying from a wise scholar: "You are witnesses that I am God, and if you are not my witnesses, it is as if I were not God." How can we interpret this? Without a testimony of God on the face of the earth, there is no presence of God there.

Someone has to bear witness. In the book of Genesis, what is God's preoccupation? That there is someone to witness his presence on the face of the earth. Why were they not supposed to eat the fruit from the forbidden tree? There can be many explanations, but the most direct and simple one is that it was a common, wild tree. It's often described as an apple tree, although according to the Talmud it was a fig tree; in a word, it was nothing special. When it says that they tried its fruit, that they opened their eyes and suddenly knew about good and evil, perhaps it refers to them opening their eyes because they defied God. The tree was in the middle of the garden, in the central spot where the man and woman always passed by. The story is very specific: *"You may eat from all the trees in the garden, except for this one."* Why? Because God says so, period.

Later, God made a pact with Noah because all of civilization had gone wrong and lost its way. God tried to eliminate it, but it was Noah who justified the continuation of humanity.

Ten generations later Abraham appears and a very strong and intimate pact with God is made, marked on the body through the circumcision of the males, a pact of total surrender. The whole story of the sacrifice of Isaac proves it. All this is to record the testimony of a God who intends for someone to remember him, that someone keeps him present.

What is it that we have to do? Show his presence through actions that show there is a spiritual dimension in each individual and, through that, to give initiative to others to discover God.

BERGOGLIO: One thing is the tradition that is transmitted to us by word, and another is what is transmitted to us through the life of a person. One can talk a lot about what they think or believe, but it's another thing to do something because they're convinced of it. That is testimony.

One text I've always been impressed by is one of the most lovely in Deuteronomy, in chapter 26, when the father of the family carries the basket with the first fruits and tells the story that goes: *"My father was a wandering Aramean and he brought us out of Egypt, he saved us and he gave us this land ... And when your son asks you: 'Why do you do these things?' tell him the story."* But it does not tell why "you say" these things. It's about a testimony of life. I do things that support history, that support doctrine.

That's why a person who says one thing but does another is not very credible. He does not bear witness or live up to what he says. There is a Latin saying, I don't recall if from Cicero or from that age, that refers to what a person says, and it's borne out by life: *verba volant, exempla trahunt*, meaning "Words fly, but examples drag you down."

FIGUEROA: There is another old saying: "Your life shouts louder than your words." Meaning, testimony is not only what one says, but rather a life that corresponds with what one does. If what a person says is not supported by how they live, they do not bear witness to their words, it's just idle talk.

On the other hand, on the subject of bearing witness to God, I think that there is a secondary meaning or another side to it. In the sense that bearing witness to God is bearing witness to his character, not just to God as a being.

Often, and rightly so, there are people who are disillusioned with faith, who say: "I can't believe that there are people who talk about faith and then go and act in a different way from what they say." And I'm not just necessarily talking about people who are ordained to the religious life, just simply people who are believers. You also hear people often say: "I don't go to church, to synagogue, or to temple, for this or that reason ..." In my case, I often respond in this way: "You can't imagine what I would be like, if it were not for God's mercy." In some way, one must bear witness to God's character, to the fact that he is the only perfect one, the only thing that is true. And in the testimony of his character, show himself to be that merciful God who pardons us, restores us, sets us back on the path, and cleanses us again. And, at the same time, to recognize my error, my bad nature, and the need to have a God, of whom I am a witness.

SKORKA: It's true, there are many places, like communities or temples where, sometimes, the one in charge does not, shall we say, behave very well. Or very often there are people who attend there and have very ritually observant attitudes and we find ourselves faced with the fact that they are really quite false. People who wear observant religious attire that speak of God and, on the other hand, behave in a manner that runs completely counter to God's rules.

To those people that say: "That's why I don't go to any temple," my advice is that they choose any temple they like, although they might have doubts about God. Because when you go to a temple you are showing your child many things: that you go in search of something spiritual and that the dimension of spirituality has a place that fits into your life and that it's relevant and important. Besides, your child can ask you: "But, Dad, if you don't do this, and you're not going to follow all the rules, then why go to temple?" The answer is: "I go to the temple to meditate, to think." And for the question: "Why don't you do that at home?" The answer is: "I also do that at home, but the meditation should be performed alongside others." That's the lesson from the Bible. The prophets were very popular, but God says: *"Go home, return to your people."*

Those of us who direct religious services or transmit a message do not have to believe that those who come, do so for us; and if they do attend for us that's lamentable—they've got to come for God.

On *Yom Kippur* what's imperative is to think about what really matters from a spiritual perspective. I cannot, neither as a Jew, nor as a human being who has a given identity, separate myself from that. If I remove myself, I'm also setting an example for my son; but a bad example.

BERGOGLIO: Bearing witness indicates the coherence of life that exists between what one thinks or one believes, and how one lives. When there is incoherence one stops thinking about how they live or believing in how they live and alters their thinking to justify the slack, lazy reality it assumes.

You were just mentioning people not going to temple because of the person presiding over the community; in each case, the priest or bishop always has this or that defect. It's true, there are religious leaders who drive some people away, not because their sermons are boring but because they're incoherent or meaningless. That's the quickest way to drive away people who are faithful.

This morning, while I was praying, I opened the book of Ezekiel and was moved. In the passage I read, God says that there are pastors that *"take advantage of their sheep, that seek the milk and wool from the sheep, but don't try to calm their fears."* This is talking about the self-interested pastor.

St. Augustine later explains, in his commentary on Ezekiel, that the milk is money, or rather, God is referring to the self-interested pastor who wants to get rich by feeding off his flock. And the wool is fame or reputation and the vanity of feeling oneself a pastor and misusing authority, not as a service and like a teacher that helps one to grow, but rather as someone that imposes their authority.

The incoherence of these leaders is probably what causes the most harm to people. People draw closer to God when inspired by a message of salvation, a word from Scripture that touched them, an episode from the story of Jesus that moved them, or the image of so many men and women who followed God and who appear in Scripture; and then they find themselves with one who is grasping after money, who is seeking fame, someone looking to get rich, and another seeking to show off or seeking power for its own sake.

Coherency is a very great responsibility for leaders and directors, especially for the two of us, Rabbi Skorka and I, who are in charge of communities, and for committed believers like Dr. Figueroa, in order to not end up driving people away who really want to live out the Word of God in a congregation or a community.

FIGUEROA: Yes, evidently the public testimony of leaders is fundamental. Reading the Gospels one understands that the true dispute that Jesus had was not with the common people or with the sinners but with the religious leaders about whom he warned the people: *"Listen to what they say, but don't do what they do, because they say one thing and do another."*

The God of the Bible is a God who shakes people up. He seems to have a vocation for shaking me up, making me uncomfortable, of provoking me to examine and improve my life, my ways, and my thoughts. He invites me to return to him, to remember where I came from, who he is, and that I must be a testament to his presence here on the earth.

SKORKA: Being coherent and consistent is a struggle because we have the truth in our hands, fully manifest, absolutely complete and fully integrated, but only God knows that. Also, life has its ups and downs and its changes. The name by which the law is defined in the Talmudic Hebrew is interesting; it comes from the verb which means "to walk" and it is mentioned in this verse: *"The rules that determine the path that you must walk."* This means that everything in life requires a constant overhaul, a touching up. Now, one thing is modifying, and the other is neglecting. That's like me keeping only the skin instead of the fruit, and touching it up, only out of necessity. Because in life there is dynamism, new contributions that give us science and technology. We can't keep the old version, only with the essence of the old version, the Bible, which continues to be the basis, and demands of us that we constantly reinterpret it.

BERGOGLIO: Yes, it's true. In that reading from the Bible, situated in the circumstances that one must live through, is where the Spirit of God acts in our hearts and leads us toward a path of greater perfection.

It's interesting, there is never a contradiction between the first covenant and the way in which we live out the covenant nowadays with our necessary modifications to it, just as long as we have walked before the Lord, in prayer, and in our searching.

There is a contradiction when we begin to negotiate with what's not negotiable from the first covenant; that, lately, is to negotiate fidelity, something that you don't negotiate. Our path through life has got to be ever more faithful to the covenant according to the new circumstances, adapting to them appropriately without ever adulterating it. That's fidelity. It is the very great work of searching, of prayer, of dialogue. That's why testimony, bearing witness, is essentially fidelity. The man who is a witness is a faithful man and this reminds me of what St. Paul says to Timothy: *"And if we are faithful to him, he remains faithful, because he cannot go back on his word."*

Finally, fidelity is imitating the Lord in a way in which he has always shown, that consists of not going back on our word nor negotiating our path, but in adapting it, improving it, or to use the Italian word *aggiornare*, which means to bring things up to date.

SKORKA: As God said to Abraham in a verse that you are very fond of: *"Walk before me and be blameless."* Or, as Micah says, *"Walk humbly together with God."* It is about walking, of not staying in the same place, at the same point, of seeing different panoramas and situations and trying to be witnesses of God.

FIGUEROA: Along that way, difficulties are surely going to arise and, as we encounter those stumbling blocks, we will again bear witness to what kind of God is the God of the Bible: the God of forgiveness and restoration, who requires of us the testimony of having been faithful, of knowing that following the path does not consist of a static life like some photograph; it is a moving picture, a film of life.

How good it is to end our lives saying: "I have culminated my days and I have been faithful. Faithful to whom I bear witness, faithful to whom I am a witness, not because they told me to, but because I desired to be faithful. I have believed and I have remained faithful. I have not been perfect but I have been a faithful witness."

2 2

The Meaning of Life

Through his symbolic parallel and normative content, Jesus' Sermon on the Mount is the mirror of the Law received by Moses on Mount Sinai. Jesus' discourse, in its version from the Gospel of Luke, contains what some Christian theologians have called "the national constitution of the new Kingdom of God."

The morning of May 25, 2012, before starting the *Te Deum* in the Cathedral, Cardinal Bergoglio commented to me, in a brief moment of privacy, that he was going to speak about beatitudes and unhappiness and that his prayer was that his message on that date* would be good for the soul of all Argentines.

The Cardinal's homily seemed to me brilliant, his exegesis impeccable, and his contextualization intelligent. I know, however, that more than a few interpreted his words rather simplistically and as a circumstantial criticism. I must say that I do not share that reading, neither regarding the sermon's contents nor its intention.

When I think of "the meaning of life"—the theme of this chapter—from my Christian worldview, I cannot avoid thinking about the beatitudes from the Sermon on

---

* *Primer gobierno patrio or* Revolution Day, the national day of Argentina.

the Mount. And when I do, inevitably, that historic day comes to my mind.

FIGUEROA: When a person reads the Bible they find key passages where it would seem that God reveals a meaning about life that, until this moment, had been hidden for some people.

He shows the stars to Abraham and says to him: *"So shall your offspring be."* He speaks to Moses from the burning bush and tells him: *"You will have to go and rescue your people from slavery in Egypt."* On the other hand, Jesus chooses the apostles from among people whom probably none of us would select: fishermen, small town folk, tax collectors for the Romans. God also calls Saul (later Paul) who persecuted the Church, and when Saul falls to the ground, God says to him: *"Now you will be my witness, you are going to set aside intellectual theology in favor of practical theology, and you're going to see how this is going to change you and give a new meaning to your life."*

Sometimes it would seem that the meaning of life is hidden away somewhere and, in a moment of life, something happens and the direction of our entire life is shown. This is a crucial fact in a person's life, the moment when they find the answers to the questions: "What is my purpose in life?"; "Where am I going?"; "What is it that I want to be?"; "Where do I want to go"; and finally, "What is the real meaning of my existence?"

SKORKA: Faced with the question about the meaning of life, I would say that there are different strata. Dr. Figueroa mentioned one of them: "What specifically does God want from me?" Maybe he wants me to be a rabbi, or a doctor, that I be a leader, or whatever. But, let's go to the most basic level: "For what reason am I here in this world?"

When we read in Genesis that God set man in the Garden of Eden, it says specifically that man was *"to work in it and care for it."* So then, Judaism's first response to this is: "Your life is extremely important; it allows God's work to continue. But be careful, there is more than just a biological continuum, there has got to be a spiritual continuum as well.

In the first verse of Genesis, chapter 2, where it begins saying: *"On the seventh day God had finished his work; so on the seventh day he rested from all his labors. Then God blessed the seventh day and made it holy, because on that day he rested from all the work of creating that he had done,"* we find something a little strange, because in Hebrew the translation would be: *"God created every-*

thing, in order for it to be finished." And who has to finish God's work? Man.

To discover where I should direct myself, and what I must do in order to unveil my existence, is a great challenge. I do not exist simply to watch and let everything happen. The first challenge that I have is the search, and that is what creates my relationship to God.

I have to give an immediate response to the first level of the meaning of life: What is my purpose? I am here, but in order to do what? We are God's partners, to complete his work. He left us something to do here. There is a reason why we call him "Father" and we are his children. I wouldn't say that he left us an inheritance, I would say that he left us an estate, understanding the concept of "estate" as what a father gives his son while he is still alive.

BERGOGLIO: The phrase "in order to" is key. God creates man in order for him to do something. He doesn't make him to be still and quiet, he instills him with movement. And so, we find a bucolic image of creation says: *"He created them to live happily in the Garden of Eden."* But he said to them: *"Grow, multiply, dominate the earth."* The meaning of life has got to be searched for there, in motion, along the way, not in stillness and quiet.

I would dare to add the little word "with." When man is alone, God makes a companion for him and this provokes the man to exclaim: *"Ah, this is what I was missing; this is my very own flesh and bones!"* Meaning, he lacked someone who could truly keep him company. So then God creates man "in order to" grow, multiply, and "with" a community.

These are the biblical parameters that make me think that one is insufficient if they try to take on the question of the meaning of life by themselves. I am myself in a community, a social being in order to complete God's work, as Rabbi Skorka was saying.

In the Gospels, one parable that stands out is the story of the servant and the talents. A man is going on a trip and he distributes talents, money, to his servants: to one he gives ten talents, to another five, and to another man just one talent. The servants were expected to put them to good use. When the man returns from his trip, the servant to whom he'd given ten talents gives him ten more that he'd earned, and the one with five returns the money along with five more that he had earned. The servant who had received only one talent says to him: *"Look, I got scared because you are a very demanding master. You reap where you did not sow, and so I wrapped up the money in a cloth, I dug a hole and I buried it. Here it is, I return it to you."* And the master's response is: *"Wicked servant,*

you failed to carry out my command that you make something of
this money I gave you."

God gives us a treasure; he puts it in our hands, in our heart,
in our mind. A treasure that we have got to make grow, in truth,
in goodness and in beauty. And if one fails to make it grow, the
treasure is worthless.

So then, to seek and find the meaning of life is to dare to have
courage. Because there are times, in certain critical situations in
life, when one does not find the meaning of life. Then they give in
and think: "Life is meaningless." In the end that person is suffering from the influences of that ugly sickness called pusillanimity,
which consists of being faint-hearted, of burying the talent and
saying: "No, I won't try that."

FIGUEROA: Viktor Frankl said that man's true concern is not to
live an enjoyable life, nor to avoid suffering, but to find the meaning of life. And he added that when he found it he was capable of
enduring almost any kind of suffering. Nietzsche said the same
thing, in that very familiar phrase that says: "He who has a 'why'
to live can bear almost any 'how.'"

On the other hand, bringing together the opinions expressed
by the two of you, in that dynamic effect of collaborating and the
danger of being conservative, fearful or weak-willed, perhaps it
might not be good to sit down to wait and wonder: "What's the
meaning of life?" The search will only be good if it implies the
courage of going, of running the risk of being wrong, and of
searching out that which we believe, crossing barriers, and assuming risks. All this, knowing that God has made me unique, unrepeatable, and with a sense of life that I have the responsibility—I
won't say "the right"—of discovering, as a collaborator in God's
creative work, in order that I then take a risk and put myself on
the line.

SKORKA: To live life, evidently you've got to take risks. There is no
safeguard against that.

Every couple that gets married and starts a new life together
represents a question of faith. Sometimes I tell fiancés: "You are an
example of faith, of faith in life, faith in God, faith in love. It's not
a mere question of instincts; there is a faith in wanting to walk the
path and build something together in life."

Then, in order to be able to answer what life is, one must live
it, and that necessarily implies taking risks and, through different life experiences, finding flashes of what is the meaning of life,

even though they might not be totally clear and explicit. Because faith and life are not presented in a totally clear manner that can be expressed with words, it is similar to touching something covered by a veil. We can perceive flashes of the meaning of existence when we make some discovery, achieve something or reach a high point in a career, but to understand clearly what life is, well, only the one who created it knows it and has the final answer.

BERGOGLIO: Another trap we must overcome—apart from a lack of conviction—is "self-referentiality." Someone who starts playing that game is never going to find the meaning of life. What's more, I would say, they are never going to be able to wonder what it is, because they'll find themselves satisfied with that game, a game in the broadest sense of the word. They can feel satisfied with nausea and with anguish, but one becomes bloated and stagnant with the game of self-reference.

That path towards the meaning of life that Rabbi Skorka was talking about, sometimes is not clearly perceived, and at last, probably, it is illuminated. I think that it's important to take into account the question: "Does this have meaning?" It usually arises in moments of crisis and greatest suffering, when we find ourselves buffeted by life.

I'll permit myself to tell a story that I've always remembered. It has no great literary value, but its message is very lovely. In this story, it turns out, there were four wise men, not three, and each one brought a present to the baby Jesus. One brought him gold, the next frankincense, the next myrrh, and the fourth one brought him some diamonds. This last of the four kings, somewhere along the road to Bethlehem, passed through a town where there was a very big emergency, and he stayed there to help, for which purpose he sold a diamond. Later he continued on his way and reached a place where there was a plague, and he stopped there to help as well. As the people there lacked the means to deal with such a great crisis, he sold another diamond. Next he passed through a place where there was great famine, and he sold another diamond to help save the economy in that city. And so, as he went along, he kept encountering different extreme situations and losing years of time in the process. When at last he finally reached his destination, the people there told him that the little baby he had been traveling to see was the man hanging on the cross. He approached Jesus and told him: "I brought a bag of diamonds to give to you, but I lost them," and Jesus told him: "No, you gave them to me along the road." And, saying that, a drop of his blood fell and turned into a diamond.

That Christian story, of German origin, tells me that there is no need to fear the circumstances of life that apparently slow us down along the way. Instead I must face them as they come, although they force me to take a detour from the path I believed that I was meant to follow.

The Gospel says something similar when Jesus tells the story of the man who'd been beaten along the road from Jerusalem to Jericho. First a priest passes by, sees the man lying there, and keeps on going. Telling it today, the priest goes on by because he doesn't want to be late to Mass. Next, a lawyer comes along, sees the man lying there, and the text in Greek says that he walks around him and keeps on going. Nowadays the lawyer would say: "No. Maybe later I'll have to go to court and testify as a witness; better not to get involved." Finally, a sinner comes along who is moved to take pity on this man and attends to him, although it delays him from doing what he had to do.

Crises make us redirect our way, and according to the manner in which we face them we are showing what life really means to us.

FIGUEROA: The idea that every crisis implies an opportunity is very well known. Oh, the poor person who's never experienced a crisis! Because crisis forges our character, it obliges us to stop, to reflect, to reconsider things—or as GPS devices say lately, to recalculate—and not only to wonder about things in life, but to let life ask us questions.

Many times, crisis is an ally in our life. Very hard moments that we experience help us to see life and value things in a different way. Sometimes, hitting our lowest point helps us to gain momentum to jump a little higher. From the point of view of the community and not just the individual, as a country, the crises that people are experiencing provide excellent opportunities for change.

I have two verses that accompany me throughout the day to make up my daily prayers. In the morning when I get up I say: *"Each day your mercies are renewed."* It is a verse that lights up my day. I start directly before God, with his renewed mercies that I am later going to use up throughout the day. And at the end of the day: *"Today's trouble is enough for today."* To put that another way, "Tomorrow will be another day." The prayers are accompanied by their own reflections. In the morning: "What am I going to do with my day today?" And when the day ends: "What did I do differently today?" Or "What did I do today that gave meaning to my life and the lives of others?"

I think that we are considering two elements. One is the importance of crisis to bring me down to earth from my idealism or elitism about life. The other is the necessity of taking one day at a time in order to move away from philosophy towards the practical part of life which is the challenge of every day, every second. Every new minute requires me to give meaning to my life.

SKORKA: The question of crisis is a very profound subject. Crisis is change and life brings changes by itself. Every person that thinks that they've got life all wrapped up in a nice neat package is, as they say, a fool. Life has many fronts about which we've got to pray to God. When I speak of "fronts," I'm talking about the relationship we've got with our loved ones, with our children: nothing is guaranteed. And don't even mention questions about money, work, or health. Nobody can ever manage to project anything, saying: "If I do this, then it's necessarily going to produce such and such an effect."

In the book of our daily morning prayers, we say: "God, do not test me, do not lead me into a trying situation." We know that the test is going to come, life constantly tests us, but when I recite that prayer my thought is: "If you are going to test me, give me strength to pass the test." It's not so simple; if we want to improve then let's not seek temptation, let's not expect to fall so that we can then rise. In short, let's try to foresee where our errors might lie in order to not commit them.

The Bible is constantly presented to us as a book of memory. One has to have a very good memory in order to keep falling into the errors of the past.

We're always headed for some kind of growth crisis. If we fall, we need not falter, we've got to keep moving forward. Let's keep going up without falling. Let's not stay where we are, although we might be very well. Let's choose between hunting for what's good and what's bad.

BERGOGLIO: In my experience, each time I passed through a crisis I realized that it was worth the trouble, because they illuminated me more about the meaning of my life, of my existence. That is when I faced them well, and when I faced them badly, things went badly for me. I think that in the relationship to the meaning of life there are partial responses by means of which one advances little by little, step by step. It's like the automobile headlight that only lights up a bit of the road at a time, as we go forward, but in the end we are going to be able to have the full answer.

On the other hand, the question: "What meaning does life have?" can be a tricky line of questioning, because it can ensnare us. Perhaps it might be clearer to ask "What does life expect of me?" or "What steps will I take so that my life might be different?" or, as Mother Teresa of Calcutta, said "This is a drop of water in the sea, but the sea is different thanks to this drop of water." Meaning: "What do those around me, my people, the world expect of me?"

In the end, the meaning of life is really quite similar to the mission. Every man comes with a mission that he goes along discovering throughout his life—a vocation, to give something, to do something—so that life might be different after my time in this world, thanks to what I have given. So, then, it's important to ask ourselves this question: "What does life expect of me?" Even in the most difficult moments, in the darkest moments, it expects something.

FIGUEROA: I would like to add the concept of otherness of life. Sometimes, the question must also be: "What can I do for the life of my fellow human being?" In what way can I improve the meaning of life for those around me? Because, as has been well said, we do not live on an island. When we close ourselves off so that we can simply seek our own satisfaction, the meaning of life for my own pleasure, we fall into a trap, because the meaning of life is found with others, in the search for making a positive impact on the lives of others.

In searching for that otherness in life by giving ourselves to others, without thinking about it, we find ourselves.

SKORKA: The fact is that life is, after all, something that we are going to leave behind to others. One lives life not only for oneself.

Essentially, the first approach to the response about the meaning of life can be that a person should live in such a way as to leave a legacy for another, because no matter how much we have we're not taking any of it with us. As our scholars of the Talmud say, we take "the good actions that we did and the Torah that we learned," understanding that studying it is not only an intellectual question, but rather something that helps me especially to work. Those who amass fortunes and who, thanks to that, believe they are successful in life, do not understand what life is.

One lives in order to leave something behind. We keep absolutely nothing from this life when it ends; nothing is ours save for the footprints we leave behind.

BERGOGLIO: My grandmother used to say: "A shroud has no pockets." And I'll add this: "I never saw a moving van following a funeral procession." We receive life so that we can pass it on, and in that dynamic we discover its meaning.

FIGUEROA: I'd like to narrate an experience of biblical translation in Africa. We had to translate the concept of "generosity" which, in our culture, is understood as someone having "a big heart." But in the tribe we were with, that expression not only meant something different but, in fact, the exact opposite. The logic of cultural thinking that impacted their language was the following: A person with a big heart was not a good person, because they had fattened their heart, so to speak, by hoarding for themselves what they had, instead of sharing it. For that culture, the person who really finds the meaning of life is a person with a small heart, because they've given away everything to others, even their own heart, finally leaving it empty of selfishness.

In the end, for us, also today, here and now, the meaning of life lies in giving ourselves wholeheartedly to others.

Joy

What sorts of things did we talk about in the moments just before we started taping each program? As I said before, we never talked about the theme for that particular session, but instead a whole variety of things. Generally, the news of the day, religious events that interested us, and a variety of things that came up spontaneously. But if there was one recurring theme it was soccer. All three of us are fervent supporters of different teams. It's well known that Cardinal Bergoglio roots for San Lorenzo, Rabbi Skorka is a fan of River Plate, and I support Club Atlético Independiente. Supporting different teams always led, at some point, to joking around and some "fierce defense" of our favorite teams. Each team's poor record did not stop us from telling all kinds of funny stories.

I always appreciated the Cardinal's broad, fine-tuned sense of humor. It typically appeared with a wide, knowing smile that accompanied some subtle mischievous remark on his part, and included his ease in telling jokes. These jokes, generally, were about religious and pseudo-theological subjects. They were evidence of an admittedly self-critical adult and consisted in dispensing with unnecessary religious solemnity but, principally, were owing to his great sense of humor.

Today I think that his sense of humor, united with his profound practical down-to-earth spirituality, is helping him bear the heavy burden of his responsibilities.

FIGUEROA: The subject we've chosen for today's discussion is joy, something important and very special. When we think about the Bible and about joy, it's very significant that Psalm 19, which is a psalm dedicated especially to talking about the Bible, says *"Your word brings joy to my heart."*

The Jews celebrate a very joyous holiday, Sukkot, an occasion when Jesus said that he is the water of life. This has a theological implication to what is referred to as the Holy Spirit and his messianic presence, but it is also an expression of joy.

For me, it is very meaningful that one of the most important festivals in our Judeo-Christian tradition, has specifically to do with joy. This question, then, is appropriate: Why does God institute a festival especially dedicated to joy?

SKORKA: Your appreciation is very appropriate. Three times a year a Jew had to go to the temple in Jerusalem to present himself before God. During those three pilgrimage festivities, one did not go to the temple in Jerusalem to see God, but rather to present himself before God.

The three opportunities are, first at Passover, the festival that commemorates the departure from Egypt and coincides with the beginning of the agricultural year. Fifty days later, on the Feast of Pentecost, which is also called the Feast of Weeks or the Feast of the Harvest, which coincides with the beginning of the wheat harvest. And the third festival coincides with the time when one must begin to ask God to bring the rain, and that is the Feast of Sukkot, when they remember how the children of Israel left Egypt and lived in little huts and shelters with thatched roofs.

In all these festivities one says: *"You will feel joy in the presence of God."* Now then, in the Feast of Sukkot there is one more commandment, that says: *"And you will find joy and you will have only joy,"* and that's why Sukkot is the feast of joy.

I think that joy is something we share; it has got to do with the spiritual aspect of Judaism in the Bible. Psalm 100 says: *"Serve God with joy"*; Psalm 97: *"Light dawns for the righteous, and joy for the upright in heart."* Joy underlies righteousness, underlies justice, and all those elements that allow us to approach God with a peaceful spirit. The person who is a transgressor, a murderer or a fraud, cannot approach God with tranquility. But the one who, in some way, is at peace with his conscience and knows how to recognize when he was wrong and ask for forgiveness, that person can approach God. But keep in mind, Judaism, unlike Christianity, has a much harder concept of God: Justice, justice, justice! Forgiveness requires a lot of thought and work, in that we have different points of view. So, the one who has acted justly can approach God with a certain peace, and I think that that peace is true joy.

BERGOGLIO: God loves the one who gives, and gives himself, with joy; there is a harmony between joy and the Lord. The phrase: *"God loves the one who gives joyfully"* that appears in the letters of the apostles, is like a synthesis of this biblical thought.

I was always impressed by a particular scene in the book of Nehemiah, when the Book of the Law, the Torah, is discovered and read before the people. Ezra and Nehemiah read it and the people hear the Word of God and weep. They weep from emotion, they weep at encountering the Word of God, and perhaps because they reproach themselves for having lost it. Later Nehemiah tells them, in chapter 8: *"Do not cry, nor be sad; joy in the Lord is your fortress."* Rejoicing in what God gives us makes us strong, while by contrast, sadness weakens and leads us to melancholy, to selfishness, to be withdrawn and wrapped up in ourselves, sulking and licking our wounds.

What a lovely thing to say: *"Do not cry, nor be sad; joy in the Lord is your fortress."* Joy is strength; it is a fortress. The scene ends with the socialization of joy, which is the festival. In the Judeo-Christian tradition, the festival is not an addition, it is a part, I dare say, even of revelation itself. If we remove all idea of celebration and festivity from revelation, then something has been amputated, something that does not end well.

This subject is often mentioned in the New Testament: *"There is more joy in heaven, there is more celebration, when one sinner is converted."* The father of the prodigal son declared a feast when his son returned. Each time that something is restored, or enters into God's wavelength, so to speak, there is celebration.

Joy leads to celebration. This reminds me of David's joy, which sends him into a frenzy, when he appears dancing before the Ark of the Covenant. That man was out of his mind. He was so happy that he transgresses the protocol of behavior appropriate to a king to such a point that one of Saul's daughters makes fun of him.

That joy from encountering the Law—that makes David sing, weep, be beside himself with pleasure and dance before the ark—also leads him to the festival. Because later it says that he distributes to each person a date cake so that they can begin their celebration.

Rabbi Skorka mentioned something very lovely: *"Celebrate you, your father, your mother, your family, the stranger in your house, and the slave."* Nobody is left out, everyone must celebrate! This says a lot to me, this fact of knowing how to celebrate well, without alienating oneself, in festivals that are linked to the joy of the Lord. Therefore, in our tradition, the servant of the Lord is a joyous man or woman, a happy person that knows how to celebrate properly.

FIGUEROA: I was thinking about a God that is happy and who invites us to be joyous and to imitate him in that way. That joy has a lot in common with the good use of freedom that God gave us. We have the freedom to live our lives with joy and to see things from an optimistic point of view. We also have the freedom of crumbling in the face of some circumstance in our lives, of sinking into sadness and despair—the famous option of seeing the glass as half empty or half full.

Rabbi Skorka was talking about the relationship between Judaism and Christianity regarding forgiveness. I understand what he means. In my case, when I read the Old Testament, I see a God that continues betting on man despite all of his betrayals, shortcomings, and transgressions. God always sends a prophetic voice to denounce, but that denouncement never ends without a voice of joy for the hope that God returns to bet again on man. It is as if he were saying: "You're going to go through this, because you did such-and-such a thing," but it also anticipates this idea: "A new dawn is coming, a new day, a new hope for this people."

BERGOGLIO: There is something that Rabbi Skorka said that seems to me to be correct and it's worthwhile to revisit it a little, with respect to true and false happiness.

There is a kind of riotous, dazed happiness that in some way is a kind of excuse or alibi.* That kind of happiness is not healthy; it is a drug, an escape from concrete reality. But the happiness is concrete. Lamentably, throughout the history of Christianity, certain currents of thought have crept in. Let's name the first one, perhaps like the Pelagianism that did not permit any sort of serene, healthy pleasure.

---

* **Alibi:** this term comes from a Latin root whose most frequent use, the judicial one, means an excuse. In a second, accepted meaning, which is the one corresponding to this text, it can mean an extenuating circumstance, and within the narrative context it describes the "soporific" effect of some unseen or uncertain reality.

Let's recall the film *Babette's Feast*. In it there is a community of people that has fallen into this type of "heresy," of hyper austerity, and has not found the freedom of God, the joy in the Lord, which is essentially free. That's why joy is expressed corporeally in so many ways, dance being one of them, but not the sort of dance that dazes and alienates you, but, rather, the dance of beauty, where the whole body offers itself in praise to God, not only a liturgical dance that is sometimes performed.

I remember when I went to Rabbi Skorka's synagogue, I was delighted that after some formal prayer and word of protocol, the songs and dances began, but as something normal, something joyous and pleasurable.

We cannot, under the pretext of austerity, amputate the unity that exists between the human body and soul; God joined them together. For that reason, joy is spiritual, psychic and corporeal; the whole body, soul, and spirit.

SKORKA: One point that you have both touched on is that of the two ways of facing life. Seeing it with pessimism and a lack of joy or with optimism and joy. Maimonides, in his codification of Jewish law, categorized this in a marvelous way, but always based on the Talmudic literature, by saying: "The prophecy is not reached, in any way, through sadness, but only through joy." For him, the prophecy signified the spiritual manifestation where the intellect is one of the expressions of man's spirit.

I'd like to add a "footnote"; in agreement with the Talmud, after the generation of Malachi, Zachariah, and Haggai there was no more prophecy and then began the age of the Talmudic scholars. Now, according to the Gospels, when Jesus mentions the quotations from the prophets, it is as if he wants to revive that spirit. The Talmudic scholars said: "No." Nevertheless, Maimonides might have seemed to say: "There is some manifestation of the prophetic voice still alive today."

The question is that under that lens there are distinct points of view between the rabbinical worldview and that of the first Christians of the first and second centuries, when really there was a very great dialogic interaction between the incipient Church and the scholars of Israel. But, independently of all that, there is the concept that only through joy can one reach the prophecy and can there be a profound approach to God. And this emerges in Judaism in a special way, in a Hassidic movement that, according to Martin Buber, is the most important religious movement from the eighteenth century onwards. That movement established dances, songs, and the banishment of all kinds of melancholy, to avoid falling into depression. A famous Hassidic rabbi had a very powerful aphorism: "Jews, do not give up." Elie Wiesel, in a very beautiful book he wrote about Hassidism and the Shoah tells how in one of those death camps he saw a student of Rebbe Nachman of Breslov repeating that phrase, even in Auschwitz: "Do not give up, do not lose hope."

Finally, I agree completely with what Dr. Figueroa said about a God that waits for man no matter that he has disappointed him so many times. Jeremiah said three times: *"There will be no more bridal songs and joy."* And in the end, in chapter 33, after the destruction of Jerusalem, it says: *"There will be joy once again in this place."*

FIGUEROA: There is an interesting concept in the New Testament that explores the theme of joy even more deeply, and which, in the majority of translations to Spanish is translated as "joyous pleasure." The Greek word is an expression or an attitude that has got to do with joy, but it transcends superficial happiness. Where am I going with this thought? It's obvious that someone cannot be happy in the face of some sorrowful circumstance in their life, and it would be absurd to ask a person to be so when faced with some personal misfortune, the loss of a loved one, unemployment, or an illness. But the joyous pleasure does not depend on what's going on around me, but rather, it is something much more profound. It is the joy that comes from having absolute confidence in the Lord, instead of depending on what happens to me circumstantially.

I think that that is, perhaps, the most intimate, profound, spiritual and intellectual place to which the man of faith can arrive: the capacity for maintaining that joyous pleasure without depending on those things that generally make people happy or sad.

This joy is permanently in the thought of the apostle Paul, especially when he says: *"I know what it means to live with abundance and with very little. I can do everything through Christ, who strengthens me."* It is about knowing how to live when I have everything and to find joy in the Lord when I have nothing, because through God I can do all things. I think the concept of joy contains a very special sense of profoundness.

BERGOGLIO: The Rabbi used a word that reflects what you are pointing towards now. He used the word "peace" and then moved on. That's the word I would like to touch on again.

There are three distinct verbs in the New Testament that refer to joy: one is the desire that one is well and at peace, and is used to talk about health. The second verbs refers to inner joy, when one feels good inside. And there is a third verb that is used for the explosion of that good feeling, which is both worship and the holiday festival. In the Bible, the festival is closely linked to worship; when people have a festival the Lord is worshiped, Yahweh is worshiped.

The first words used for greeting, which are a bit aseptic, are "All right, I hope you're well and that everything goes well for you." But as regards the feeling of pleasure mentioned earlier we meant a very basic kind of joy, the peace that I might feel even though I'm going through some very bad or difficult times. Peace is the basis of all joy. There is a fundamental peace that lies at the heart of a true joy.

What is the basis on which a woman or a man of faith, according to our Judeo-Christian tradition and what God taught us, can be at peace, feel pleasure, celebrate, and worship? The fact of feeling that they are chosen by the Lord, feeling promised—because we received a promise—and being in alliance with the Lord.

And we return to the base of our entire life of faith: being chosen, the promise, and the alliance. The basis of our peace lies in resting on the certainty that God chose us and promised to accompany us united along a path, sometimes through the desert, but without letting our feet get swollen, as it says in Deuteronomy. God made an alliance with us and he is not going to break it. And it's interesting what the Apostle Paul says: *"And even if you prove to be unfaithful to the Lord, he remains faithful, because he cannot forswear himself."* For me, the choice, the promise, and the alliance, are the basis of this peace and of all joy.

SKORKA: Dialoguing about God with nonbelievers, many times the concept of "I'd like to believe, but I don't believe. I envy the person who can believe," emerges. It's as if they're saying, "You have something—that peace people talk about but that I don't have." I feel that the overarching message is: "I can't have that enjoyment or that joy of existence." And, certainly, an existence without God alongside man is very hard; it's that confidence from the twenty-third Psalm: *"For you are with me; your rod and your staff—they comfort me."* In the moment when one has that tranquility of spirit, there really can be a pleasure in existence.

When we understand that not everything begins and ends with the things that we possess, or the power that we can end up achieving, it becomes clearer that that is not the essence of life. In that moment, we can enjoy life and experience a distinct joy, that joy that costs a great deal to achieve, that one has to work towards along the way, to grow closer to and feel the presence of God.

It's a matter of what we always say in prayer: "This is our life and the span of our days, and it is also our joy." It is our life because we conceive it through a very spiritual joy, a joy that is so different from what all the different media, sadly, try to sell to us in our lifetimes.

FIGUEROA: There probably exists a popular thought or imaginary idea that's mistaken, of which I form a part because I come to my faith from the position of atheism. It's about the false sensation that if I approach God, a church or a temple, it's the perfect formula for that God to rain on my party or spoil my happiness. There also occurs the thought that in some moment I'm going to get closer to God before life comes to an end, but now I want to enjoy that joyful happiness, because God is a party-pooper who wants to pull me away from all the things that make my life happy. Later, one discovers that it's not so. That God—as we said at the start—is a joyful God who invites happiness, who invented it, and who wants his people, his faithful people, to live within that joy. But it's not a superficial happiness, not just some mask or outward protective covering, but a profound joy, a sense of intimacy with God. One discovers that in God and in our fellow men and women there is a true joy.

Enrique Santos Discépolo says in his tango song "Cambalache"—which means a junk shop: *"Herida por un sable sin remache, ves llorar la Biblia junto a un calefón."* ("See the Bible wounded, crying, hanging from a spike in the bathroom by the hot water heater, its pages sliced out.") The story behind those lyrics is very interesting. Around the start of the twentieth century most houses had no bathroom, just an outhouse, and only the richest people had hot water heaters. But the one thing that was truly a luxury, that was not to be found anywhere, was toilet paper. So, for that reason, the wrapping paper for apples was highly coveted. In those days, the evangelical ministers of the Bible Society gave away for free, or sold at a very low price, copies of the Bible printed on very thin paper, which we nowadays call "bible paper." Many people collected those Bibles and, making a hole in the book's cover, hung them from a spike in the wall called the *sable sin remache*, or sword without a handle, next to the hot water heater. And so, as the song says, the Bible cries because it's so far from being used properly, so far from occupying a central place on the family table, and it's being used in a way that Discépolo sees as one of life's scandalous mix-ups.

It's an anecdote about how such a popular tango comes to be, but it's also a teaching for us about how the Word of God, the Bible, occupies a central place in our heart and how it gives us that joy that is mentioned in Psalm 19, with which we began our dialogue today: *"Your word, Lord, brings joy to my heart."*

24

Solitude

It was not too long after my tremendous emotional experience of seeing Cardinal Bergoglio greeting the crowd from the balcony of the papal palace in Rome, now as Pope Francis, that a personal doubt started to invade my thoughts. Would he feel lonely? How would he endure, all by himself, the enormous pressures and significant decisions that he would have to take?

Of course the Cardinal was already rather accustomed to live in that solitary way. His very public pastoral activity at the head of the Church in Argentina had shaped his character to help him face the most difficult moments, in that way. One might say that he even sought out and longed for those moments of solitude in the presence of our Lord Jesus Christ, a great normative example of how one is to live in that unique condition. Often, he shared a Bible passage with me. He told me about a moment of prayer or a thought that had helped him to make an important decision, the fruit of his moments alone with Christ, very early, at four or five in the morning.

But a new ingredient now had to be added to all of his enormous experiences and finely honed spiritual nature. The distance from his friends and loved ones and his being suddenly uprooted from familiar places. This new solitude concerned me.

Only a week after he was named Bishop of Rome, while I was eating lunch four blocks from the Metropolitan Cathedral in Buenos Aires, my cell phone rang: "Hello, Marcelo." "Yes," I answered, "Who's calling?" "Jorge," answered the voice on the other end. Trying to overcome my surprise, I asked: "Jorge who?" "Bergoglio," he said to me. With his soft, quiet voice, and in response to my question about how he was doing, he interrupted me, saying, "No, the reason I called, really, was to see how you were doing."

Today, months after that call, and knowing the large number of others that he had to make, letters written and sent, and visits from friends, the answer to my question becomes clear. Like Jesus, who withdrew from others in order to speak to his Father in solitude, but came down to earth to meet with his friends and loved ones, Jorge exhibited the humility and humanity of great historical figures by maintaining ties of friendship and brotherhood.

FIGUEROA: We've spoken many times about the passage in Genesis in which God invites man to not live alone because that is not good. And the whole story of God's creation continues with the creation of a people—the people of Israel. It speaks to us about the need for man and woman to live together in a community.

After Pentecost, God wishes the Church—and of course I don't mean the edifice, but the community of faithful believers—to develop a community-based Christian life, which also implies an invitation to not be alone.

The majority of the commandments have got something to do with other people; obviously, if I've got "no one else" around I cannot fulfill them. Nevertheless, that great crisis that we're experiencing today, especially in big cities, is the large number of people who are completely disconnected from what it means to live in a community. Because it's perfectly clear that you can stand in the middle of Florida Street in Buenos Aires at twelve noon, surrounded by hundreds of thousands of people, and still feel absolutely alone.

SKORKA: There are many facets to the theme of solitude. There are certain settings in which only a man who is alone can find solitude.

There are different types of solitude. When we talk about solitude, we must first define, to my humble understanding, what we mean. There is a type of modern solitude which borders on the alienation of the individual, but there are other types of "solitudes" described in the Bible, and they are very interesting.

There is a solitude that man needs to know when he is stuck in his life, for example, the solitude of Moses when he saw the burning bush. Many others, surely, also saw the bush, but only he said: *"I want to go there and see what this is all about."* First, surely, there was a whole process; I think that all the prophets had a moment of solitude in which they worked out many things, where they had a real dialogue with God and then later came back and he said to them: "This talking between us is all fine and well, but now return to your people, because your being a prophet, a saint, and a wise man serves me not; you have got to take all the spirituality you've found with me and lay it on society. You've got to share it with others."

One of the most marvelous scenes in the Bible that reflects that type of solitude is when Elijah goes in search of God on Mount Sinai. When he gets there, he finds God, who manifests himself with a faint, silent voice. The two of them are together! The same thing appears in the book of Exodus. When Moses goes to search for God it says that all the people were gathered around Mount Sinai, *"but Moses approached God all by himself."*

Rabbi Joseph Soloveitchik, who lived for many years in the United States, and who was the director of a famous rabbinical school, wrote a very lovely article in a book titled *The Lonely Man of Faith*. In it he discusses those times and places where one is with oneself and in that moment God appears. It's a way of saying, "Alright, God, come to me, intervene in my life, a part of you is in me." I think that that is a type of solitude necessary for man. We cannot all share it. We have got to dive down deep into ourselves, but we cannot remain in that solitude. God himself tells the prophets to go back to their people, that life consists of sharing it with other people.

So, I see two types of solitude. One, from which something emerges; the other, very dangerous, which can lead man to his loss and ruin.

BERGOGLIO: God saves us from solitude. Creation, in some way, is saving man from solitude so that he might enter into communion with God and with others.

And on the other hand, God leads us to another kind of solitude, to the solitude that Rabbi Skorka first described, so that we give something back to the community. He rescues us from the bad kind of solitude that leads us to perdition, as the Rabbi said, in order to lead us to a positive kind of solitude.

I think that in Deuteronomy it says that God saved his people from a solitude filled with howling; from a harmful, strident solitude, meaning the solitude of a desert. In another instance, in the book of Hosea and in Jeremiah, God speaks of his people as a woman, saying *"I will take her out to the desert and I will seduce her."* In relation to solitude, the desert can be aggressive, full of howling jackals that can devour me when I am alone. But there is also a fertile desert, to which the Lord leads me to speak to me in my heart and to tell me things that only he can say to me in the desert. It is the solitude of Elijah that Rabbi Skorka mentioned, that of Moses or that of Jacob wrestling with the angel. It is the purification that the desert offers which then allows one to go back to their people and proclaim.

It's curious; bad solitude has got to be full of stridence. It does not know silence. It is not a silent solitude. That's why Scripture says, *"filled with howling."* By contrast, solitude in God, that profoundly human solitude where God speaks to us, is an open solitude where I leave everything aside and I open my heart to what he has to say to me. This even implies a discipline to help us find ourselves alone with the Lord. And sometimes, the Lord, as if we were simply moving from one stage of life to the next, separates us from all human consolation, so that we can come face to face with him that he may speak to us in our hearts and seduce us, in the good sense of the word.

FIGUEROA: The cruelest moment of solitude or the most dramatic one in human existence is death. In that moment it doesn't matter where we might be or in what circumstances. One always dies alone, in an instant of profound solitude, although we might be surrounded by people. But even in that moment, in the twenty-third Psalm it says, *"Although I walk through the valley of the shadow of death, you will be with me."* God is present there, close to the human being, and accompanies him and carries him towards death.

There is also that solitude of feeling alone, even away from God. That's why it seems good to me that we dedicate some time to talk about the company of God. That is not only related to God's plan for us to live in community, but also to a God who is our companion, who makes sure that man is not alone.

SKORKA: What comes to mind is the verse from the prophet Amos which is the response to this question of solitude: "*Thus says the Lord, Seek me, remember me, and you shall live.*"

I think that feeling abandoned by God is a very delicate and profound feeling that the people who have talked about living it, evidently, have experienced as a result of a very great pain that was smothering them.

When someone who has experienced a terrible misfortune says to me: "I felt abandoned by God," the only thing I can do is accompany him with silence. There is nothing I can say to him; it's something very intimate. And perhaps the only thing I can express is: "I'll accompany you. I am with you in this moment. I understand your pain and even, to a certain point, I share that pain with you."

Now, when someone who was not affected directly by some great drama feels abandoned by God, at first I would remain silent and then try to ask these questions: "How much are you really looking for God?"; "What does looking for God mean to you?"; "What does God mean to you?"; and "What do you expect from God?"

BERGOGLIO: Sometimes it's difficult, in an abstract way, to begin to search for that encounter with God, and some people might get distracted or bored because they don't find the Lord in solitude. But there is something that attracts my attention, and it is the active part. In the Bible, God asks us to care for those who are most alone: the poor, the stranger, the orphan, the widow; they are people who are suffering a certain social solitude. Now, a person who does not make the effort to try to get closer to those who are alone is going to have a very difficult time solving the problem of his own bad solitude. And that's how life delivers that harsh "backlash." If you approach the person who is alone, you are going to reap the reward of a richness of an encounter with God, in a positive solitude.

I'm impressed when, in Matthew 25, it talks about the end of the world and how a final judgment is going to take place. The judgment will be based on whether or not: "*When I was hungry you fed me; when I was thirsty you gave me water to drink. When I was naked you clothed me; when I was in prison you came to visit me. When I was sick you came to see me ..."* Meaning, I am judged by how I behaved towards those who were alone. Wondering how I behave with those who are alone is a good form of learning the right path towards solitude, given that God is very jealous of those children of his who are alone: the poor man, the orphan, the widow, the stranger, the one who is hungry, or who is in jail. As we take charge of the solitude of others, we make our own solitude fertile for living it well. It is not a question of worrying about what I can get in return. Rather, it is as Jesus said: *"When you have a feast, don't invite the rich men, or your friends, or those relatives who later, when it's their turn, are going to invite you to another feast. Instead invite the poor man, the one who cannot pay you back, the one who can't give you another big party in return, the one who cannot pay you back."* Here there is a science, a divine wisdom toward one's fellow man that consists of being concerned with that person who has no means to pay me back. And for that reason my action leaves me alone, but alone with God, taking care of someone who is also alone, in solitude. This is a very interesting paradox that we find in the Bible.

FIGUEROA: One of the great paradoxes of the communication we have today is that through the social networks a person believes they have hundreds of friends while, in reality, they are merely contacts. And one can have the illusion of being hours in front of the computer "dialoguing" with "friends," but be isolated and alienated, without realizing how profoundly alone they are.

SKORKA: In Talmudic literature there is a paragraph that says that a man should "acquire" a friend—but be careful, because acquire here means "to become friends with," it's not a question of buying or possessing—and it says: "Eat with him, study with him ..." and then at last says: "reveal all your secrets to him." I think that the concept of having to reveal secrets has got to do with opening one's heart.

Solitude has got a lot in common with our capacity and courage to be able to tell someone else what is really going through our minds. True friendship doesn't make me want to stay with the person who sits down next to me and tells me all about his great successes; that's not friendship. No! Tell me what you really feel, who God is to you, how you speak to him. What would be, in a word, stripping bare the heart and removing all the makeup, all the disguises. Friendship happens in the moment when one can share all that with a person.

BERGOGLIO: One expression I like from what Rabbi Skorka said is: "Remove the makeup"; and of course, if it's a true friendship it must be without makeup. The same thing happens on the road to our encounter with God. One has to pass through a purification—a path that begins with being stripped bare. According to the Bible, God always demanded of his people that they cast off their idols. There are people incapable of being alone because they are preoccupied with idols. And sometimes—or many times, or always, I don't know—there are people who are not happy, who feel embittered because after all of those false idols give what they can of themselves, they find themselves feeling empty. Also, they find themselves with people that laugh a lot, and they make a big noise about life. They're very sociable, but they have the "face of a pickled pepper." And one says: "You're not happy, you're missing happiness; you haven't stripped yourself bare!"

The path towards the encounter with God, or the encounter of a friend as a paradigm of God, supposes stripping away what's unnecessary and my listening to what God tells me or what my friend tells me. Friendship supposes listening, opening the heart. And sometimes there's nothing to be heard, because God makes us remain a while in silence—that silent solitude which requires patience and the ability to wait until God speaks. Elijah, for example, felt like he wanted to die because God was not speaking. He was escaping from the threats of the queen who wanted to kill him for having beheaded almost four hundred prophets of the idol. He was scared; he was alone. He did not speak and he felt God's silence.

God speaks but he leads you along a path where you strip away things and leave them behind yet stays silent. In some way, it is like he is falling in love with you and wants you to seek him out. This is so because we're incapable of looking for God on our own, if he doesn't attract or draw us towards him. There is a psalm that says God attracts us when he makes our hearts swell, but he can only make our hearts swell when we cast off all of our idols. That's the way to make the heart grow bigger.

Bad solitude is an idolatrous solitude, self-referential, a coquette with makeup, as Rabbi Skorka said. True solitude is stripped bare of all extraneous things. It is brave, humble; it seeks and it finds and is fundamentally characterized by its capacity to listen. It encounters God the way one encounters a friend.

FIGUEROA: I think that the capacity for listening is reached when one learns to listen to what they don't like to hear. Because when one only listens to praise or pleasantries, they're only listening to themselves, and it fans their egocentrism. But the true friend is not obsequious; he's one that one day says to me: "Look, pardon me, but you're blowing it. I'm your friend and I'm telling you alone, but it seems to me in this that you're wrong"—because he wants what's best for his friend. And God also helps us in that way, and sometimes we reject God or that true friend because we're afraid.

SKORKA: Speaking of the fear a person has in asking these questions, in the Jewish ritual of prayers we learn a morning prayer that goes like this: "What is our life?" "What do we possess?" "What are our strengths?" The act of praying itself teaches us, in agreement with the way in which it was structured thousands of years ago, that it is not only an act of speaking to God, but to begin by speaking to oneself, asking oneself these questions, and then God will enter the picture. Why? Because they are questions that we must always ask ourselves, not just in the sunset of our life—we should always be asking them. And when we remove the makeup or mask from all these things, meaning, when we have the courage to ask ourselves those questions in distinct moments of our lives, we will probably find the answer—a sincere answer that helps us to overcome, face up to, and better yet, make use of those moments of solitude that we're inevitably going to encounter in our lives.

If we always ask ourselves, "What is life? What is existence? What do I want?" and, as the Book of Prayers teaches us, suddenly we realize that the real answer is: "Life has deeper dimensions and within those dimensions is what we call God"—we stop being afraid. Then, when that inevitable moment of solitude comes, which, I agree, is death, perhaps we can face it like the great Spanish writer Alejandro Casona said when he wrote the very lovely play called *Los árboles mueren de pie* (The Trees Die Standing Up). To die standing up on one's feet, means knowing how to confront that solitude.

BERGOGLIO: A line from Deuteronomy that I like says: *"I led you through the desert to test you and to see what there was in your heart."* The truth of what we feel, of what we are, only blossoms in solitude, when God makes us see what there really is in our heart, not in disguises, makeup and masks, nor in idolatry.

FIGUEROA: At the moment, God appears to be absent or silent within the science of communication. Nevertheless, even there the silence is communicating something. In music, for example, silence forms part of the melody, and it would be impossible to compose that melody without silence. And God, in his melody of life, also leads us through places of silence, but that does not mean that he is absent. It means that he is more present than ever, but he is waiting for us to make the next move—for us to look inside ourselves. And in order to look inside ourselves we need to be alone and have the courage and resolution to discover that we are neither as perfect nor as imperfect as we thought.

We need, on one side, the good kind of solitude; and on the other, be sure that other people don't end up alone when they need us.

2 5

Inclusion

The day was Monday, July 30, 2007. I showed up, as scheduled, at five o'clock in the afternoon, at the offices of Canal 21 at the archbishop's chancery in Buenos Aires. The Canal 21 management had made the enormous gesture of inviting me to record a program about the Bible, to be broadcast in September, the celebratory ecumenical month.

A few minutes later Cardinal Jorge Mario arrived. He greeted me affectionately and even had the courtesy to express his appreciation for my contribution to an article published that day in *La Nación* newspaper.

When I got to the recording studio I was surprised to see that only two chairs were set up in front of the cameras! How would the program go? Who would be the participants? After my initial surprise I became very nervous when the producers sat me down face to face with the Cardinal, both us of now wearing clip-on microphones.

It was not just going to be a simple program about the Bible. Archbishop Bergoglio himself played the role of reporter, and with his questions and comments he set about directing the program.

I had not seen the tape of that show for six years, but I recently reviewed it before writing this introduction to the program about "Inclusion." I was profoundly moved.

The man who is now Pope Francis included me on his TV channel. He made room for me at his table, in his place, with real humility and brotherly love, to engage in a dialogue about the Bible and the work of the United Bible Societies.

In these last months, some international journalists have named me as the only television host to feature a Pope throughout a series of thirty-one consecutive programs. Frankly, I am a little embarrassed by such a label. But now I think that I was, in my own humble way and in the company of the greatness of Cardinal Bergoglio, an interviewee on a television program that showed a previously unknown side of him—that of television host.

FIGUEROA: Let's talk about inclusion because, clearly, we understand that there is exclusion. That person who was once included and was later excluded for some reason must be included. And the decision should be made to include that person who was never on the inside.

Probably we find that there is an active subject, that person who perhaps excluded someone else and then takes the decision to include them; and a passive subject, that person who is, or who feels, excluded and is later invited to be included.

Let's take, in some way, something that for me is a profoundly theological concept: that the God presented to us in the Bible is a God of inclusion—from the individual, especially widows, the poor, the marginalized, and the sick, to groups—the people of Israel, from slavery to liberty, or the Christian people who went from anonymity to form part of the Kingdom of God and his justice.

SKORKA: To my humble understanding, the theme of inclusion is based on a verse in chapter 25 of the book of Leviticus, verse 36. But before citing the verse let's look at the context. The whole chapter talks about the help that one must lend to the person in need. It says that each family of Israel must have its own territory, its own parcel of non-transferable land. In a word, each one must have a source of dignified labor; and if they do not manage to work that land, what they can do is lease the land to someone else to farm and harvest it until the Jubilee Year when all the lands must return to their original owners. The land was worked for six years and then it had to lay fallow for a year; during which time the fruits of the labor belonged to all and nobody could stock-pile food. Each man went with his hoe to the common land and worked the harvest, and from that they all lived during the seventh year. When the seventh year of the seventh cycle arrived, after for-ty-nine years, the people celebrated and rested—from that comes the word "Jubilee." Those who are enslaved are set free. In biblical times slavery was a reality, an institution—to use a legal term. It was spelled out in a very special way in chapter 25: *"You will not set your brother to hard labor, he who became a slave because he had to sell his labor or his capacity to work."* All of chapter 25 talks about the help one has to give.

But within that frame appear two key verses, one of them is: *"And you shall help the foreigner, and he will live with you."* There were two kinds of foreigners in biblical times; one of them was the kind who was partially allowed to become integrated with the people of Israel and who was circumcised; and the other was the foreign inhabitant like the one who comes to live in a another country. The other key verse speaks directly about the one who shares everything with you: *"And your brother shall live with you."*

In a word, if we share a nationality we must share, theoreti-cally, many other things, too. What defines the Argentine nation-ality are the rights and obligations specified in the Constitution, the law, a common language, a past, a history, a present, a future, values, and so many other things that constitute our folklore.

The text says: *"And your brother shall live with you."* This means that you've got to live a life in common with the other per-son; he cannot live in a totally different sphere from your own. In short, the sense of brotherhood, the call to brotherhood, is not something so simple. We can study almost the whole book of Genesis from the perspective of: "What can we do so that people live together in peace?"

BERGOGLIO: It's like a test of existence where it shows people's capacity for understanding one another and becoming broth-ers and sisters. They are like two existential extremes; they come together in moments of pain and sorrow and one puts himself in the other's place and knows how to overcome the other person's sorrow. The same is true for moments of joy and celebration.

And here I want to add a parable from the Gospels. When Jesus talks about that man who gave a party but the guests let him down and didn't come, one told him: *"Look, I just got married yes-terday and I can't come."* Another one told him: *"I've just bought a field and I have to go and measure it."* Another one said: *"I've got to see how well my new oxen works."* As we would say, "excuses," they "put on airs." They didn't accept the invitation and each one excused himself from participating in a common joy, because they couldn't or didn't have their heart prepared to participate. Then they excused themselves, they excluded themselves. And the man that had organized the party—for his son's wedding—then tells his servants who were preparing the feast: *"Look, please, go out to the crossroads, and bring everyone you can find."* And out there they found all the homeless people, the ones who walk the road, who just happened to be there and who, lamentably, had to live outdoors. These are the kinds of people whom someone with bad intentions might call "nasty looking people." And this father invites them all to the celebration in his home, and they all come.

Participating in a party is a test of brotherhood, because here is the symbol of the party: participating in joy. What in some way demonstrates our capacity for inclusion, for inclusive brotherhood, is my being able to rejoice with another who rejoices. And in the parable, there is a detail that is sometimes misunderstood. It says that the master greeted all those his servants had gathered together in the street and finds one who did not have the right clothes for the party. But if all these guests had been street people how then were any of them going to have party clothes? What it really means is that this person did not have a sincere attitude about inclusion; he was there to see what was happening or for some personal interest. And the master of the house makes him leave because he did not have his heart ready to be included and to include the others. He stood out, he distanced himself from others.

What's inclusive, from the existential point of view, is to always approach others and also let the other get close to you. Inclusiveness is that "solidarity," a feeling of fellowship that the Gospels talk about.

FIGUEROA: There are two or three very important concepts that you spoke about, and which contradict, a bit, that temptation to think that the person that takes the decision to include the one who has been excluded, does so from a position of superiority or power: "I have the possibility of including or excluding you, so it's in my power to include you as far as I want, and I set the limits." Often, we don't totally include the other. We don't go as far as our heart adopting the attitude that we're on equal footing, of sitting down to talk like equals, of breaking bread together, or celebrating together.

I would like to introduce an additional element, bearing in mind this concept of inclusion, but on a national level. I think about needing to include those who do not have the opportunity to study, who are born into a poor home where children have to work. They are born into a situation of injustice simply because they are born into one home as opposed to another. So, the question is: "What is the concept of inclusion towards that person who is excluded? Is it about having an attitude of mercy and everyone having the same benefits, or does it consist of everyone having the same opportunities?

SKORKA: I would say that the very minimal step that the Bible demands is that we help orphans, widows, and all those in society who are weak, but that is the bottom line. When a prophet like Amos has got to come to a society and say: *"You covet even the dust on the head of the poor man, whom you would sell for the price of a pair of sandals,"* it is because we are already in a terrible state of social decay. The step is to bring social equality into being, but the mere fact that social equity might exist is no guarantee that society will reach a state of brotherhood.

Figueroa mentioned something that was, for me, a key idea: "Include the other, not from a position of power." I don't believe in authoritarian powers; not even on a family level, for example, when a father gives orders that may not be discussed or disputed. In some way, the father has to have a feeling and a reality of brotherhood with his sons to be able to speak freely about all subjects with them and so that the son can say: "He's my dad. He lived many more years than I did. He knows more than I do, thanks to his life experience; and I can't just argue with him about any old thing for the simple sake of disagreeing," and so on, at every level.

But in the moment when one tries to destroy the other, when feelings and passions like envy and the passion for power enter the picture, inclusion is not going to be a brotherly inclusion. He will live with you, in some way, but he will not be your brother. In order for him to be your brother, he's got to live with you and be one more of you. I've got to share the power with him; I cannot impose things upon him arbitrarily. There must be leadership, but you've got to try to make it a leadership of teaching. Perhaps I'm asking for a utopia, but that really recalls Moses and other leaders who were unique because they were so upright and well-integrated under this perspective that is, perhaps, a bit utopian. In the degree to which the Bible is a utopia, although I don't believe that it is, it is a great challenge for humanity.

BERGOGLIO: Inclusion means that one tends to accentuate the active role: "Alright, I'm going to include this person." But there is also something to which the Bible refers, in some way, and it is to that passive role that Figueroa mentioned at the start: the wish to be included in the life of the other. Life is something that transcends all those things, and this person matters for who and what they are as a person, as a child of God. So then, I include him, but also I'm asking him to include me in his life. To be included in a poor man's life, a person who has needs, a person who, humanly speaking, would not have the same kinds of possibilities that you have, is a very great brotherly grace. It's not that I become concerned with him simply so that he finds a better condition in life, but rather that he is also concerned with my life and my life is included in his life; that's brotherhood.

FIGUEROA: That double sense of inclusion leads me to understand that in the process of including or excluding, I must recognize that I also have to demonstrate in my attitude towards my brother, that I want to be included by him.

SKORKA: Inclusion is a job for both parties. We have got to look at ourselves and there must be a mutual acceptance in order to achieve real inclusion. When we put ourselves in a superior position over others, we're lost. In the end we return to the profound sense of dialogue that appears in the Bible. What Martin Buber spoke about so often, with respect to the idea of one's neighbor, is a profound concept. What does dialogue signify in the biblical sense? In order to be able to include we have got to learn to dialogue, and that means: feeling the other, listening to their silence, analyzing what they have, and putting ourselves in their shoes.

BERGOGLIO: Your comment about dialogue leads me to talk about what happens there. What is it that's happening around this table? Are we here to talk about religious matters, through our various positions? Is it playing at being civilized through these visits?

From the doctrinal point of view of inter-religious dialogue we are two Christians "against" one Jew. It's not about coming together to socialize. The purpose is to publicly affirm, as Christians, that our identity is not to be understood without recognizing that it's intermeshed with the Jewish identity. And from that we understand that antisemitism is a monstrosity for a Christian because it means wiping out his own identity. A Christian who is anti-Semitic has ceased to be a Christian because he's wiped out his own identity. A Jew is not someone who is professing a different religion or, in this case, the minister of a different religion, he is my older brother! And the Christian identity cannot be understood without looking at my older brother and learning from him. And that is inclusion.

In such a way, we Christians are included and we are not superior, although from our point of view we affirm that the Messiah did indeed already come, and you are still awaiting him. But we are both waiting; we are waiting for the Messiah to return, and you are waiting for him to come. That does not make us greater; that maintains a truth that we say liturgically in our prayers: "God does not renege on his chosen people; the people of Israel continue to be the Jewish people, and are included in our faith, and we ask them to include us, and that we walk together." This is something that is clear; it's not a question of education or of exchanging opinions about our theologies, but rather it is about God's choice. We, Christians, are chosen by God because we participate in their selection. Here there is inclusion. I think that we are giving a signal, an example of what it means to include ourselves mutually, on the path that God gives us.

SKORKA: If someone could manage to really think about what it is that we are doing here, he or she would realize it is not what people used to say before: "merely tea and sympathy." The truth, I subscribe totally to what you say and I believe that I was principally inspired by you, in your beliefs.

Soon they'll be celebrating the fiftieth anniversary of the Second Vatican Council, which justly tried to include the Roman Catholic Apostolic Church in the worldwide reality, from a different perspective. It tried to be a response to the Second World War, to the spiritual rupture in Europe that led to the Second World War. Because *Nostra Aetate* and other documents like *Dignitas Humanae* have a really strong force and message with respect to all peoples and all persons. And especially *Nostra Aetate*, which is directed to many religions but, principally, as Cardinal Kasper says, often specifically to the Jewish people.

FIGUEROA: I think that, in some way, after more than two dozen programs that we've recorded together, and some "coffee breaks" between ourselves without the TV cameras running, we're not just speaking for the occasion or the benefit of the camera, we're not just saying the right things to sound good.

From my position as a Protestant or Evangelical, I also feel included in a discussion in which we can speak freely with the liberty of understanding that we are part of the same family. And to understand that for the Evangelical, Christianity was not born with the Protestant Reformation, it was born with Christ. We have got all this in common and, in its turn, as the Cardinal said so well, one cannot understand Christianity nor Christ himself as a Jew, without understanding the history of the people of Israel, our older brothers.

Then, I think that there is a dynamic, something that was present in this program, which consisted of mixing, without us realizing, the active and passive subjects of inclusion and exclusion, where we can all be excluded or, perhaps, we exclude the other.

Our task consists of finding the profound sense of inclusion: being a family, being oneself, putting ourselves in another's shoes, sharing, and feeling that we are equal to one another, that we need to include the other in order to be more united, and that we also need the other person to include us too.

After all, inclusion is a work among all people, because we all need the other in order to be living participants in an inclusion that overcomes exclusion that does not favor anybody.

May God help us to become protagonists of an ideal and, why not, of the utopia of inclusion in which we all really feel that we can share like one great family, just as God dreamed it from the first moment.

Fear

It was hot in Buenos Aires, mid-afternoon around the end of February, 2007. Cardinal Bergoglio had proposed to me that he would return my visits to his office at the Archbishop's Chancery by coming to visit me at my office. As was his custom, he walked like any other person the twelve blocks that separated us. When he arrived he told me that along his way, a young man had insulted him rather aggressively. I did not bother to advise him that the next time he came he should take a taxi, because I knew what his answer would be, but I did ask him: "Weren't you afraid?"

His response was enlightening: "Not at all. God knows why these things happen to me—circumstances in life that help me to lower my pride and not listen too much to people who say nice things to me."

I remembered that occurrence when I was on my way to record our program about fear.

FIGUEROA: The theme of fear always has a negative connotation. Fear by itself implies an imminent risk, real or not, about something—it can be past, present, or future—that tends to enclose us and paralyze us.

But fear can also have a positive connotation, in the sense that I can have a healthy fear, for example, on taking a decision that can affect a third party. In that case, fear is transformed into something proactive, because I'm motivated to avoid something that can produce a bad outcome.

Seen from the point of view of faith, when one talks about the fear of God, in general, one thinks about the fear of a God that can do us harm. Nevertheless, the Bible shows us that when we talk about the fear of God, it is about the reverence with which we direct ourselves towards a loving God. It is an attitude of recognition of his authority and that under the care of that fear we can live a wise life. The Word of God affirms it in Psalm 111: *"The beginning of wisdom is the fear of God."*

SKORKA: It's interesting that from the linguistic point of view, there are basically two terms in Hebrew to define fear. One refers directly to fear as something that paralyzes, as in the example found in Psalm 91: *"You will not fear the terror of night"*; and on the other hand, there is the concept of temerity, for example, in the verse that Dr. Figueroa has quoted: *"The beginning of knowledge"*—or wisdom—*"is the fear of God."*

So, what does "fear of God" mean? The Talmudic interpretation puts it this way: "All those things that you alone know in your heart that you are doing, for those things have a fear of God, because he too knows it." Another element that we find in rabbinical literature is the fear of being wrong, making a mistake, or doing something wrong.

BERGOGLIO: It's true that there are two different kinds of fear, and we must distinguish between them. The healthy, holy fear of God; fear of that someone who is guiding me. And there is the other fear that is not healthy, that is morbidly unhealthy, which paralyzes me.

And it's curious, the book of Ecclesiastes says in its opening words: *"If you want to serve the Lord, prepare yourself for battle."* And this means, prepare yourself to get involved in something where you have got to fight. Fight against whom, besides the enemies of all things? Fight against those fears that fantasy itself exaggerates and which can become overwhelming, crushing.

A phrase most often repeated, both in the Old Testament and the New Testament is, *"Have no fear."* In Isaiah 7, for example, it says: *"Have no fear of those two smoldering firebrands."* Before, it says that the king and the people *"began to tremble with fear, like the leaves in the trees when the wind shakes them."* In a very lovely description of fear, God says: *"Do not fear them, for I am the very cause of all this."* God wants to give us strength to conquer those paralyzing fears.

FIGUEROA: Madame Curie said: "There are not many things to fear, but there are many things to comprehend." The question is somewhat linked to this thought. "Isn't fear sometimes related to our incapacity to understand or to manage what is really going on, distinguishing what's real from what is not, and also including God as company? I think that in our exaggerated imagination, which often generates our fear, lies the failure to comprehend or understand what it is that's happening; and I think that if we had understanding it would help us to handle our fear.

BERGOGLIO: In general, regarding this paralyzing fear, fantasy takes root when there is some area of insecurity, and what grows is the lack of comprehension that Figueroa mentions. When I don't understand something, I feel insecure, and then that's when all the phantoms and fears of my imagination start to swirl round inside my head.

There is an ignorance that allows fantasies to take root. And fantasies are an enemy that we carry inside and which are at the root of many fights and wars. Because fantasy separates and divides at heart, fantasy is the offspring of idols. Our God is a God of reality, not of fantasy. When fantasy presents things to you, it presents you with idols that make you sick, that diminish and destroy you; it cannot present you with anything that has a relationship to the living God, the God of life. It presents you with something powerful, but something that is not true, that has no importance. And that is the essence of an idol—something that presents itself as powerful but which has no meaning, and yet it is respected as if it had some powerful significance.

SKORKA: Speaking about the concept of the true God, there is a prayer which is one of the central prayers that we pray. It is a declaration of faith that begins with the verse in Deuteronomy: *"Listen, Israel, the Lord is our God, the Lord is One";* and it ends with a paragraph from the book of Numbers where it talks to us about the strands that we must weave into our garments. Then, the celebrant that finishes reading those words, has got to continue with a paragraph that says: *"I am your true God."*

In the moment when I really want to get closer to God, I must keep studying to rid my mind of preconceived ideas, phantoms, and the lies on which theories are constructed that really, pathologically endanger humankind—those ideas used in the past and in the present to move the masses.

One of the ways to move the masses is to create for them a non-existent enemy. As Jews, we suffered through this terribly when the book *The Protocols of the Elders of Zion* was published. We know perfectly well that this book was based on a lie created by the Czar's secret police, in order to create a hoax and foment antisemitism in Russia.

The masses are also controlled through fear; dictators always need an enemy and it's usually a fictitious one. Sometimes they have to be unmasked, but sometimes it's a matter of an invented enemy.

Now, there are fears that are about falsehoods that we ourselves buy into. In Psalm 49 it says: *"Do not be overwhelmed when other men grow rich, when the luxury of their houses increases."* How can we interpret that verse? Don't think that someone with their money can do everything. If he is a man of integrity, he will not exchange his integrity for all the money in the world. The powerful man cannot buy it, and for that reason one need not fear.

The only way to overcome those terrors is to remember God. I am not talking about God as a placebo or a palliative, but rather as something very strong, as the font of inspiration in order to maintain my values.

FIGUEROA: I think that when Jesus said: *"And you will know the truth and the truth will set you free,"* in that freedom of knowledge he's including everything that produces fear. In the daily reality one sees more and more how fear has advanced—fear of what's going to happen in the street, fear of an assault, of an accident, of getting fired from work—although in reality it's not an advance but the complete opposite—. There has been an enormous increase in the sales of all kinds of medications to prevent panic attacks or anxiety; that is also the source of a lot of fear.

In my experience, 99 percent of the things that I was afraid of that might happen to me in my life never happened. And for the ones that did happen, I found a way to solve the majority of them. Sometimes the solution to the problem led to something better, but I always believed that God was by my side.

SKORKA: It's a totally complex theme, because in certain cases I would not call it "fear," but "anxiety." What happens is that when the anxiety has a basis in reality, the words to calm that anxiety are difficult to find.

There are many people suffering because they find themselves in solitude. There has to be a greater effort to find more restrained, secure channels to say: "Alright, remain calm." There are people who need to find work, not only to stay alive, but also to find a way to feel useful. So many people have been turned out of their homes and come for help, and no matter how much we help, we sometimes feel that whatever we can do to help is actually very little. For example, if a person comes to us afraid because they don't know how they're going to find something to eat tomorrow, I can give them something and help to mitigate that fear a little, but their fear is not unfounded, it's a real fear. The system that has been created—at least in a great part of the Western world that we know—is very hard: you're either inside the system or you're out, excluded and without possibilities. And if you find yourself outside the machine then it's very difficult to get back inside. All that, evidently, brings anxieties that are also, if you will, fears. There is a Talmudic rabbinical concept that says: "You cannot trust in a miracle. Go knock on a thousand doors, but at the same time you know that there is a Father up there who is going to help you; but you've got to do something first." What happens is that each time it takes more effort to move through realities that are so insensitive.

BERGOGLIO: I like the fact that you've brought up that fear of being marginalized, which is the fear of being plundered and left destitute. It is the fear that one feels when one is deprived of any close connections, of justice, of attention, or by age itself, marginalized and deprived simply for being a certain age, for being too old.

At bottom, the current socio-economic systems that are imposed on us give way to what I would call a "throwaway culture." Lately, it's about the anxiety of feeling that one is on the road to ruin, about to get dumped, because they're considered disposable.

That is when, as the rabbi said so well, we must not lose hope in a God that is on our side and who accompanies us while we go knocking on a thousand doors. As the saying goes: "God helps those who help themselves."

There are so many people living in anxiety right in our midst! How many men reach the age of fifty-five—I heard this myself— and they tell me: "I no longer have the right to have a job because I'm old." Fifty-five years old! It's the dispossession that results from a worldwide socioeconomic system that leads a man to his anxiety. And yet, there, we always find God's voice saying *"Do not fear."* It's what Jesus says very clearly in the Gospel of Saint Matthew, in the Sermon on the Mount: *"Do not be anxious about what you'll eat tomorrow"*—that is, do not be distraught— *"because the Father in Heaven feeds the sparrows, the Father in Heaven dressed the lilies in the field, and Solomon in all his glory was not arrayed like one of them."*

Now, how do I open the path towards hope in a God who tells me: "Do not worry, I am here, by your side; I am your Father," in the very midst of so much dispossession? It's very hard. I think that there is a great lack of solidarity and compassion for one's fellow humans and a need for closeness to the one experiencing anxiety to help him begin to knock on those doors, also on Heaven's door, in order to be able to get out of that situation.

FIGUEROA: There is a verse in the first letter of Saint John that says: *"True love expels fear."* It speaks about the love that fulfills the role of scaring off the fear, and also adds: *"The one who fears has not grown perfect in love."* I think that the word "love" acquires an important dimension in the two concepts that were mentioned, in terms of self-restraint, and of rejection.

It's important to know that God did not forget about me this morning, nor was he looking the other way, but instead he has his arms open wide to love me, and one—and here I'm going to use the passive voice that the Cardinal often uses—can let himself or herself be loved by the Lord. But something else that acquires importance is that those who surround that person who is experiencing a fearful situation, or one of anxiety, or the loss of a job, are family members or friends, and that they know how to keep that person feeling secure, and how to love them. Often what is troubling that person is low self-esteem, lack of self-love, and they really need to receive love as much as possible—the love of God, of course, but also the love of God seen in others. It's there where it is explained that love expels fear.

SKORKA: The affection that the individual receives from the moment when they see the sunlight, the care that their parents give them, real love, the development of their capacity for love during their lifetime, is what is going to enable them to get closer to God in a profound sense. If you did a very objective analysis of the Bible, of the Pentateuch, you'd see that we must respect God's work and have a healthy fearful respect for him. But also, the final link to reach God—which is greatly emphasized in Deuteronomy—is: *"You will love the Lord, your God."* In this case, this fear is not a paralyzing fear of God, but rather the manifestation of a mature love towards God and towards his work; and that same manifestation has also got to be directed towards one's neighbor.

BERGOGLIO: Temerity is also love, it is being careful to not be lacking in respect towards God. It does not reduce neither my confidence nor my courage—the same courage that Abraham had to spar with God whether they were forty, or thirty-five, or thirty. It is a respectful courage: "Don't be angry, my Lord, don't be angry. Don't take this badly, but please listen to me." It's like seeing the intersection of Corrientes Avenue and Pasteur Street in Buenos Aires as a biblical location. It's about the respectful courage of speaking with God, what our people, in some way, in their common wisdom sum up in a single phrase: "Be careful; don't toy with God!" It's like an initial respect for love and for the dialogue with God.

SKORKA: You know that we Jews like to laugh at ourselves. So regarding your reference to Abraham, I wouldn't say that it's Pasteur and Corrientes, because I have a better analogy. When Jacob escapes from his brother Esau, who was going to kill him, and he dreams of the ladder, God tells him: *"I'm going to help you, and I'm going to bless you."* And Jacob responds: *"Good, listen to me"*—that's literally what he says—*"of all that you're going to bless me with, 10 percent of that belongs to you."* That's the birth of tithing, and that's what the intersection at Pasteur and Corrientes represents.

FIGUEROA: One of the beautiful things about the Bible is that it tells us about real life events, about reality, about real people, flesh and blood, about people who struggled against their own difficulties, including the biblical heroes.

I was thinking about the writer of Ecclesiastes, who was, according to tradition, Solomon. The truth is that when one reads that book one discovers a person who is going through some very difficult moments, profound moments of anguish, depression, and decline. The writer begins by saying that all is in vain, that everything he has tried and experienced in life is worthless, and that all pleasures are vanity, they are meaningless, just a question of wasted time. But at last he says: *"This, then, is the conclusion of the whole matter: "Fear God and keep his commandments, for this is the whole duty of man."*

Peace

It was a great honor to receive Cardinal Bergoglio's invitation to prayer, as a representative of the evangelical peoples, during the *Te Deum* Mass on May 25, 2012. I never imagined that it would be the last one that he would celebrate. His invitation, he knew, was a gesture that filled me with peace and pleasure.

I was very nervous as I prepared for it and I expressed it with all my heart. I also remember that our "big brother," and outstanding participant from the TV program, Rabbi Skorka, prayed for the Jewish community. All of it was a symbol of peace between the religions.

The significance of this gesture was not only that the Cardinal invited other creeds to be present, but that he would include them in the celebration in an active and visible way: praying together. As if that were not enough, in the afternoon he called me to thank me for my participation. Again his words brought me the peace of knowing that my prayer had been a blessing.

I recall the words of Hans Küng: "there will not be world peace without peace between religions; there will not be peace between religions without dialogue between religions." Let me take the liberty of transcribing a few paragraphs of my prayer, related to the dialogue for peace, which is the theme of the following program:

TO YOU, GOD, who taught us through your word …

When brothers live together in harmony we see your blessing: Show us the path of agreement and dialogue, where our differences may be an opportunity for growth and not an excuse for confrontation, in order to discover together that harmony is not uniformity, but rather the symphony of diversity.

You are a God of peace: We say to you today that violence, in all its forms and in any place, brings us sorrow. Violence both in word and in deed. Violence with what is provoked and with what is ignored. Help us to make the teaching of Jesus Christ our own: "To work for peace and, in that way, to be called sons of God."

FIGUEROA: "Peace" comes from the Latin word *pax* that contains the component of thinking that peace is explained by things that do not exist, like the absence of conflicts, wars, and divisions. In some ways, peace is defined is terms of negation.

When one analyzes history, principally the beginning of Christianity, after the time of Alexander the Great came the Roman expansion and invasions that imposed that sense of the *pax*, which was the "peace" of the dominant empire that collected tribute and oppressed the people. The *Pax Romana* created a certain feeling of peace in some areas, because they had a certain complacent tolerance. They allowed the Jewish religion to be practiced and even the building of some synagogues. But it was a fictitious peace; if there were no greater conflicts or wars, it was because the Roman Empire dominated everything. For that reason, the *Pax Romana* is an example of a peace that was not quite real.

From a biblical point of view, both the Hebrew word *shalom* as well as the Greek word *eirene,* in Christianity, conceive of peace from a more positive, more proactive perspective. In this sense, it's believed that peace is not what doesn't exist, but rather the construction of a state of complete well-being for both the individual and society—complete well-being that involves health, care, justice, and truth. It is an ambitious idea for things that do not exist.

There are two kinds of peace: an apparent *pax*—which in reality is not peace, but an absence of visible conflict—and a peace that provokes the construction of ambitious things for man and can exist amid conflicts.

SKORKA: That's a very good distinction you make between the *Pax Romana* and the Hebrew *shalom. Shalom* comes from a Hebrew word that means "what is whole or integral." For example, we are told that after Jacob made peace with his brother, they embraced, they greeted each other as brothers, they forgave each other, and they went on with their lives, even though they had not resolved everything. So, that's very good that you mentioned that there can be peace without having a complete resolution of conflicts, but at least no wars, no massacres. Then, the key verse says that Jacob arrived "whole," in peace and safety. What does "whole" mean? The simple rabbinical interpretation is that he arrived safely on a physical level and on a spiritual level; and he also arrived with the small fortune that he was able to make from the material point of view. I think that this was a way of saying: "I finished one cycle of life with my brother, now we don't hate each other as much as before. We're not going to kill each other; we'll rise above this a bit."

The Bible applies the concept of peace to the individual level, for example, when Jacob talks with Joseph before his brothers sell him, and tells him: *"Look after your brothers' peace."* Or rather, when someone uses the biblical greeting of peace, it would be something like: "Are you at peace?" "Have you achieved peace?" "Are you in good health and well in all things, integrally?"

BERGOGLIO: "May God bestow his peace" means may God shed his grace upon you, that he be familiar with you, that your life allow him to enter into your heart and not reject it. Such a peace only comes from the Lord. Jesus says: *"I give you peace, not like the world does."* The peace of God comes to us completely free, a gift, not something one can buy, not something one can acquire, however many spiritual exercises and virtuous acts one performs; he gives it freely. And I would like to emphasize this, because the blessing that I always use in the Mass ends with *"And I grant you peace,"* so that it might enter into you. It is given to you, in some way, but I bring it to you, and that is grace, our salvation given to us freely. One can work for peace, and make space for peace to come, but to receive the kind of peace that Rabbi Skorka referred to, what we can do is open our heart, make a space to receive it, because it is a pure gift.

SKORKA: When the priests were going to bless the people—and this continues today in many communities—they had to say this: *"Blessed be you, our God, King of the universe, who have consecrated us with the sanctity of Aaron and you have commanded us to bless your people Israel with love."* The one who invokes the blessing so that there might be peace has got to do so with a feeling of love. But I want to also add on this concept: love is a special relationship with respect to one's neighbor.

I'm going to give an example of the Arab-Israeli conflict and what it means to establish a loving peace with respect to one's neighbor. When Anwar Sadat arrived in Israel it was something that, really, shook up a lot of people, and he said: "I've come to Israel to make peace." He came to the Israeli parliament and said: "We have many conflicts to resolve,"—there were many questions about borders that were eventually resolved—"but a decision has been taken; no longer will there be any disputes between Israel and Egypt that will be decided by war." And they fulfilled this promise. And I hope that they continue to fulfill this promise thorough eternity.

Once, Golda Meir said: "When Arabs have more love for their own children than hatred for us, in that moment they will be able to recognize the other as an individual." And in that meeting in the Israeli Parliament, she made a gift to the Egyptian president of a pair of booties because he had recently become a grandfather.

I think that the basic question to begin to make a path towards peace is to think about the other person as an equal who has rights, a family, dreams, who wants to live life just as much as I do.

One of the books of Talmudic literature asks: "Who is the hero?" In one Talmudic version it says: "He who restrains his impulses." In another it says: "The hero is that man who knows how to turn his enemy into his friend."

FIGUEROA: It's very easy to start a fight, anyone can do it, but what's really difficult is to build peace. The words of Jesus really speak to me when he says: *"Blessed are the peacemakers,"* and he adds: *"... because they will be called children of God."* In some way, there are two concepts there: one, that peace, besides being a grace from God, demands work, and needs to be constructed; and there is a blessed happiness from God in that. But also, the second part clarifies that he who works to achieve peace will recover his identity as a child of God.

BERGOGLIO: Why is the peacemaker, the one who works for peace, going to be called a "child of God"? If we look to the elementary facts of the Bible, everything begins with a war, a rebellious disobedience against God. And in the second place, something concrete occurred: someone who killed his brother. All throughout Scripture, God's work consists of restoring the peace in the heart of his people. There were attempts to establish hegemony—like the *Pax Romana*—I think there is something of that to be understood, as well, in the myth of the Tower of Babel: "*Let's go that way, let's be powerful! We all speak the same language*," and then they end up throwing stones at one another.

By contrast, the Lord was working for peace with that mystery that humbles me every time I think of it: his patience. Talking about God's patience would seem to indicate that it's something contradictory, yet, nevertheless, God has had patience with us, from the time of the first fall until now. Why? By demonstrating that patience, he makes peace. Faced with so many other disasters that we keep on making, God continues working for peace. That's why the words of Jesus reflect history: "*Happy, blissful, blessed are the peacemakers, those who work to establish peace, because they do their Father's work, they are children of God.*"

A person who does the opposite is a destroyer of the peace, creates conflicts, and divides. In our popular language we say that they are "sowing tares," an expression from the parable Jesus tells about the enemy who went by night to sow tares in the wheat field. That person cannot be called a child of God because he does not follow the work of his Father or, as Jesus says: "*He does what your father, the devil, does.*" The devil always sows mistrust, hatred, scorn, contempt, and pride.

He who works for peace and creates peace, besides having a truly noble nature that consists of being a child of God, has something else from God: humility, because our God is humble. Ascribing adjectives to God is sometimes petulant, but God is humble because he accompanies and walks with a people hard to understand that mutters against him, like the people of Emmaus, about whom God said to Moses: "*They did not mutter against you, but against me.*" That's why, the greatness and the nobility of the one who works for peace is humility.

FIGUEROA: It's very interesting to add important qualitative concepts that are related to peace, because you spoke about love and about patience and humility being needed to reach true peace. But there is an element that seems significant to me and it's what is mentioned in Psalm 85: *"Righteousness and peace kiss each other."* And in Isaiah 32 we read: *"The fruit of righteousness is peace,"* meaning that justice is integral for that peace to occur.

SKORKA: Yes, where there is injustice, intrinsically, there can be no peace. We said that peace is something complete and harmonious, and that there is nothing harmonious about injustice, because it creates conflicts and causes wars. When conflicts become suffocating for some reason, then they begin to spiral out of control, and that is when, evidently, justice is a condition *sine qua non* for reaching peace.

Undoubtedly the concept of justice is found indissolubly linked, in the Hebrew Bible, to the concept of peace. If there are injustices, there is not going to be social peace. And when there is none, people will search for a scapegoat or some excuse, but that conflict will explode in an unpredictable manner.

When someone is discriminated against, for whatever reason, they have three options: leave that society, accept the discrimination—something that we consider aberrant—or fight to eliminate that discrimination. When we talk about the fight that generates that discrimination it means that there is no longer any peace, no longer that sense of completeness to which we have alluded.

BERGOGLIO: Discrimination is distance: "You're there, and I'm here, because you're not worthy"—I'm simplifying—"of being where I am," meaning, "you're beneath me." Generally, powerful people discriminate, but resentment is also another kind of power. The one who feels inferior and generates envy practices self-discrimination or, in turn, discriminates against someone else in order to escape from feeling small. That is, certainly, a serious sin: envy. That attitude of not accepting that I have got to approach the other person instead of creating distance; that's why the key is that sense of "neighborliness" that leads us to create a culture for encountering one another.

Let me return to that other figure we see on the Cathedral of Buenos Aires, on the main facade, that shows Joseph being reunited with his brothers, showing "brotherly compassion," coming together, embracing, and recreating their family. The encounter between Joseph and his brothers creates peace.

FIGUEROA: Considering the biblical story of Joseph, the reality is that when he is reunited with his brothers he has an enormous amount of power. And he is face to face with them, who have misbehaved quite badly. They sold him as a slave and told their father that he had died. Joseph had every argument he needed to take vengeance against them; and he might very well have thought about it this way: "All right then, life is circular, everything returns. Now I have all the power. Who is going to say anything to me? Who can question me if I take vengeance against those who did so much harm to my life?" Nevertheless, Joseph shows a different conception of power, in which power is not an instrument of vengeance, but an instrument of justice, where love, reconciliation, and peace make justice. And he says something very interesting: *"How could I presume to take the place of God?"* He knew exactly who and what he was.

There are two concepts there: vengeance is not the pleasure of the God of the Bible; and people who have a certain amount of power—it doesn't matter how much—must keep in mind that power is not for taking vengeance, but rather for justice and peace.

BERGOGLIO: Twice, on two different occasions, Joseph had to hide because he began to cry. He was overcome with emotion, and I find that very significant. Joseph, with all his power, never lost his capacity to cry. What point am I trying to make? I think that to the degree that one engages in wars—whether they be domestic conflicts, neighborhood disputes, international clashes or any type of war—and sows discord, it's because in their heart they lost their tenderness for their fellow man, their capacity to cry. Tears are purifying when they spring from tenderness, from that compassion for one's brother that consists in suffering "along with him," and sharing in what he is going through.

Peacemakers are women and men full of tenderness, of "compassion for their fellows," of the capacity for feelings and for grief.

We have a very lovely liturgical prayer that asks for the gift of tears: "You, Lord, who, through the rod of Moses made water spring from the rock, bring forth tears of repentance from my heart of stone."

SKORKA: The image of Joseph, his story, is one of humility, to borrow a word that the Cardinal used when he referred to the humility of God.

God's humility is infinite. Because if God, who is infinite, creates man and speaks with him, then it is as if God were—and this merits the anthropomorphism—approaching, bending down, or shrinking in order to be able to speak with man. What happened with Joseph? He learned to be humble. Primarily, he was a very intelligent person, and then what happened? He was arrogant and petulant when he told his brothers: *"You are going to prostrate yourselves before me."* This caused a conflict. Their father also had something to do with all this. He made Joseph a present of a special robe, and there were distinct family problems that caused envy, an imbalance that caused problems. They sell Joseph as a slave he ends up imprisoned in Egypt. And in that moment he acquires a complete humility; he is conscious of his intelligence. He knows where he wants to go, but he learns to be very humble. And that is why he responded to his brothers in the way that he did, rising above the just and understandable fear that they had of him: *"Father has died, now let's see if he takes vengeance against us."* And Joseph did not take vengeance because he had absolutely overcome what had happened; he was not possessed of a "mean, childish spirituality."

Only great people know how to achieve a real peace, one that is sincere, and is the only possible peace—looking one directly in the eyes, taking them by the hand and saying: "Well, let's walk together through life, let's put our hatred aside. We do not feel love for one another, but at least we are showing consideration for one another, the love will come later."

FIGUEROA: I think that the elements added to the concept of true peace or *shalom*, like love, patience, tenderness, humility, compassion, otherness, and justice are very interesting. And like the other side of the coin, sadly, it's easy to destroy, incite war, create conflicts, seek vengeance, and sow hatred; and for that reason it's a great temptation for the one who considers it—no matter how much or how little power he has.

May God help us all to be builders of a true and lasting peace!

28

Happiness

In mid-2012 the three of us decided to meet to make our own critical evaluation of our program *The Bible: Living Dialogue*. Our host was Rabbi Abraham Skorka, who received us at the offices of the Benei Tikva Jewish community in the Belgrano neighborhood of Buenos Aires.

Seated around a simple table, amid tea, coffee, and pastries, we spent about two hours reflecting on what we had done up to this point and thinking about the future. It was a very serene and spiritual meeting. Each one of us wore a yarmulke, and we kept up the same level of dialogue and friendship as usual, but this time without the television cameras running.

Beyond settling the topics and ideas for the upcoming programs, the three of us reached a conclusion. We felt happy to be working together on this television project. And the next chapter has to do, precisely, with that theme: "happiness."

FIGUEROA: The theme of happiness is very important as it is relates to being. "What does being happy consist of? What does happiness itself consist of? Is it found in what I have or in what I give? In what I am or what I am not? In what I want or what I'm able to do? In what I have found? Or does happiness consist of a search?

As this dialogue among friends focuses on the Bible, it's very important that I cite a book of poetry par excellence found in the Bible—the book of Psalms. It begins with a verse concerned with happiness: *"Happy are those who do not follow the advice of the wicked, or take the path that sinners tread, or sit in the seat of scoffers; but their delight is in the law of the Lord, and on his law they meditate day and night."* In some way, it marks out the path for a happy life and perhaps that way we might be able to begin to find what happiness really consists of.

SKORKA: I think that when we speak about happiness, we are talking about two realities: one of circumstantial happiness, and one of deep happiness, of existence itself. There are things that produce in us a certain happiness and have got something to do with the small events of daily life, small passions that are the salt of life. But when we talk about happiness in a more profound sense, the kind we need to keep moving forward and not fall into depression, it's about the peace that the human spirit experiences.

Happiness has much to do with the peace and tranquility of the spirit. Let's look at that first Psalm. What does it tell me? That the person who does not join up with evil doers nor follow the paths of corruption, that one who honors life by following the paths of justice, goodness, and mercy, will be like the tree planted along the banks of a good river—a tree that knows how to give fruit in due time; its leaves will not dry out and wither, it will go on living. But the person who is impious and wicked will be the leaf that withers and dries, blown here and there by the winds, and on Judgment Day—that's how the first chapter ends—will not be found among the congregation of the just. Another psalm that speaks to me about happiness is Psalm 128: *"Happy is everyone who fears the Lord, who walks in his ways."* Then it moves on to practical matters: *"You shall eat the fruit of the labor of your hands; you shall be happy, and it shall go well with you. Your wife will be like a fruitful vine within your house; your children will be like olive shoots around your table. Thus shall the man be blessed who fears the Lord."* Then the psalm continues: *"The Lord bless you from Zion. May you see the prosperity of Jerusalem all the days of your life;"* and then ends: *"May you see your children's children. Peace be upon Israel!"* According to the vision of our prophets, we understand the phrase "Peace be upon Israel!" to mean a universal peace.

It's important to be happy about our achievements and not let our worries about success strip away our enjoyment—our happiness—of contemplating what we were able to do. I think that society today, lamentably, does not know how to enjoy many things that are the real basis of happiness: children, one's spouse, the struggle to carry oneself well and to be able to offer something to the other person. Who is rich? Or to put it another way: "Who is the rich man among the rich?" The one who knows how to be happy with what he has in this earthly reality.

BERGOGLIO: I'm very moved by Psalm 1 because it's the one that the Pope cited in his analogy to Jeremiah when he named me, "bishop." And it touched me! I've got to be the caretaker of God's Word, following his path, etc. That's why I was happy to begin our discussion with this psalm.

I want to return to this idea about the fruit of his hands. There is something that is the basis of happiness, and that is to collaborate with God in creation. This is related to work; work anoints us with dignity. The dignity that a person has is not obtained through inheritance or because you won the lottery. Neither is it because you made a great business deal or because you own a lot of stuff. Dignity comes exclusively through one's work.

The one who does not work has his dignity through play. There are those who don't work because they have no job, and in that lack of dignity they have got to go through the humiliation of begging or asking for handouts. Then, their self-esteem deteriorates. But it's not only a question of self-esteem, it comes down to a question of ontology.

Work is what makes us most similar to God. God creates, and we are "co-creators" with God in his work. For that reason, unemployment eats away at the dignity of all those people who cannot put bread on the family table for their spouse and children. So, the person without work cannot experience that very lovely description of the holy abundance of Psalm 128: *"Your wife will be like a fruitful vine within your house; your children will be like olive shoots around your table."* And they remain unfulfilled.

In terms of social justice, this creates an obligation for all people to have a job because that's the way a person achieves dignity., Following the path of creation, *"Fill the earth and subdue it,"* work it in order to gain dignity and happiness.

FIGUEROA: Kant said that happiness was not a goal, but rather a construction of actions and intentions in which three elements intervene: liberty, willpower, and truth. In some way, in biblical terms, happiness is always associated with doing something, with building or causing something good to happen. Perhaps the goal, if it does exist, has got something to do with a situation of peace. Happiness, could well be a construction of movements. It is never a time of stagnation; it always invites us toward action.

I greatly admire those old people who continue doing things. They don't need to, but they keep doing things for other people. They commit themselves to some activity in solidarity with others because they've realized that the secret to happiness—or one of the secrets—is not being stagnant, but in being active and doing so for the good of others. Perhaps that's why the person who believes that they have reached a place where they don't need to work, and says that they have found happiness, soon realizes that they are in fact a profoundly unhappy person.

SKORKA: Undoubtedly, the state of peace in life depends on the dignity with which I earn my daily ration of bread. These are situations that are linked and they must be the primary concern of all those who are managing the world.

I think that it was John Paul II who spoke about savage capitalism. He described the drama that we are living in, in very concrete terms. We saw that among the different economic and socio-economic systems, capitalism achieved many things. But a capitalism that knows how to respect the individual, where the goal is well-being, is related to the happiness of the individual and not the mere accumulation of assets, which to a great degree is exactly what we have been witnessing in recent decades.

BERGOGLIO: Also the person who simply accumulates assets is not honorable and not happy. What comes to my mind is Jesus' parable in the Gospels, about the man who had excellent harvests and who was so rich that his granaries were overflowing and could not hold his harvest. Then he said: *"What I'm going to do is build more granaries, so that I have a good reserve, and then I'm going to take a rest and enjoy myself."* And Jesus says: *"That man did not know that on that very night his soul would be called to make its final reckoning."*

Working simply to "scrimp and save" does not bring dignity and, therefore, does not bring happiness. So, which job confers dignity on the worker? The job that is separate from the selfishness of possession. It consists of a gentle ownership. There is an aggressive kind of ownership which is what we see in the parable that I just mentioned, and there is a gentle ownership that consists of earning one's bread. God gives us intelligence so that we can do things well, but with that meekness not possessed of the aggressive desire to accumulate more, and more, and more.

Jesus has other advice for people who are only concerned with accumulating and who believe riches to be the source of happiness: *"Do not store up for yourselves treasures on earth, where moths and vermin destroy, and where thieves break in and steal."* Happiness, therefore, is not found in that savage work—let's consider a moment more the idea of capitalism—of wanting to accumulate. That does not make me happy. By contrast, what does bring joy is some noble work that allows me to grow.

SKORKA: This makes me think of Rabbi Meir, one of the most famous Talmudic scholars, who divided his income into three parts. He used one part for his own sustenance, another part to help his students, and another part to buy firewood for the school and to provide heat during the cold days of the winter. So, they said to him: "Teacher, why don't you save for your children?" And he answered them this way: "If they turn out to be good people, God will then provide for them. If they turn out bad, do I have to provide for bad people?" You've got to be very careful. Sometimes we like to fool ourselves with an excess of love: "Because I've got to leave something for them, I've got to protect them!" No! Let your children struggle in life. If you're going to give them everything, that won't help them either.

Talmudic literature says: "When a baby is born his fists are clenched. Do you ever wonder why? It means, 'The whole world is mine.' When someone dies, they die with their palms open, as if saying: 'I've not taken anything with me from this world.'" What I think is that it's best to follow a middle path. To live with dignity and struggle to have what one needs to live. As the prophet Jeremiah says: *"Woe to him who builds his house by unrighteousness, his upper rooms by injustice!"* Eventually, as time goes by, he will have to leave it. In some way he will lose it and will end up being an unworthy person, a bad person.

FIGUEROA: It's interesting because, when Jesus delivers the first parable that Cardinal Bergoglio mentioned in the introduction, the Lord said: *"Man's happiness does not consist of the goods he possesses."*

And thinking about what you mentioned about the general idea of leaving something for one's children or grandchildren, I'd like to share with you a personal experience. A few months ago I finalized the inheritance of a small house my parents owned.

There I found myself facing a great deal of family mementos and things from my childhood. But I found something, and I thought: "This is really the most important inheritance that my father left me." There was an old picture frame that didn't have glass in it. My father was a customs inspector, and that frame was like his greatest trophy. It contained an old yellowing diploma that read: "In recognition of your honor and service." He did not leave us significant material wealth; he always lived thinking that the most important inheritance he could leave behind for us was the example of a noble life. He lived with dignity in a place where the temptations were very strong, he never accepted any favors, he never got mixed up in any funny business, and he went to sleep with a clean conscience. That old yellowed paper is worth much more to me than all the material possessions that my father might have left to us. That was his idea of a happy life. Viktor Frankl said: "Happiness is not an end in itself; happiness has got to do with a person finding a purpose for being happy."

SKORKA: When people are at peace with themselves, they stay that way, "even in death." Those who live in peace throughout their life and know they are at peace with themselves, leave this world peacefully, as if saying, "I've fulfilled my purpose." I think I understand that's how my father left this life; he ended his life happy. In a given moment, when he saw that the end was coming, he told me: "I'm not complaining, I built a dignified home, I have two worthy sons"—worthy because we worked, my brother and I—"we live from our work, we live an honorable life, a pleasant life thanks to our spirituality, we have good grandchildren." We don't pretend that life should be something that it's not. I think that the person who searches like mad for happiness, does so because he or she loses the dimension of simplicity.

BERGOGLIO: It's the trap of wanting to paint life a different color. Life is how it comes to us and you've got to make the catch from wherever it's thrown to you, however it comes.

I want to think again about Psalm 1, about happiness being related to the dignity of work and the image of that tree planted alongside a good, clear-flowing stream, which is peace.

The happy person has that inner-peace no one can take away; although on the surface the wind moves the waters and there are storms, family problems, illnesses or some distressing situation. The happy person, or rather, the one who assumes biblical happiness, has a deep, lasting, inner-peace no one can change. It is the peace of the one who has been pacified by God's grace, and the one who brings peace to others because they always opt for peace. For that reason, Jesus says in the Beatitudes: *"Happy are those who work for peace."* I refer to the peace of the heart, to the happiness that necessarily involves a deep peace that no one can demolish, even though the person passes through moments of sorrow, of pain, of illness, and all the difficult circumstances of life that we know.

Sometimes when I've gone to visit some elderly person in an old folks' home, I've noticed that some of them have such a clear gaze. Those people are saying goodbye to life yet, nevertheless, they have a clear, transparent peace about them. It's like a gift from the Lord, the death of the just. Something that is "amassed" throughout life. A gift that God gives when one makes the effort to live with good conduct, to walk the straight path.

FIGUEROA: Kierkegaard said that "Happiness is a door that opens from inside."

Returning a bit to some words from the beginning, when we were wondering if happiness was the sum of happy moments or a state of being. It seems to me that we are reaching a consensus in which we understand happiness as a state of the character that has inner peace as an inevitable component or beautiful partner. Borges said: "I committed the worst of sins: I've not been happy." I don't know if unhappiness or the lack of happiness might be a sin, but I do believe that one can live in a state of happiness even in spite of losses, of mistakes and disasters. If one clings, like the tree mentioned in Psalm 1, to a life of dignity, of working for the good, of searching for peace, of humility, of meekness, one finds that happiness is indeed possible. This is happiness that does not depend on what is happening all around me, but rather on what's happening inside me, in the place where God usually works very well if we make room for him.

29

Ends and Means

The times off-camera when the three of us wondered about the future of inter-religious dialogue, we ended up taking the words of Cardinal Bergoglio: "Let us walk, let us walk together, let's not stop for anything; God is walking by our side."

In the interconfessional encounter—that was how we defined it because we were brothers in the Judeo-Christian confession—the means and the end feed, define, and qualify one another and dialogue between themselves.

The next episode of the program is about ends and means, a theme to be explored together.

FIGUEROA: Today's program begins with a question: Do ends justify means? I'm going to give three postulates to begin the debate. The first is: "Yes, the end justifies the means." What's important is to reach a goal, and the way one reaches it is less important; that's the Machiavellian vision. The second postulate could be: "The end qualifies the means," in the sense that if there is a good goal, the means to reach it must also be good. And the third would be: "The means is the path"; it's not so important to have a goal, but rather that the primordial emphasis on life is to make good ways, means, or methods and later, surely, the harvest will be a happy ending.

Also, I want to give an example from the Acts of the Apostles that has always struck me. In the story there is a woman who follows the apostle Paul for three days, telling everyone: *"These are sons of the living God who are here to tell you about the road to salvation."* Theologically speaking, this woman was absolutely correct, but there was only one problem: she was a fortune teller who worked to bring riches to the people who made use of her prophetic abilities. On the third day Paul loses his patience and vehemently silences her. In some way, it did not matter if her message was correct or not. What mattered was whether the one pronouncing this message had the right to deliver it or not.

But, the initial postulates, once again, would be: "Does the end justify the means?" "Does the end qualify the means?" or "Is the means the path?"

SKORKA: From the point of view of the Hebrew Bible, the means is important. The rabbinical interpretation, faithfully following the message of the Hebraic text, says that there is a conduct from which I can never separate myself, and that has got to do with justice. The end cannot be good if I, in order to achieve it, have got to move away from justice.

After the eighteenth century, a religious movement took shape with its epicenter in the Ukraine and later spread throughout Eastern Europe. This is the Hassidic movement. It included great teachers who interpreted the biblical verses in a very special way. One of them, in the city of Peshischa, was named Simcha Bunim and when he read the verse: *"Justice, you shall seek justice,"* he said that it must be interpreted in this way: *"You shall seek, you shall pursue through justice."* In a word, we cannot stray from this path because we would be distorting what is good. It may be that the goal is a marvelous one, but if I obtain it by following corrupt paths—and corrupt means that it is unjust, it has no relationship to justice—then the goal becomes distorted.

BERGOGLIO: When Jesus and the apostles were going to Jerusalem, the night overtook them and they passed by a town in Samaria where two of the apostles went to look for lodging—James and John, who were both very high-spirited—and as they were Jews no one offered them a place to stay. They came back and said to Jesus: *"Look, they won't give us rooms, because we're on our way to Jerusalem. Do you want us to call down fire from Heaven to destroy them?"* or more literally, *"Do you want us to burn down the town?"* And Jesus tells them: *"You do not understand your own spirit."* Jesus wanted to make them see that although the Samaritans had treated them unjustly, one should not do anything to punish such an attitude. In the Gospel, evidently, no end justifies the means.

So the Bible itself shows us that a good end can never justify a bad way to achieve it. God punishes the one who uses bad means, for example fraud and entrapment, for a good end. He punishes exploitation, and I think about sweatshops in this city. God punishes those who become rich, who take possession of something, one who hoards goods, or one who achieves any goal, by means of some wicked method.

And I repeat that interpretation mentioned by Rabbi Skorka that struck me as so very good: Justice, by means of justice!

FIGUEROA: Clearly, there is a consensus that the ends do not justify the means, because the means must be just or legal. But what can happen is that they have an appearance or dressing of legality and they're still not legitimate from the moral or ethical point of view. For this reason, the end that will be pursued is going to be an illegitimate end.

I think that concept is very important, because one can enclose oneself in a legal fundamentalism and say: "It's correct, the law gives me the right to do this," however, in my heart and in my intention what I'm doing is something illegitimate. From the biblical point of view, someone can also take a Bible passage that seems convenient to them to justify something illegitimate. This is fundamentalist use, manipulating and twisting the biblical text, in order to be able to say: "What I'm doing is something biblical"— but it's not moral, it's not ethical, it's not legitimately biblical.

That phrase of Jesus which Cardinal Bergoglio mentioned is extremely important: *"You do not understand your own spirit."* Or to put it another way, *"You have no idea what you're saying."*

SKORKA: Nahmanides was a scholar who was born in Girona and lived there in the thirteenth century. He was active in the early period of Jewish mysticism, the Cabala, and he wrote a very lovely exegesis of the Bible. Leviticus 19 contains many laws, and it begins with: *"You shall be holy; for I, the Lord your God, am holy."* Then, commenting on the spirit of the laws he says: *"Someone can fulfill every law and still be a bad person,"* but if you had to translate "bad person" literally, the translation would be "filth." Someone can be spiritually unclean even within what is permissible in the Torah or within the laws and legal code of the Torah.

In the rabbinical interpretation of the Hebrew Bible that contains legal concepts, like when it speaks of one bull striking another, what does the Talmud say? "Well, it is nothing more than the example of a case of damages and losses; everything is written in a terse language where I have got to deduce the applicability of the law." The Talmud is completely open and its final version was completed somewhere between the years 500 and 600. So, if I want to know how to apply the law I have to go to Maimonides, in the twelfth century. And the "million dollar question," the challenge that Deuteronomy sets before us is: *"And you shall do what is correct and what is good."* To what extent? How do I make what is good match what is legal? For example, in some cases, where they say to me: "According to the law it's this way ...," the Talmud clarifies: "But I am adversely affecting the poor, I cannot apply the law in this way." In each case, the rabbi, just like the Talmudic scholar, has got to analyze all the ins and outs, and to the person who claims: "The law is on my side," respond to him: "Yes, just a moment, the law is on your side, but goodness is not. You've followed the law but let's now see how we should proceed in order to not distort the concept of goodness."

BERGOGLIO: What's good is precisely what leads us to a good end. If what's good is distorted or falsified, although it's dressed in the garb of legality, it cannot generate a good outcome.

In the Gospels, Jesus is also very clear about this: *"No good tree bears bad fruit, nor again does a bad tree bear good fruit, for each tree is known by its own fruit."* Good means produces a good end, bad means produces a bad end.

Let me use a fictitious dialogue: "I managed to develop this company," someone says. "And how did you do it, by what means?" they ask him. "By bad, tricky methods. You see, things have got to move ahead, and I'm over budget, so now I'm hiring people under the table," he argues. "You're doing damage to your life by getting involved with a bad company and putting your heart in a situation of injustice and wrongdoing. You're using bad means to try to cut costs and meet your company's budget, because all those people you're hiring under the table have the right to social security, and to retirement benefits, and you're depriving them of that right and you're exploiting them by doing things badly."

I'm going to tell you something very painful that can scandalize some people, but this did happen, many years ago now. A group of women from a certain Catholic association, women who worked for the common good, were talking about domestic service and the various difficulties involved in it. Of course, it occurred to none of them, in that moment, to think that a housemaid had the right to a vacation and to a retirement deduction. No, that was precisely out of the question. But one of these women said: "And of course, they have to be in good health." And she insisted: "Because I've got sons, and I want the maid to be healthy, so my sons don't have to go looking for sex outside the house." The woman was Catholic, and very observant, but she employed that maid not only to clean the house, but to be a prostitute for her sons, so that they did not go looking around on the streets for sex and end up catching some social disease. Shocking! I'm not making this up, this is a true story, involving someone who belonged to a group of Catholic women working for the common good of the Church, in a church organization, using these unjust means, making selfish use of human flesh.

Sometimes, under the appearance of a justification we are really exploiting our fellow brothers and sisters, committing an injustice or using a bad means to an end. We've got to be very aware of how we make use of things; our methods must always be respectful of other people's dignity. A person cannot cheapen someone else's dignity to achieve some end. The other person is inviolable, they are the image of God. I can't use someone else!

FIGUEROA: The Cardinal's anecdote is a painful one and there is another one we must be sure to hear: some top-line name-brand clothing is manufactured using slave labor. We're talking about human trafficking, women, whole families that work in conditions of slavery; and knowing this, people often turn a blind eye. Why? Some people, perversely validate this, and say: "Well that kind of employment is for people who are used to living that way." No! Social, human, and spiritual responsibility guides me to say that all people have the right to live and work with a high degree of dignity.

And, of course, this is going to come back to haunt the person who acts this way. One person cannot strip away someone else's dignity, or treat them badly, or use them in some illegitimate way to take advantage of them, and simply not have to pay for it in some way. If I do, I'll have to pay for it in this life, because I live in a spiritual world where God's law applies. That's why, when we talk about means, we're not talking about some ephemeral, philosophical concept, but about flesh and blood human beings who are going to receive dignity or suffer according to the means we employ. And that makes it incumbent on us all, not just the clothing manufacturer, but also on everyone who buys those clothes and wears them.

So then, be careful. When we talk about means we're talking about people, not only about ourselves or about papers. I think that's where we apply all the biblical learning we have so that we look out for, care for, shelter, protect, and love in order to bring dignity to our fellow human beings. If we don't do it, we cannot even talk about God, because he joins those two concepts in the great commandment: *"You shall love your God and you shall love your neighbor."* And what does this mean? In practice, it means not just giving him a hug, it means being involved with him, making him a part of your life.

SKORKA: I'd say that what you've just pointed out is a syndrome that occurs in many religions. There are people who think that just because they make a point of praying to God, invoke him, or follow certain religious norms, they can justify or permit themselves certain licenses for other things. They think: "It doesn't matter, this is secondary, what comes first and foremost"—in the Jewish case—"must be to honor Shabbat, eat kosher* foods, and strictly follow the rules and regulations prescribed in the Torah and Talmud."

There was a scholar, a great thinker and fighter for human rights in the last century whose name was Abraham Joshua Heschel. He and the students in the movement he created reached the conclusion, for example, that certain kinds of wine must not be consumed, even though it was strictly kosher, because the vineyard workers were being exploited. It ceased to be kosher because the first norm of kosher food is that it involve no exploitation of one's neighbor.

And that is a phenomenon that usually happens: since I'm on good terms with God I can twist the human rule, I can make contraband or some other act that runs counter to the determined laws of a country. Not at all! One must comply with the Talmudic concept of respecting the laws of the place and the laws of God. One rule does not cancel out or annul another; they complement one another.

The biblical frame of reference is simple: one can only reach God through a good relationship with one's neighbor. The final words of the Ten Commandments—I often repeat this—is the divine "I" that is directed to the human "I": *"I am the Lord, your God."* This is not expressed in the plural, "the God of you people,"

---

* **Kosher:** Part of Jewish religious precepts about what foods observant Jews can or cannot consume, drawn especially from the book of Leviticus.

it is directed to the individual, to each person. And what is the final word? *"Your neighbor."*

The example that the Cardinal mentioned happens in many religious circumstances, and it is what, lamentably, projects a negative image that make many people speak scornfully about religion without even having any introduction to religious matters. They say: "If this is what religion is, then I detest it." That's why, the religious person must always be careful and think: "If I have religious clothing, and if I put on such clothes along with my beard and my long sideburns or locks to show that I am very religious, the person out there watching me is going to expect some special attitude and is going to judge my religious conduct." The same thing for a Catholic priest, for any of the Christian denominations, for an Imam, a teacher of Islam, or for someone of any other religion. To wear a religious garment and not respect it is to doubly falsify God.

BERGOGLIO: This makes me remember the Latin phrase *corruptio optimi pessima*, which means, "the corruption of the greater one"—the one who wears the garment is the worst and does much harm. The teacher, or the minister that is corrupted, harms his people. The same is true for the Catholic leader—although they may not be a priest or nun—or the faith leader that starts to lead a double life with a double set of rules for himself, whether things suit him or not. They provoke a scandal because of what Jesus condemned so strongly: hypocrisy.

FIGUEROA: We've got to conclude today's program, but while you were talking, as a Protestant I also made an analysis and I remembered that the United States, a "land of Protestants," that founded black slavery, exploited and tortured blacks all while reciting verses from the Bible.

I recall some words from Anglican Archbishop Desmond Tutu: "When the whites came to our lands, we had the land and they had the Bible. They asked us to pray, and now they have the land and we have the Bible."

By way of conclusion, we could agree that not only do the ends not justify the means, but that the means must be legal as well as legitimate.

To live a life that is not hypocritical, even being men of religion, it is necessary for us to understand our own spirit, the spirit inside of us, which is the spirit for good; and not lose heart or grow tired of living inside of that spirit that works for the greater good.

3 0

Human Trafficking

Cardinal Bergoglio was no stranger to the theme of this program, neither in his thoughts, prayers, nor actions. I remember having attended several masses and acts of awareness about this scourge of modern slavery. In particular, the Mass one spring afternoon in September 2012 in the Plaza de la Constitución in Buenos Aires. There, facing a group of street workers—men, women, and children recovered from sweatshops, and young women rescued from prostitution rings—he offered his valiant homily.

The questions that he started with continue to resound in the urban cosmos and in the memory of all those who were present that day and now, surely, roll round the whole planet: "Today, in this city, we want the cry to be heard, God's question: 'Where is your brother?' So that question that God asked is repeated through every neighborhood in the city, and echoes in our heart and, above all, enters into the heart of every modern 'Cain' among us."

FIGUEROA: The theme that we're going to discuss today is a true worldwide scourge. We're talking about a tragedy from which no country in the world, unfortunately, can claim to be excluded. We're going to talk about a system of modern slavery: human trafficking.

When we talk about "trafficking" we're talking about people who, due to their vulnerable situation, are led into situations of servitude or slavery, through trickery or with offers of imaginary jobs which are enticing to them because of their poverty.

Basically, we know about three main forms of human trafficking. Firstly, exploitation through slave labor. We're talking about the use of illegal, hidden sweatshops used by major clothing brands. Secondly, we're talking about the sexual exploitation of women. This happens through brothels that keep them in captivity. Lastly, the third form, sadly, is exploiting children through forced labor. Child labor is never considered to be within the bounds of normalcy but, additionally, we're talking about slave labor. It is a terrible, sorrowful evil. And when one reflects on this subject, on this program of inter-religious dialogue, with its focus on the Bible, take note that there are moments in which the Old and the New Testaments engage in dialogue with one another.

What just came to my mind is Jesus' first public sermon in the synagogue in Nazareth, where there is a text from Isaiah 61 that, according to the Christian concept, Jesus takes for himself: *"The spirit of God is upon me, because he has sent me to bring good news"*—and he says clearly—*"to set the captives free."* He is delivering a very strong message in which, I insist, he speaks to the prophet Isaiah in what amounts to a clear denunciation of the situation of slavery. Freedom for the captives, to those subjected people *"to announce the year that is agreeable to the Lord,"* or rather, to announce the Jubilee when the slaves shall be set free.

So this is how I would like to begin today's dialogue. From a biblical perspective we can speak about this terrible evil that exists today throughout the world.

SKORKA: The Torah, in the Pentateuch, twice mentions, in explicit detail, the punishment reserved for someone who takes another captive in order to take advantage of them: in Exodus, chapter 21, and in Deuteronomy 24. If someone kidnaps another to sell them—into a state of slavery, we suppose—what is the punishment? Death. Beyond relating that act of abduction for the purpose of profit or exploitation, with the death penalty, I think that what needs to be seen in all this is the underlying concept. And what is that concept? The one who abducts another person, deprives them of their liberty and takes them away to sell them later, deserves the death penalty.

There is a hermeneutic rule in the Talmud that says one must understand the verses based on their context. If the Ten Commandments says *"You shall not kill"* and later says *"You shall not steal,"* the latter does not refer only to a thing, a cup, or some possession belonging to your neighbor but to stealing the physical body of your neighbor himself.

I want to comment on a very important concept. When we examine this subject, the Talmudic interpretation tells me that when someone kidnaps someone else to use and abuse them, the guilty party deserves the death penalty, because it's clear that, to a great degree, that person is committing a kind of murder. Furthermore, I believe that it is a terrible crime because it is a crime that is committed in phases. It's not the kind of crime committed by someone who goes and simply kills someone in a fit of rage or madness. This is a crime that destroys a person little by little; because to take someone and to exploit them through forced physical labor is a way of killing. If I do this, I am killing the other person's being; I am preventing the total development of their soul, of their affective capacity. I am murdering them.

BERGOGLIO: We don't really realize what it means to use a person. Therein lies the germ of abuse, of abduction, of selling a person, of that gradual assassination that you mentioned. And using a person means not recognizing the dignity they have as a child of God, the image of God that he placed within that person and, for that reason, one can reason—by extending the logic, but without lacking in truth—that they are using God himself, in his image, in the image that he chose to embody, which is man. Use is the basis of abuse, and to prepare a society for avoiding abuse and, thus, exploitation, and slow death, it means educating children to not use their neighbor for their own personal gain.

The one who takes advantage of situations of suffering or moments of illness, for example, in order to get some monetary benefit, is using or profiting from the life of that other person who is made in God's image. I was really struck by seeing, once, in the waiting room of some hospital, where I had to help someone who was sick, seeing some hearse drivers from a funeral home take advantage of another person's grief in order to do some business.

I would ask this question. Are you using your neighbor for your own personal profit, to do business? Well, if you do that, you are creating a basis for abuse. Using someone else is the basis for abusing them.

FIGUEROA: In this subject we're discussing there are two fundamental principles that are clearly violated: dignity and liberty, where one concept speaks to the other, depends on the other, and needs the other; they go hand in hand. There is no dignity without liberty and there is no liberty without dignity.

You spoke about a process. When you start reading a little about the different problems and forms involved in the subject of human trafficking, it seems that there is a sort of "intelligence" work; you might call it a kind of spy ring that is involved with finding people to exploit. Some of them are abducted, but others become captives due to their financial needs, from their poverty. Some are tricked by advertisements and promises of a better life or phony ads for imaginary jobs. Then with duping people there is a whole process known as "softening up." What does this mean? This is the denigration of the captive person, and it involves trying to break the person's will by means of drugs, violence, or torture. And when these people lose not only their dignity and their freedom, but also their willpower, it is as if they've gone from being a person to being a thing that is used.

If we read the Bible, it will lead us to an identification in which that person who is suffering, who is being abused and mistreated, is not some stranger apart from us, it is something that is happening to humanity. Because if it happens to only one single person on the planet, it's like it is happening to me, and it's as if all of humanity were enslaved, tortured, and mistreated. The biblical principle of identification calls to me to not withdraw but to think about my brother's suffering as that of my child, or even myself.

SKORKA: I want to go back to the introduction. Let's look at which "cultural" questions lead to these aberrations. In Leviticus it says: *"Never place an obstacle in a blind person's way."* If a person has some problem, don't make it harder on them. Why choose to denigrate someone by making jokes so others can laugh? What's happened in our world today is that a culture of aggressiveness has taken root. And everything becomes objectified and, worst of all, people become objectified; one's neighbors become objectified.

BERGOGLIO: Objectification is when man is viewed and treated as an object. And it's one of the main facts of human trafficking endured by women, because women are not only the object of trafficking in the field of prostitution, their objectification extends to the world of advertising. Scantily clad women are used to sell toothpaste! Women are probably most roughly handled, most mistreated in daily life. I've always wondered: Why have women always been used in this way, disrespected, scorned, used as a propaganda device? I think that the answer, perhaps, tends towards the idea that woman is the one who gives life, she is the mother, and trivializing women destroys life.

In Isaiah, chapter 58, verse 7, in the first lines, God speaks about what kind of sacrifice he wants. And he finishes by saying, and I'm going to mention the first translation, the most imperfect one: *"Do not be ashamed of your brother's flesh,"* meaning, "Look, treat him well, do not exploit him, because he is flesh and blood like you." But later, the more accurate translations, which adhere more closely to the text, change the word and say: *"Don't be ashamed of your own flesh, because you and your brother share the same flesh."* The most precise translation goes even further, and uses two verbs indistinctly: *"Don't stop worrying about your brother's flesh,"* or *"Don't ignore your brother's flesh."* Here, God makes us realize that the flesh and blood of that person who is being victimized and exploited, a victim of human trafficking, is *my* flesh and I cannot approach the drama, the error, the crime of human trafficking, without recognizing that that person who has been objectified is my flesh and blood; they are my brother or sister because we share the same human flesh. This idea made things very clear for me.

FIGUEROA: It's necessary to understand it in that way so as not to run the risk of seeing this hard and heavy subject as if you were watching a film that's happening in another world; like someone who turns on the television, sees that, and then changes the channel and watches a soccer game, and that's it. That's the great risk of these subjects. For that reason, it's important for us to look deeply into them and utilize a means of communication like this in order to bring a different focus to the issue.

There are two strong elements under consideration. One is the clearly economic fact because when we talk about trafficking we're referring to a system that participates strongly in the world economy, especially through money laundering. In some European countries, studies say that the money that is generated through human trafficking represents between 1.2 and 1.5 percent of the gross national product. What's more, some other countries would start to go broke if they did not exploit people. For example, in some Asian or African countries, if they dismantled all of the sweatshops, and did away with human trafficking and slave labor, the economy would immediately collapse. There are three "markets"—again the words have a double sense—that strongly influence the world economy: arms trafficking, drug trafficking, and human trafficking.

But, besides that monstrous system that is such a big player in the world economy, and that directs its course, one also has to look at the other side. This market, this system, exists, and there are individuals who demand this. Recently I was reading an article from an international magazine that mentioned that there is a large amount of prostitution that operates out of all the big hotels in the world, where business executives stay. They traffic in captive women and even young boys because the "clients" are ever more "demanding" and "sophisticated" about the services they require. We're talking about people with families, money, economic status, and a high level of culture given the positions they occupy. This all goes unpunished. There is a very clear motto that people everywhere say: "Without clients there is no trafficking." The client of this system, in some way, has cauterized their conscience and believes that not even God sees what they do and therefore will not judge them either.

There has been a loss of the fear of God. In some way, humanity is falling into the self-deception of believing that what it does in private goes unpunished, even before the eyes of God. And the Bible clearly says that this is not so. Someone once said: "We are nothing more than what we are when we're alone."

SKORKA: There is another detail I would like to mention, returning to the verse: *"And do not ignore your flesh"*—that would be the literal translation. When someone is with a female prostitute—although we know that there is also child prostitution—that person, that "client" is also lending their body to engage in that act, not only the prostitute! Let's not even mention the soul that is inside that body, the spiritual part that is inside a person. In the moment when one person degrades another, they are degrading themselves, because they are using their body for a degrading pleasure, for an act that is an aberration, one that springs from destructive instincts. They are making an offering to *Thanatos* as Freud defined it, to the death instinct.

I cannot just do whatever I feel like doing, because the moment in which I am destroying the other person, I am also really destroying a part of myself. Someone that forces a boy into prostitution is not only prostituting him, but they are prostituting themselves as well.

BERGOGLIO: Let's think, for example, about harvesting blueberries, a task that requires a special and gentle touch. Well, let's suppose I'm a farmer and so I want to get women and children, exclusively, to do this job, so I collect them, and I subdue them; I bend them to my will. I'm not saying that all growers do this, but there are certain crops that require a special touch in order to be properly harvested—I used the example of blueberries, but there are quite a few others, too—. And so by being forced into this specific job that requires a delicate touch, these women and children are exploited. Also farmers who raise special kinds of chicken or quail eggs, so delicate they need to be handled by a child, and so this child is sacrificed to the god of money. We're sometimes horrified when we read that in ancient civilizations children were sacrificed to the gods. But that's not gone out of fashion! In today's world—with the trafficking of children and adults—human beings are sacrificed to various gods: call them the gods of luxury, the gods of ambition, the gods of money, and the gods of power. At bottom, the parts of the first Commandment that says, *"I am the one true God,"* is being denied. Why? Because we are living in a situation of idolatry. All human trafficking distorts the image of God in the human being and an idol is created. These people become human sacrifices to the idols that have been fabricated by our passions.

FIGUEROA: I'll allow myself to finish today with something stated at the beginning. In human trafficking the principles of liberty and dignity are being wagered. And when these values are attacked, we are all in serious danger.

3 1

Family

Buenos Aires was largely deserted on the afternoon of December 26, 2012. This was perfectly normal for the week between Christmas and New Year's Eve, and it was a favorable date for the topic we would explore: Family.

None of us three imagined that this would turn out to be the final program in the series. When we finished recording we set the date and topic for the next program, and at the same time we recognized that 2013 would be the third year of the series. But God had other plans for the pastoral ministry of Cardinal Bergoglio, plans that would of course impact our own and the continuation of *The Bible: Living Dialogue.*

Today I allow myself to think that our presence in that last program represents the broadcast of God's great family plan as revealed to Abraham: *"And I will make of you a great nation, and I will bless you, and make your name great, so that you will be a blessing. I will bless those who bless you, and him who curses you I will curse; and by you all the families of the earth shall bless themselves"* (Genesis 12:2–3).

FIGUEROA: Today we're going to talk about family, as well as intra-family relations. I'd like to begin with an anecdote, not necessarily a true story, but one that will serve to give an introduction from the place that I, at least, would like to focus the discussion. Once an evangelical pastor was invited by his congregation to let them pray for him and his family. With the pastor's whole family around the pulpit, one of the deacons prays for them and gives thanks to God for what they all mean to the community. But it turns out that when his prayer is over and he invites the pastor's wife and children to return to their pews so that the pastor can begin his sermon, they don't want to go sit down. The congregation begins to get restless and then the daughter says, speaking with the truth that children don't fear: "We want to stay here, because here Daddy is very different from Daddy at home."

In the way that we don't talk about our families as if they're perfect, we speak about the Bible from a perspective of knowledge, not from idealism.

Family is one of God's marvelous inventions, far beyond its nature as a civil contract and, as such, a basic institution.

The Bible has countless examples or counterexamples, because what's marvelous about the Bible is that we almost don't find cases of perfect families and saints. The Bible is a book in which we read about the virtues as well as the low points of human beings, and that is what makes it such a large book. To name just a few examples, the families of Jacob, Joseph, Isaac, David, and Saul were far from ideal.

SKORKA: The family is a basic institution in the sense of the child's contact with a mother and father who, as parental figures, transmit values to them. For Judaism it is an extremely important institution, because that's where we see the most vital manifestation of Judaic tradition. The family is where the child begins to experience it, for example on Friday nights as we receive Shabbat, the Shabbat supper, the lighting of the menorah in the festival of Hanukkah and so many things that must be done in the heart of the family home. Now, that doesn't mean—as has been well said— that the family is not a crazy mess of conflicts that we must try to resolve. The point is how we resolve them—conflicts between the couple, sibling rivalries.

The whole book of Genesis has various focal points, one of them consists of God's desire to make a covenant with man. Firstly, he wants to make a covenant with the first man, Adam, but he cannot do it because Adam eats of the forbidden fruit. Later, he makes a covenant with Noah because all of humanity has gone astray; and finally he ends up making a very profound covenant with Abraham. What is the essence of that covenant? That the human reality contains a consciousness, a knowledge, a contact with that total, omnipresent God, who creates everything out of nothing and of whom we carry a divine spark with us in our human condition. So the first focal point is that God searches.

Another one is a question: How do we develop a family whose heart will shape the people who will maintain that covenant with God? Then we see that Abraham had many children, but only one of them—Isaac—would make a complete commitment to that covenant. Later, Isaac fathered twin sons: Jacob and Esau. Between them we have a war between two brothers, which finally ends in reconciliation. And the book of Genesis ends with a great event: Jacob manages to get all his sons to exist in a state of brotherhood, after all the problems he had with them due to his excessive love for Joseph. And Joseph, in the moment that he sees all his brothers, tells them: *"I am your brother, Joseph."* We might say that Genesis concludes by showing that God's struggles end in triumph, as from this family comes the people of Israel; and that leads to the beginning of the book of Exodus.

BERGOGLIO: This brought to my mind the covenant of Abraham when he divides the animals for the sacrifice. And the Bible says that he is there awaiting God's signal, with the animals ready for the sacrifice, and the day ends, and nothing happens. And the vultures and birds of prey came swooping down on the carcasses, and I imagine that man, now old, with a stick in his hand, because the Bible says that he drove them off "by striking hard with a stick," fighting against the vultures that were trying to destroy the offering of the covenant. That pact that was going to be the family, the children, descendants as numerous as the sands of the sea and the stars of the sky. And at nightfall, when Abraham was tired and sleepy, the fire goes out and a horrifying darkness descends on him.

Similarly, family unity, fecundity, and posterity are also attacked by vultures, both from inside and from outside of ourselves. As if there were a conspiracy against God's plan to create his children in a family so that the line of descent might continue. These are the trials a family must pass through in order to maintain its unity.

God made us family so that we might love one another and help form one another, like kneading dough, you might say, because in a family one helps to form the other members, helping them grow, modeling and shaping them. Siblings help form one another through their conflicts. This is presented by Scripture itself, without any shame, as a human path. It is a path of struggle against all that wants to batter and break the family unity. It is a creational path, because that is how God, through love, shaped us from the clay and infused us with the spirit. And in the family we grow and help each other to grow, "kneading" one another's personalities. The child develops and strengthens his powers of personality in relation to his mother and father, and there his psychology grows and matures so that he can become an adult.

The family is that creational act of God that is perpetuated through us. God makes us a part of his creative work. For that reason we must, in some way, care for the family the way one cares for a great inheritance: our inheritance from God, because by carrying the family forward we are participating in his creation.

FIGUEROA: When we talk about the family, the concept of construction and building is very interesting. Traditionally, and I think this happens in all three faiths, marriage ceremonies involve an exchange of rings. It might be a good idea, though not a very aesthetically appealing one, to also give the bride and groom a pick and a shovel. Because family is a construction project that requires sweat, sacrifice, effort, self-abnegation, denial, and understanding. I was thinking about that passage in Deuteronomy that says: *"And give these teachings to your children, at night when they go to sleep, in the morning when they rise, when you travel along the road, when you leave the house, when you come in, all the time."*

I was also thinking about a line from the writer Jaime Barylko: "People ask me, 'What right do I have to teach my children a religion?' and my answer is: 'The question goes the other way: What right do you have to not teach them a religion?'" Understanding that teaching a religion is not simply teaching dogmas and precepts, but also transmitting the spiritual nucleus and the value of the religion, of the relationship that must exist among the family, and between the family and God, the creator of the family. And that is achieved through teaching, but also by example.

There are very clear concepts in the biblical faith, such as forgiveness, for example. I can show my son all the Bible verses that have to do with forgiveness, but I have to be capable and have sufficient humility so that when I make a mistake as a father, I can sit down with my son, look him in the eyes and say: "Dad was wrong, and I ask your forgiveness. Do you forgive me, son?" That teaching is worth much more or, better yet, it goes better with all the Bible verses than anything I can add.

There is something that I always say at the family table. Information is power; or rather when one has information about certain things that no one else knows, he has a certain amount of power. And the reality is that in a house, in a family, one knows the information about all the weak spots, and the strong ones, the place that hurts someone more than another, the defects, and the virtues. And I can use that information to protect, to care for, to complement, to accompany, to develop, or I can also use it to wound and destroy. But it is a beautiful decision to say: "I have the information I need to end the argument by putting you in your place with one quick comment, but I'm not going to use it because I know that it will hit you where it hurts the most. I have that information and I'm never going to use it against you, because I'm going to use it to protect you."

SKORKA: Regarding the respect that happens in the heart of the family. In Hebrew, the word "father" has the same root as the word "teacher." The instructive part that falls to the parents is enormous. Once someone asked me about circumcision, which is very important for us. It's really a sign of our covenant with God, Abraham, and his descendants. I reached the conclusion that can be applied to what we're discussing here: if you're going to circumcise your son, you are marking him, but you're also marking him if you decide not to. In a word, who is going to give him a message about life? We are formed out of nothing, there are centuries of civilization and centuries of existential experience. So then, who is going to transmit that message to him if it doesn't happen in the heart of the family?

And the last comment refers to the reality that we're living, where so often, in so many places, people are talking about the breakdown of the family institution, something that really is very sad, very painful.

It's an enormous challenge to try to live with dignity. It means learning, first, and before anything else, to put aside our selfishness, our "I," our immediate pleasures. So many couples split up, so quickly, and get divorced. The section of the Talmud that deals with divorce ends with the words of the famous Rabbi Meir, who says, "When a couple divorces, even the altar in the temple of Jerusalem"—where sacrifices are made—"weeps, and sheds tears." Divorce is accepted in Judaism, but be careful, it's not like someone choosing a new pair of shoes, or what they want to drink. It's not as simple as: "Well, I'm with you today, even though tomorrow our love is finished." Wait a minute, there are children in the middle. What image are children receiving about life, about love? What is the impact? But the underlying idea is: What is it that I want to leave to my family? A seal of honor, of goodness, that others follow in my footsteps, the example of someone that made the effort to live with rectitude.

BERGOGLIO: You've both raised two very interesting ideas. One is: "What right do I have to pass on my religion to my children? Because when they're older they can choose for themselves." That's the same as saying, "What right do I have to pass on my language to my child?" or "What right do I have to pass on my culture to my child?" My religion forms part of my culture, of my spiritual language, of my way of being, and I must give everything of myself to my child. These are ideas or questions people sometimes bring up in order to avoid the importance of religious responsibility. The other idea that came up is the destruction of the family—that image that even the temple altar is going to cry when a family falls apart. I would add that it gives the impression that behind a breakup there is always at least one, or several, conflicts; and that nowadays conflict is privileged more than unity. Privileging conflict is privileging the atomization of society. Privileging unity above conflict is to seek the solution to the conflict for the sake of unity.

And the Bible shows us a very beautiful text, which consists of advice about how to deal with the family, given by St. Paul in Ephesus, and I want to read it. These words don't require commentary. They speak for themselves: *"Husbands and wives, submit to one another out of reverence for Christ. Husbands, love your wives as Christ loved the Church, and gave himself up for her, to sanctify her. He purified her with the water of baptism and the word, because he wanted a splendid, shining church, without blemish or wrinkle, without any defect but only holy and immaculate. In the same way, husbands must love their wives as they do their own body. The man who loves his wife loves himself; no one should despise their own body but instead nourish it and care for it as Christ does for his Church, for us, we who are the members of the body of Christ. For this reason, the man will leave his father and his mother to be united with his wife, and the two shall be one single flesh. Children obey your parents in the ways of the Lord, because it is just, as the first commandment that contains a promise is this: 'Honor your father and your mother so that you might be happy and live a long life on this earth.' Fathers, do not provoke your sons to anger, on the contrary, teach them, correct them, and counsel them, in the ways of the spirit of the Lord."*

This guidance includes advice for relations between men and women. And here is where tenderness grows, as St. Paul says: *"With the same tenderness with which Christ loves the Church, so must you love your wife; love her like your own flesh."* And the first thing that is lost when a family has a conflict is, precisely, tenderness. When one loses tenderness, shouting takes over, rage, misuse of authority, institutionalized disobedience from the children.

That text tells us a lot about how to safeguard unity in the face of family conflicts, and it does so from a Christian perspective, which comes from the Old Testament, from the biblical tradition, from God's first revelation to man.

FIGUEROA: Different behaviors, in some way, are taught, and they can cause a lot of harm. If the typical solution to conflicts in an area as important as the family, where there are always going to be conflicts because we are conflictive human beings, is to "kick over the chessboard," that thoughtless response is going to be reproduced in different areas of life.

In the New Testament, or second testament, there are three different Greek words for love, but when talking about relations with one's peers and relatives the only one that is used is *agape*, which is about a surrender, a commitment to another. When I am worried about another person's well-being, in this case that of my wife and children—putting them before myself—that is the true love a commitment demands. It is a commitment that nobody says will be easy to take on. Getting married and having children is, in itself, not complicated; the complicated part is forming and shaping the family. Building a house is not so complicated either. What's complicated is having a home. It is the effort as a family to shape individuals for the common good, and that they develop in a wholesome way as people, with their dreams and with their own personal relationship with God. I was thinking about the words of Joshua, in chapter 24. It's a family decision when he says in front of all the people: *"You choose which God you're going to follow, but my house, my family and I, we will follow the Lord."*

SKORKA: There are so many parallels to be drawn between the Bible and what Cardinal Bergoglio read to us such as learning to love God through love and, specifically, the love of the couple that is examined there. And among those parallels, the quotation from the letters of Saint Paul and the verse from Genesis: *"And you shall be one flesh."*

The concept of unity in the Hebrew Bible is very subtle, and I think that it guards one of the most important messages with respect to the theme we're discussing. For example, in the book of Exodus we read about the instructions for the portable temple the Israelites had in the desert, what's called the "tabernacle," and the story ends in a very special way: *"And all the tabernacle was one."* The idea of being one before God: *"On that day"*—says the prophet—*"God will be one in your name."* What does it mean to "be one"? Trying to live with the other person, trying to have a common language, a lexicon, an affect. That is the basis of everything.

BERGOGLIO: When Mass is finished, I stand at the door and say hello to the parishioners as they leave. Frequently I'm approached by some old couple and they say to me: "Father, pray, because we've been married forty-something years, or fifty years—give us a blessing for this." And I usually ask them: "And who puts up with whom?" And the answer is always the same: "Both of us, Father, half and half." That's love that lasts to the end.

Good wine doesn't turn sour, it ages well. Good love, when one cares for it, ages well. Well-aged love is the source of wisdom for others.

One woman, married and with a child, brought her grandmother to live in her house. Then an uncle asked her: "Now that you've got your grandmother, who is your son's great-grandmother, don't you think it's important that she goes to live somewhere else, because it's a problem to have an old person and a young man together in the same house?" And she answered him: "No, I want my son to know what it's like to grow up with a grandmother in his life." Now, that's a true sense of what family means!

FIGUEROA: I think that we chose this subject today, not because it was easy, but because it's a crucial theme for our society. An individual, as such, never fully develops or matures far from a family, neither in their relationship with the family nor in their relationship with God, because from the time he is a child, he sees God in the image of his mother and father.

And no society in the world, in any civilization, can develop strongly and in plenitude without united families. If we want a better society, strong, solid and with well-developed individuals, we need to strengthen the family.

We hope that our simple, humble contribution, our thoughts and prayers, will allow this program to help strengthen the family in our country.

Epilogue

The program *The Bible: Living Dialogue* was a special grace from God. I confess that, even today, I have not managed to properly put into perspective what it means to have shared this experience with the first Latin American pope. I feel a certain nostalgia for the conversations the three of us shared, and I also miss hearing the wise words of Rabbi Skorka, although I still do so in an informal way.

Also unexpected were the television awards: the "2013 Marín Fierro Honorary Prize" and the "2013 FunTV Award." I'm aware, of course, that Pope Francis' presence was a determining factor in receiving those awards, but I also permit myself to consider them as awards for a program of inter-religious dialogue and as the just recognition for all my friends and colleagues at Canal 21 who, in silence, anonymity, and humility, work devotedly at what they rightly consider to be "The Pope's Channel."

We had agreed to film a program which explores the theme of "Friendship," but distance and the circumstances recognized by everyone did not make that possible. The times when Rabbi Skorka and I talked between ourselves, and also with Pope Francis, about this unfinished program and the feasibility of completing it to bring closure to the series, led us all to the same conclusion: "Let's leave it in God's hands." If it couldn't happen, the friendship strengthened by so many conversations, and which runs through all the programs, will stand as a parabolic testament to our thoughts on the friendship between people from different ages, contexts, and religious faiths.

Once again, the Bible speaks to us about these sorts of friendships. I conclude this book with a quotation from the Holy Book that brought us together: *"A cord braided from three strings is not easily broken"* (Ecclesiastes 4:12).

So may it be.

Marcelo Figueroa

Acknowledgments

To God, the only one who can make us all his children and before whom we can recognize ourselves as brothers.

To my wife Emilse and my children David and Carolina, who supported me with infinite love and patience throughout this program and during the time it took to write this book.

To my friend and brother, then Cardinal Bergoglio and now Pope Francis; although his titles and appointments have changed, for being the same person and same faithful disciple of the Lord.

To my big brother Abraham Skorka, for his enthusiasm and selfless contribution to make each program unique, and in whom I discovered a friend and a wise man of G_d.

To Julio Rimoldi, producer at Canal 21 who, selflessly and lovingly, made available to me all the material from the television broadcasts necessary to make this book possible.

To Andrés Eidelson, who carried out the enormous job of transcribing our conversations from every program, with a thrilling pastoral commitment and a meticulous intellectual zeal.

To Malva San José, for her patience and dedication in correcting literally every line of this book, pouring into it her enormous professional skill and spiritual understanding.

To Horacio Salas, for his sincere and great friendship, and for encouraging me on this "publishing adventure" with his advice, criticism, and heartening words at the right moment.

To all those brothers and sisters who travel the path of inter-religious dialogue and who have paid, as only they know, a high price, but one that is incomparable to the pleasure of feeling themselves united in fraternity and sisterhood before one God.